MW00450256

Getting to Here

A memoir of promise, passion, and despair

Lorraine Bouchard

Getting to Here

A memoir of promise, passion, and despair

©2022 Lorraine Bouchard

All rights reserved. This book or any portion thereof may not be reproduced or used in any manner whatsoever without the express written permission of the publisher except for the use of brief quotations in a book review.

print ISBN: 978-1-66785-655-1
ebook ISBN: 978-1-66785-656-8

Contents

November 2013, Sanford, Florida

Shall we start with a fine *whine*?

I'm 58 years old and I've had four different jobs in three different states in the last five years. Before taking this job in Florida, I had been unemployed for a year up in Ohio. I moved here this summer, signed a one-year lease, then got fired after 90 days. Let's just say that these stats do not make me sparkle in the eyes of potential employers. Now here I am in Central Florida, with a bunch of debt from the move, no prospects, and an octogenarian husband who grows more crippled and confused by the day.

This is a pickle.

How did this happen to me? To *me?* I was the good girl, the high achiever, the one who could figure things out. I've been in leadership and managerial positions for the last 35 years. I've presented at international conferences, my doctoral research won a national award, I started my own school and ran it for over 20 years. I take calculated risks and usually end up just fine, no regrets. Now I can't even collect unemployment.

What the hell happened?

Spring 1985, Houston, Texas

The steamer hissed at the front of the store, behind the display window where the amazon-sized mannequin posed in her polyester pants, plaid shirt and casual cardigan. Shoppers in the mall regularly stopped to make rude comments about Big Betty. Woman's World was for middle-aged, plus-sized women and prided itself in its realistic, size 14 mannequins. Other stores displayed those big sizes on size 8 dummies and pinned them like crazy so the skirts wouldn't fall to the floor. However, to keep Betty from looking dumpy, they made her six feet tall. That polyester-clad woman loomed over the mall's customers like an inhabitant of a theme-park haunted house. The bug-eyed gigglers got on my nerves. Meanwhile, one dowdy woman cruised the racks of the clothing store. A bored, teenage salesclerk steam-stroked one shirt at a time from the new shipment, easing out the wrinkles, occasionally casting an eye to the customer, alert to a sign that she would want a dressing room unlocked. I sized a rack, pulling errant size 20s from the size 16 wedge of the rounder, putting them back with their fellow 20s.

"Looking for anything special?" I asked, sizing her up and down. I knew how to estimate her size, determine her style preference, and find her buying trigger, thanks to the training I had gotten at my last retail management job. But I also knew how not to be pushy, to let her feel that she was in control of the experience. If she just wanted to browse, so be it.

If she didn't want to chat, I would enjoy the peace and she would know that she didn't have to be assaulted to shop in my store. I was the manager and could focus on the long haul, on the repeat customer who, if she didn't want to buy today, knew she could return and be welcomed. We were not on commission, so the pressure to be obnoxious was off.

"No, just looking."

"Love this spring weather we are having. Sure beats being up north! We have a great clearance sale on heavy winter coats."

"Oh, I know about winter, and I don't miss it! I'm from Wisconsin."

"No kidding! So am I! Whereabouts?"

"Kenosha. Know where that is?"

"No way! I'm from Kenosha!"

"How about that."

"Yes, I headed south two weeks after I turned 18. I wanted out of the cold and the small town life. What did you do there?"

"I was a school librarian."

"Cool. What school?"

"Lance Junior High."

"No! That's where *I* went! What years were you there?"

" I was there from 1967-1980."

" I was there then! We probably saw each other! What a *small world!*" What were the odds of running into your junior high school librarian 1500+ miles away? Probably as great as the odds of my ever having spoken with her when I was there for seventh and eighth grade from 1967-1969. Students spent almost no time in the library, except to learn to copy down the bibliographic information onto 3x5 index cards for the resource section of the paper we had to write for RLSS (Reading, Library, and Study Skills.) RLSS was a required class taught by a homely, ever-cheerful woman. She was hyper-organized and determined to see that we were all launched into our high school paper-writing years armed with organizational skills, replete with color-coded index cards, outlining skills, and reading comprehension. It was the most agonizingly tedious class, exacerbated by her wrong-headed belief that there was anything remotely interesting in her many, many personal stories or well-intentioned lessons. Teens are only interested in personal stories if they are told by hip, young teachers fresh out of college.

Lance Librarian Lady warmed up and bought a shirt from the sale rack. I wondered about the pointlessness of it all. Here I was, a store manager with a great track record. This was the fifth store that I had opened, having worked for four different companies; the turnover in retail management is quite high. The job had gotten me to Texas and as close to the ocean as I could get: Galveston was just a 90-minute drive down I-45. When I wasn't opening new stores, I was being transferred to stores where the previous manager "accidentally" forgot to make the night deposit. I kept the staff honest and increased sales. But who cared? What was the point? Is this what all my education and passion was for? I had raced through college and graduated Magna cum Laude, earned a Master of Arts in Teaching, and I was selling elastic-waist Levis to housewives.

I fell into retail out of desperation. It was January 1980 in St. Louis, a slushy time. I was just back to teaching after the holiday and my 6-week maternity leave. The Satellite School was a little storefront alternative school, started by fellow Webster College students and home to 15 rowdy adolescents who, like me, were no longer willing to put up with the public schools. I was burnt out after five years of public school teaching. Rich Vejvoda and his tiny Italian girlfriend, Toni, started the school and made all their dreams of fun learning happen. I taught math and reading, and I set up a photography lab in the basement. But switching from public school to an independent school did not come without its challenges. I cringed when a student climbed a utility pole during PE at the neighborhood park and Rich just laughed and said that he would be fine, while I had visions of a fried boy fallen at the base of the pole. I shuddered when the giant student, Ben, got angry when I required him to sit down and do his math and he picked up his chair and threw it across the room. I was nine months pregnant then, which added to my fears, and Rich counseled that perhaps I did not need to push him quite so hard to work if he did not want to work. My jaw dropped when I was in the hospital, having delivered my baby, and Toni delivered hand-drawn cards of well wishes from the students, one of which was a very graphic drawing of me screamingly delivering the baby while other characters cheered me on. I remember one sad morning when, thanks to the baby refusing her breakfast feeding, I had to lock myself into the dirty little unisex bathroom to express my engorged breasts into an old coffee cup, then had to dump the precious cupful down the sink. I wondered if this job worth that, but did not have to wonder for long because Rich called me into the office, softly and apologetically, to explain that they simply could not pay me any longer. The school was out of money. They didn't have money to pay him and Toni, either, but they would get by with help from her folks.

So there I was, unemployed, and my husband was unemployed, too, having resigned from the college where he was a dean. His generous severance was nearly gone, we had a baby, and we needed money. One doesn't easily find a teaching job mid-year, and as burned out as I was on public school, I did not even consider applying to another school. I went on a hunt for something to help us scrape by. A big new Hallmark Crown card shop had opened down the road. It sounded much lovelier than fast food or a convenience store. When I dropped by on that snowy day, the store was hopping and their sidewalk was covered with the slippery stuff, so I asked at the desk if they had a shovel. I went outside, shoveled the walks, and returned the shovel, asking if I could speak to the manager. I asked her for a job. She looked at the walk and could tell that I was a person who could see what needed to be done and would do it independently, and she hired me on the spot. From that day, I spent five years in retail management.

It was so different from education! It put my talent for organization and my midwestern work ethic to good use, and it gave me a respite from the frustrations of working in schools. It was an easily portable talent, as no matter where we lived, I could get a job. That was important because Richard, my husband, was searching all over the country for a college job. And with a baby and a husband at home, I could work the odd hours that retail demanded. He was home during the day, applying for jobs while I was at the store. It was the right fit at the right time. My days off could be midweek, so once he went back to work, we would only need daycare a few days each week.

"Why on earth would you want to leave teaching?" folks would ask. "You get to play with kids all day, the hours are short, you can be home with your own children in the afternoon, and you have the summers off. You get insurance and retirement." I never strangled anybody who said that, but I was tempted. They were ignorant.

"Let me explain it to you in terms of this business," I would say to my retail colleagues. "Imagine you are a salesperson here, and twenty-five customers walk into your store at the same time. You are expected to sell something to each and every one of them. Each one has different wants and needs, and you are expected to uncover those, however reluctant a shopper she may be. Some come in hungry and would rather be at the food court. Others are busy socializing with the other shoppers. One is a thief. Several find the store's styles uninteresting, and share those opinions with their fellow customers, but you have no say in what the store sells — your job is to sell whatever they send to your store. You get as many into the fitting rooms as you can, exchange sizes, restock their discards, offer suggestions, try to build the sale. You ring up the purchases. You make every customer feel special. You are the only salesperson in the store.

"The next hour it begins all over, but with 25 different customers. You have one hour to sell each one something. But you must also deal with the customers' families. They want to discuss Susie's sense of style and her lack of motivation to try new things. They want to complain that last week's purchase cost them too much or that it interfered with their home life. They want to explore a rumor that you said something unkind to their precious child when their angel interfered with another customer. They are disappointed because the neighbor's wife, who shopped at a different store, came home with two dresses, but his only came home with one, so why wasn't she given the same opportunity?

"And the next hour, 25 more customers come in. And the next hour — you guessed it — another 25. You estimate that 1 in 10 of your customers have ADHD and are frenetically picking hanger after hanger off the rack, rushing around the store, unable to decide on anything. They can't find their purse or their keys. Your sales pitch is interrupted at random times by a public address system that calls for certain customers to come to the office. Another hour is cut short by a special presentation in the mall center court, attendance mandatory. A loud bell clangs for all the customers to leave, and another bell clangs to announce the arrival of the next batch.

"That metaphor describes the hourly changing of classes in secondary school, but does it apply to the self-contained elementary school classes? Yes, but instead of a different batch of students each hour, imagine a different sales focus. As all the customers enter, you are to direct all their attention to slacks. In an hour, you redirect their attention to shirts, then an hour later you point them to the dresses. Some customers make their choices in five minutes and then must be entertained for the next 55 minutes as you wait on other customers. Some still haven't made up their minds after an hour, yet they really need a dress, but you must move on to sweaters. You try to help them connect those sweaters to the slacks that they perused three hours ago. The selection is disjointed, perhaps beyond their means, yet you must form a judgment about how each customer is doing: Are they listening to your sales pitch? Do they wear the clothes properly? Do they come to the store prepared, and do they get along with the other customers?

"Now imagine that you must take home all the day's receipts and record them there because there is no time to do that at work during the day. And imagine that every quarter, you are to send reports to all your customers' families describing all that was offered for sale, all that was actually purchased, and make unique, individual comments of encouragement or admonishment—not too harsh—for each customer. At home, between family demands."

"But you have the summers off. It all balances out."

Teachers are still teachers in the summer, but the hours are different. Show me a teacher who isn't always planning, always ferreting out cool activities, keeping up with the professional reading, taking the workshops that are required for continued employment or certification. Many teachers are visiting their classrooms in the summer and putting the infrastructure together, creating bulletin boards, writing rubrics, decorating to create a nice atmosphere to turn the cinder blocks and harsh fluorescent lighting into an interesting, comfortable place in which to learn. Or maybe they are spending days studying to learn the new math program, or trying to internalize the new schoolwide discipline procedure. *This year I will reach every student! This year we will have fun!* They try to wash away the disappointment that Johnny's test scores were not higher, the annoyance at the demanding parents who complained to the principal. They refill their well of energy and enthusiasm for the very long 10 months ahead. It is teacher comp time and they are in recovery.

In my first couple years in retail management, people asked what I did before, and when I said that I had been a teacher, they would say, "Yeah, I thought so." Really? And the way that they would say it was not complimentary. It had the flavor of that old adage: You can always tell a teacher but you can't tell her much; it is an occupational hazard. My authoritarian aura annoyed adults. They had endured 12 or more years of (mostly) women running their lives, and they were glad to be away and in charge of themselves.

With determined effort, I went about trying to shed that skin. I wanted people to be surprised when I told them that I used to be a teacher. It took time, but I got there. It meant approaching people with greater humility. This was quite a trick—to be a manager, to give direction without being too bossy or acting superior. To this day, I disdain being around teachers who act like teachers—the ones who have an inflated confidence that what they say is The Truth. They Who Know So Much.

But despite the ways in which retail management fit for me, it was dawning on me that the job did not matter. The stop-gap job had lasted years, and there was no endgame plan. I was a child of the '60s, an idealist, so selling bras and counting plastic-wrapped shirts was not what I was supposed to be doing...whatever that was. What was it? Surely somebody out there knew. Surely someplace could make better use of my gifts.

I saw a headhunter that spring of 1985. Quest Personnel's ads were the biggest in the Houston Chronicle. They were searching for people with skills, talent, and ambition. After my interview, they sent me to a few potential jobs. I recall visiting one of the largest law firms in Houston, Vinson & Elkins. I was on the 52nd floor, and when I walked up to the floor-to-ceiling glass windows, vertigo hit me and I flashed back to the movie *The Towering Inferno.* Sure, employees could get endless free Diet Cokes from each floor's lush break room, but did I want to die leaping from those windows to escape the flames? I interviewed with a charming and friendly attorney in the admiralty department. Did I know what admiralty is? he questioned with a smile. I had visions of captains aboard navy vessels and wondered how often they needed lawyers. I admitted that I did not, and he explained it to me. What would the job be like? He said that the paralegal job would have endless variety. I should keep a bag packed because I might need to jet off to Europe on two hours' notice. That was appealing! Visions of transatlantic flights, Parisian cafes, and nice-smelling men in expensive suits lit up my pleasure center. I would have to have a babysitter on call. Or I might spend days shut in a room with boxes of files, digging out the pertinent facts of a case. That inspired a mental picture of them opening the office door and finding me in a hollow-eyed, foggy-headed, rumpled heap on the floor. No, thank you!

Several other interviews did not lead to a match, but they led to an offer from Sharon, the personnel firm's founder, to come to work for them. I was offered a draw against commission. I would place candidates whom I had interviewed, and I could see the best jobs as they came to the office and perhaps move on to one of those jobs. Why not? I knew that I was great at sales. How different could it be to sell well-qualified candidates to an employer in need?

The cactus on my desk should have been my first clue. The agency was in a beautiful suite of offices just outside The Loop, in the Galleria area of Houston: Fancy! Sharon was proud that the offices had earned an award for their interior design. Six spacious offices flanked the perimeter, with Sharon's in the prime corner spot. There were two interior, window-less offices, one of which held the copier, and the other—my desk. All the offices, the reception area, and the testing spots had lush, green plants tended by a special service each week; mine had a 7-inch cactus.

I interviewed applicants who responded to the generic, enthusiastic classified ads. I asked questions designed to assess their skills, flexibility, capacity for learning, and reliability. I uncovered their level of profession-alism. I met with dozens of women. I went on both cold calls and warm calls to companies to try to convince them that we had the perfect employ-ees waiting for them, somebody just right. We would save them hours of investigation, interviewing, and reference checking. I sat through hours and hours of meetings with the other placement team members. These were sleek, coiffed, well-dressed women who had connections to the executives of the city's biggest manufacturers, oil companies, law firms, and accounting firms. They pitched the jobs, and they pitched their hottest candidates.

I placed no women. I secured one job lead, but the company backed out.

It was a muggy, oppressive July day, the kind of day that visitors to Houston describe as knocking you backward with a wet towel as you step off the plane. Sharon called me into the office and explained that she was letting me go. I was not making the company money, and my income was costing them.

I was stunned! I had never been fired in my life! I was the high achiever, the woman who folks wanted on their team because I worked hard and got the job done. I was friendly. How had this happened?

Here is what I learned too late: I was interviewing these women for their professional qualities, their drive, and their talents. That was a mistake. I had not caught on to the fact that I needed to differentiate between Pretty, Cute, Beautiful, and Front Office. My candidates ranged from Plain Janes to Lower Middle Class. None were destined to assist the movers and shakers of River Oaks, however competent they were.

My job at Quest was over. My own quest was not. My unrest of months had come to a critical juncture, and now I had to figure out what to do with my life.

About nine months before that assaulting July day, I had been a passenger in the car of the district manager for Woman's World. I loved working for this man. He was funny, fair, and told great stories. He was interested in all his managers as people. We were driving back west from visiting a store on the far east side of Houston, rising up and over one of the many I-10 overpasses that pass as hills in that flat part of the country. As we crested the hill, he asked how I felt about being in retail. He knew that I had a master's in teaching and a background in the arts. My response is vivid to me to this day: I said that I felt that my time in retail was a time of creative incubation. I felt guilty about not leading a more meaningful, creative life, because even though a well-laid-out store with attractive displays benefited from an artful eye, it did not matter to the world. I told him that I had this sense that something big was going to happen, and that I was getting ready for it without really knowing. Telling him that made the whole concept of An Interesting Future seem like an inevitable thing. Fate was headed my way as I was heading out the Katy Freeway.

And now fate was hitting the fan—or *was* that fate?

What did I want to do? I knew I still could not bear to go back to the disappointment of working for public schools. Retail held no meaning for me. My art was not good enough for me to make a living it. I had failed as a headhunter. So I looked into my heart. I used creative visualization.

My husband, Richard, taught me the power of creative visualization. In the college classes he taught about Affective Education (now it is referred to as Social-Emotional Learning), he would use guided exercises to help folks to learn about themselves. He frequently used one called "Stump, Stream, Cabin." You sat quietly and comfortably, eyes closed, and listened as he slowly talked through the visualization.

"Imagine yourself in a beautiful forest," he would say. "Look around you. See the trees. What kind are they? Can you smell them? Feel the forest floor beneath your feet. Now see a stump, a tree stump. Approach it, touch it. Sit on it if you like. How does that feel? Now imagine you *are* the stump. How does the forest look from your vantage? How does it feel? Are there animals around you? People? Are you a fresh stump, or a weathered one? What is your bark like?

"Now leave the stump. Look over and see that there is a stream. Walk over to it. Can you hear it? Smell it? Touch the water. Is it cold? Do you taste it? Is the water fast or slow? Now be the stream. Feel yourself moving along. Feel the bottom of the stream. Is it sandy, or full of pebbles, rocks, or boulders? Do you have fish or other animals? Is there anybody around you? How do you feel?

"Now leave the stream. Look over and see a cabin in the woods. What does it look like? Is it large or small? How is it made? Is it occupied? Walk up to it, into it. Now be the cabin. What is inside you? What can you smell? Are there people? What is it like outside? How do you feel?

"Now come back to this room. How was your journey? Did one of the visits—the stump, stream, or cabin, feel better or worse than the others? What did you learn about yourself?"

Dewy-eyed students would look calm but amazed as they revealed their journeys. The visualization uncovered feelings through this poetic journey, and we found a way to ourselves. There were times when I experienced "Stump, Stream, and Cabin" and flat-out rejected the cabin as mildewed, stuffy, and confining, and embraced the stream as my place to be free, to be traveling, to be fresh and unbound. Those were my undergraduate days, my early days of freedom in my new life as an adult. Later, I shocked myself when I found the stump a gratifying place to be, to be a nice place for somebody to seek rest and comfort. And as a young mother, I loved my cabin and the cozy home it created away from the madding crowd. Each journey was revelatory.

So I took an important journey that July after I was fired. I had just turned 30 that month, and it was time to Figure Out Life. I took a journey into my heart, using creative visualization. I wanted to find my heart's desire, my passion, and let it guide me to my next career step. I looked inside at my heart.

And what I found horrified me. It is vivid to me to this day. What I saw, where my heart should be, was one of those little black plastic capsules that was used to hold cartridges of 35mm film. I went to find my heart and found it encased in plastic. Out of touch. I had spent so long in retail, in the unnatural world, in a land of plastic hangers, shiny chrome, and mirrors, that what was real inside was shut away. But it was not gone. I had to pry off the lid of that container and get to what was inside. What did I care about? What had I always wanted to do but had not had the time, the opportunity, or the courage?

Oh, my god. The answer hit me like a tsunami. After all these years, I was still passionate about education. I thought that I had jubilantly left the world of the classroom behind me, but what I felt that I had to do was to show how school *could* and *should* be. I looked around to see what was happening in the world of schooling, to see if I could align myself with someplace that was getting it right. And because I could not find one that met my standards, I would have to do it myself. I would have to put my money where my mouth was and make it happen. I had bitched and moaned for years about how awful schools were, and I had failed to make any big changes or contributions. I had set out to show them how it should be done, but I had gotten burned out. Burnout doesn't happen to people who have no fire to begin with. My fire was an ember in that plastic, which once exposed to air, caught flame. I had to do it: I had to start a school.

Where to begin? Ideas were racing through my head. Where would it be? What would it look like? How do you start a business? Would it be a nonprofit? Where would I get the money? What were the rules and regulations? That tsunami had me swimming and splashing and crashing into ideas, diving into research. It was a vast, murky, sparkling mess. Here I was in a state far from my home, with no education connections, and no family, other than my husband, to support me. We had no savings. What the heck: Why not? There was a lot to be done. But where to begin? My mind had been racing for days. When Richard got home from work, he would go to his walk-in closet to change out of his tie and work clothes into shorts and his trademark short-sleeved shirt in a Hawaiian pattern or vibrant plaid. I followed him in and sat on the floor of his closet, blocking the door. He was trapped into listening to a manic cascade of all the thoughts that I had been having. I had to talk this out! What did he think? What should I do? "That sounds great!" he would say, or "good question."

He suggested that I write down a vision of the school, a vision in which it is already established and successful. From there, I could work backward. And that is what I did. Before I got to the nuts and bolts, I created a vision. A vision that would be the antithesis of my own abhorrent education.

1969, Wisconsin

I let my parents know: I was not going back to school. Not to Lance Junior High School. I was 13 years old, finishing off the eighth grade before it finished me. And it almost had.

Anybody who knows recent American history knows that 1969 was a flashpoint, a crazy, critical time in the life of this country, and a 13-year old was not immune to the viral changes happening in society, especially not for someone as political as I was. Everything was changing, happening fast, Moore's law on speed, on acid. Psychedelic times. Overdoses and the war on drugs. Miniskirts. The race to the moon. Women's Lib. Civil Rights. Martin Luther King. All in the Family. Questioning the old, questioning everything. Don't trust anyone over thirty. Vietnam. The military-indus-trial complex. The medium is the massage. Burning draft cards. College sit-ins. Revolution.

My flashpoint was a nervous breakdown, if you could call it that. I was with my NuTheater gang. We were delightfully smashed into Greg's old sedan. Were there six of us in the backseat, and three in the front? We were a teenage jumble of gangly legs and young flesh, enjoying the ride offered by our theater buddy who drove around town and deposited us individually to our homes after rehearsal. We were too young to drive ourselves, so we depended on the two or three folks in our group who could both drive and get permission to drive others. It was fun, and risky, and intimate without being intimate, which made it safe. We were a close bunch.

Suddenly a Taco Bell semi tractor-trailer towered dangerously outside the car window, up so close, so fast, so threatening. I screamed, and crumbled to the floor, terrified, shaking. "What?!" My friends had no idea what prompted this. "The truck! It was going to hit us!" I told them ,and I could not stop crying and shaking. Whether there was truly any danger I do not know, but none of the others were reacting. The rest of the ride was quiet, and I was the last to be dropped off. Greg dropped off the others, saving me for last. I was shell-shocked and limp. Greg was soothing, leaning me against him, carrying my things into the house. He greeted my surprised parents and told them that he thought I was exhausted, and did they want him to get me upstairs? My parents did not allow guests to the upstairs bedrooms, especially not boys, but something about my disheveled appearance and Greg's cheerful, safe attitude threw them off and they waved him up. I collapsed.

The next day, I made an appointment to see Mr. Leisemann, the guidance counselor at Lance Junior High School.

It was embarrassing, the way that I met Warren Leisemann. I had been flirting with him a few months back as he hung lights at the theater where we were preparing a show for the adult Little Theater in town. He was tall, lanky, and sported a jaunty black beret. I asked him inane things about the lights, and did he help out often, and who did he know, and did he like the show, and all the while I was smiling and paying him lots of attention. He acted charmed and behaved like an adult gentleman should around young teenage girls. Harmless fun. But that next week, I saw him walking the halls of the junior high, and my jaw dropped. "What are *you* doing here?" I demanded of him. My theater life did not show up in my "work" life. He was as out of place as if the Titanic had just docked in front of the school. And the jig was up: he would now know that I was not only a teenager but a severely underaged one who should not be flirting with a guy his age.

"I work here," he smiled at me.

"As *what?*" The slick was run out of me.

"I'm a guidance counselor."

"Whoa," I regained my control. "Can I come see you sometime?" And so I began to visit him. Our safe, connective tissue was to chat about theater and local productions and how those were coming along. He would listen with his long legs splayed very wide, a body language that was appallingly open. He was an excellent listener, and I began to open up to him about how pointless school was, about how stressed I was. It was taking me hours to do my homework, usually until well into Johnny Carson blaring up the stairs to my desk in my bedroom. I would write pages and pages for social studies, for English, for RLSS, for science. None of it was interesting. At all. How did other students manage to get As and still go to bed at a decent hour? Was I doing too much? Overthinking everything? Stretched too thin with theater? I had to do it all, and I had to do it well.

My parents did not push me. They were grateful to have a child who did not need pushing and incentives. Each report card A was worth a dollar at my house, but my dad pulled me aside one day and said that I didn't really need those dollars to do well, did I, so could he just not pay me like he would my brothers and sister? They didn't get the dollars anyway because they did not get the As, except in choir or PE. Sure, I said, because I knew that I got a generous allowance and could earn extra cash if I needed it. My compulsion to get it right and do it well was innate, fed from years of getting it right easily and being the top of my class in elementary school. The only time my parents were compelled to go to school to speak on my behalf was in fourth grade when I got all As in school with the exception of a C in physical education. My father went to the school and let them know that that was unfair because I had put in an A's worth of effort. Just because I couldn't pull my chubby body up for a pull-up should not have brought down my grade. The school changed it, and I had no say in the matter.

Warren's solution to my stress threw me for a loop: Take a Bath. "Why, did I stink?" I asked.

"No," he chortled. "You'll feel better. You need to relax."

"In a bath?!" I asked. "Sit in my own dead skin cells? Baths take so long! The water gets cold!"

"Add more hot water," he said.

"A shower is faster!" I objected.

"That's the point." he argued. "You need to just sit and breathe."

And so I took a bath. Mind racing, lists ticking off in my head, I took a bath and bided my time until I could bounce out and get back to work. But the bath worked, and I slogged out, wrung out, not as tense, but still with a long to-do list of pointless, boring work to do.

So by that day when I entered the junior high school office and requested an appointment with Warren, that day after my nervous breakdown, he knew what had led up to my crisis. He labeled my experience as an "identity crisis," which made little sense to me because I knew who I was and what I cared about—and what I loathed. I hated school and the effort that it took for me to jump through all their stupid pointless hoops.

I was called out of typing class on the public address system to report to the office. Classmates glanced with detached curiosity: What did *you* do? I gladly gathered up my books and trekked down the long, linoleum corridor, past tile walls and safety-glass doors, rows upon rows of metal lockers, and found a place on the bench in the office until Warren summoned me back to his office. My back to the glassed door, I cried and cried and cried. I was done. I could not do it anymore. I had no hope. When I had broached the subject of finding another school with my parents, they ruled out each of my suggestions. They would not consider The Prairie School, a private school where my theater friends were excited about their learning and where their projects reflected the students' interests. Just because Jeffrey goes there, that does not make it a good school, they said, and would not give it further consideration. They did not like Jeff.

Jeff was a brilliant genius, no doubt about it, and I came from parents who were skeptical about brilliant, artistic types, especially those with long hair and blue jeans. And he was half Italian, which made him even shadier in their eyes. Jeff was three years older than me, with a mop of brown, curly hair, and wire-rimmed glasses that framed his startling blue eyes. We had met through the summer traveling children's theater sponsored by the city Parks Department. He was charismatic, creative, funny, and prone to moods. He understood what it was like to deal with idiots, and he too found a wonderful release through theater. In Cinderella, he played the king and I was the fairy godmother. The director, Anna Antaramian, was a college student of theater and a force of nature despite being barely five feet tall and only 100 pounds. She had a dramatic Armenian nose and a full head of wild, black, wavy hair. Her large, brown eyes looked intensely and her tiny hands and thin fingers darted expressively. She took all of us young theater babies under her little wing and fed our love of the stage. She would host play-reading discussions in her basement. We'd share snacks and break into show tunes. She was, essentially, the adult sponsor of our little group. And our little group became a theater company, NuTheater Productions, graduating from the Parks Department-sponsored summer plays to become an independent company. Kenosha's adult Little Theater had gone bankrupt, the victim of grandiosity and overreaching dreams. I was in its death-knell production of *Little Me*, an ironically misnamed musical that lasted four hours and had a cast of 50 or so; that is where I met Warren Leisemann. So our energetic little band of teenagers strove for the opposite of that bloated production. Alternatively, we wanted to fill the void with our counterculture productions. We wanted to avoid "romp and stomp insanity" and produce shows that were smaller, artsy, and had a message. Jeffrey appointed himself president, and I was vice president. He had the charisma, and boys and girls flocked to work with him and bask in his attention. I had the organizational skills and the follow-up to make sure that rehearsal spaces were arranged, phone calls made, money raised, and bills paid. I designed advertising posters, sold ad space, and sang in the chorus while better divas took lead roles.

We started with *The Apple Tree* (Jeffrey had the lead, teamed with the gorgeous voice of Sandy Neuens), followed by *Stop the World, I Want to Get Off* (Jeffrey had the lead, teamed with gorgeous voice of Sue Cibrario). Then came *Celebration* (Jeffrey had the lead, teamed with the gorgeous voice of Renee Hammond). We rehearsed on weekday evenings or weekends, bouncing to whatever free spaces we could beg, like church meeting halls, or—my favorite—the basement of the KYF (Kenosha Youth Foundation), all old linoleum, knotty pine, and strange nooks and crannies in a building that housed men down on their luck, a swimming pool, badminton courts, and architecture that looked more like a big sandstone castle than a community center. I made certain that ashtrays were empty, the accompanist's pages were turned, and the chairs were folded up and put away before we left.

It was tough to find guys for plays. These were the days just before Gay Pride made it to the Midwest. The adult Little Theater would recruit men from the Great Lakes Naval Station just across the border in Illinois. Part of my father's disdain of Jeffrey was certainly partly because Father was convinced that Jeffrey must be gay because of his passion for musical theater and artsiness — an accusation against which I vehemently argued, because I said that one did not indicate the other. I told him that Jeffrey had lots of girls after him, but that I was not one of them. Back then, it was a very negative thing to call somebody homosexual. It was considered deviance. At the time, homosexuality was just coming out the closet. *The Boys in the Band* was a Broadway hit, bringing homosexuality into the public consciousness and discussion. Those were the days of *Free to Be You and Me*, in which it was championed that there were all kinds of ways to be, that you did not have to conform to how others felt you should dress or behave, or who you could love. Like I said, 1969 was a watershed year for revolutionary change.

Marty Andersen was one of the straight boys in our casts. Slim, dark, Italian, and cute, the other boys liked him, and he was an intellectual equal. He was in the ensemble, and he played a stillborn baby in *Stop the World*. Jim Kurz was a close friend of Jeff's, a tall, thin, mop-haired funny guy. He had been a thalidomide baby—one of the infants born with malformed limbs in the 1950s and 1960s to women who'd taken the drug thalidomide during pregnancy—and he sported a fascinating, scissoring hook that he controlled with two little nubs below his elbow. Louie Mattioli was the other main boy in our company, and Louie had terrific talent. He had a pitch-perfect, mellow baritone, and despite his giant feet, he moved with as much loose-limbed grace as a white adolescent could muster. He and I were an item when we were twelve. At theater parties, we would sometimes sit and make out for an hour while the others chattered away manically. My favorite mash note ever was from Louie: he had typed a heart with LM & LL in the middle—no easy feat with a manual typewriter! He was the good father in my stage debut as a witch in the summer children's theater production of *Hansel and Gretel,* and he was the sheepdog, a pirate, and milquetoast father in *Peter Pan;* I played Wendy. Once Jeffrey went away to college, Louie got the leads in NuTheater productions, starting with *The Roar of the Greasepaint, the Smell of the Crowd,* which I directed. We listened to Broadway cast albums on my little portable record player and shared rides to rehearsals.

Back in the counselor's office on the day after the breakdown, I was wrung out. I had cried for hours, the students had long gone, and the school was locking up. "Should you call your parents?" he asked. I couldn't bear to go home. They wouldn't understand. I needed to be with somebody who understood me, somebody who could listen with empathy, not with confusion. I should let them know not to worry, but I wanted to go to Jeffrey's. I wanted to talk to his mother. I could take a cab over to their house on the other side of town. I had never taken a cab in my life, but it was the only escape I could imagine that would not involve facing my parents. If it had been today, I could have texted friends for help, but communication was not so easy back then. I called Jeffrey's mother, and she said that I could come over. I called my mother to let them know not to worry, but she told me that I could not go, that she was coming to school to pick me up. I sighed, resigned to black despair, and went home in mute catatonia.

"What is *wrong* with you?" My parents cornered me. There was no way that they could understand. How could their star student—the only one of six kids to do well in school—hate school? It had to be something else, probably that damn theater and those crazy hippie kids she was hanging out with. What could she be mixed up with?

"I'm not going back to school. I'll finish out the year, but please help me to find someplace else."

I asked them to consider Interlochen Arts Academy in Michigan, a college prep boarding school with a famous arts program, a place where I could get an education *and* do theater. My parents did not look at books or promotional materials. They had heard all that they needed to know: it had theater and the arts, so it could not be good for getting a real education. So my father asked around and found a neighbor who had considered sending his daughter to a boarding school up north. We drove up to Beaver Dam, Wisconsin, for an interview. I went down to Lake Forest to take an entrance test. Teenagers lounged around on the floors of the elite prep school, clinging to one another in lazy, disinterested piles. I passed the test without a problem, and Wayland Academy would welcome me in the fall. The hardest thing to leave would be my theater family, but the school had a theater department, so there was hope.

So I trudged through the soul crushing of the rest of the school year, going through the motions and suffering its impersonal indignities. For example, PE continued to mean getting graded on dressing out for class in our snazzy blue one-piece playsuits that snapped up the front. Part of our grade included taking a shower, and teachers stood by with a clipboard to mark that you had showered after class. They would only allow a certain number of showers behind a private shower curtain during your "time of the month." Scofflaws who claimed to have a period more often than the allowed quota were disciplined.

Another junior high modesty challenge was that the days of the miniskirt had begun, but unfortunately, they began before the days of pantyhose. I remember the daylong wrestling matches to tug my skirt down to cover the garter snaps on the pretty little flowered panty girdles that held up my thigh-high stockings, purchased with my allowance from the discount store at the local strip mall. Girls were not allowed to wear slacks to school, not even in the sub-zero Wisconsin winters. Dad would drive me to school so I would not have to walk the mile in the cold, but he would not heat the car first. He scoffed when I complained about those cold vinyl seats on my bare thighs. It is no wonder my sister and I each headed south as soon as we could after high school, while our brothers remained in the North.

Hair was another struggle. I was born with wild, curly hair, but without the talent to do a thing with it. My big sister was a natural, and she could be bribed to set my hair on giant rollers and beer cans to give it the stylish, smooth look. When I did it myself, my hair sported errant road bumps from the hairpins and misdirected chunks of hair that had been improperly wound around the cans. So it was worth it to me to give her a dollar or write a paper for her in exchange for her deft work with a rattail comb and a big jar of Dippity-Do. We shared a bonnet style hair dryer, and it would take at least an hour to dry our hair; that hot air, secured with elastic around our forehead and the nape of our neck, would dry out my eyeballs if I tried to read while baking away the frizz. We would emerge with what looked like a red zipper around our hairlines from the elastic.

The roar was too loud to be able to speak on the phone at the same time. When we didn't have the patience or time to sit under the dryer, we would sleep in those big cans and spiky curlers, waking with a headache and a stiff neck. We tried Curl Free, a stinky hair relaxer, and that would help for a while. I did not go so far as to iron my hair as my sister did. But those humid weather sent us diving into our drawer full of scarves, handmade headbands, and cute little triangles of fabric that matched our outfits. Hair was a very big deal and a big time waster.

Despite the fact that I would be leaving Lance Junior High, the school insisted that I register for their 9th grade classes for the fall. This led to my small but important victory in junior high school: I battled the sexism in the course offerings—and won! In seventh grade, every single girl was required to take home economics, a class where we learned to cook and sew. All the boys took industrial arts, where they learned drafting and woodworking. This adherence to sexist pigeon-holing continued in the 8th and 9th grade course offerings. I petitioned to be allowed to take the boys' drafting class in ninth grade, and the school board changed its policy to allow me and any other girl into those classes previously reserved only for boys. A new era had begun. I did not stick around to take advantage of it, however.

I did keep talking with Jeffrey's mom throughout my teen years. Virginia Hunter was the mother I thought I should have had. She read books and learned all she could to help her son. She fought the schools to do right by him. Once a teacher accused him of plagiarism, saying no junior high student could have written the paper that he turned in; he was deeply upset and his mother raised hell with them. She got him admitted to the Prairie School on a scholarship. She nursed him through his bouts of depression and supported his artistic efforts. She allowed him to host parties for his theater pals and ran interference with his macho father, a firefighter. It was from Virginia that I learned about giftedness, that I learned about an alternative education movement, and that I learned about myself. She decided that I was gifted and convinced the school to test me. While I was no genius like her son, she helped me to understand why I was having such a hard time with schooling. She and I spoke a lot, because if Jeffrey was busy, or too depressed, or out whenever I called to make our theater plans, Virginia was interested in speaking with me. Sometimes her ideas were a little off, like when she declared that my excess energy was because of my strong libido. I was 13 years old and didn't have a boyfriend—what did I know of libido? Wasn't that just a sex drive? She persuaded me to take a community college course that used Eda LeShan's taped programs about early childhood as their discussion base—my first child-centered education class before I was even in high school. With Virginia, I could pour my heart out to an adult who understood about the foibles of public school, who could see that my despair was not just adolescent drama. She knew what I was up against. I did not baffle her as I did my own parents.

That summer of '69 was the summer before boarding school and it was the summer of *Mother Courage*. Anna had the lead in Brecht's dark play about war, and she was believable, all raw bone and love and hardened oak, pulling her wagon through despair. Jeff's little sister Nina was stunning and heartbreaking. Eric played the priest, with a haunting deep voice—a tall scarecrow with big eyes and long, tortured fingers. "In the first hour of the day, our Lord Jesus Christ was...." I can still see and hear him. Jeff must have played a soldier, but he was struggling *not* to be one that summer. His draft number had been drawn, and it was a scary low number. He would not go to Vietnam. What would he do? He would go to college in the fall, to New College in Florida, an ultra-liberal school that attracted artsy students and political free thinkers. But that summer was about Mother Courage, and they took that show on the road to campgrounds and to Kemper Hall. They touched the nerve of everyone who was struggling with the war and with the anguish and wrenching it caused the country.

It was also the summer of the moon walk. Jeff's parents were glued to the TV set, in amazed awe at the first step for man, the giant step for mankind. Why weren't we watching with them? they barked in annoyance, then turned back to the TV. His dad's eyes had tears in them. Didn't we see how important this was, how proud we should be, how amazing it was?! To us, sure, it was cool, but we had life and death and art in front of us. We had grown up with the space race. It was always going to happen. We had sat with our elementary classes and listened to the radio as the Gemini capsules splashed down. We had worked the "new math" that was to prepare our generation to have the skills it needed to beat the Russians in the space race. Walking on the moon was supposed to happen. We were not supposed to be sent to Southeast Asia to die.

That summer before, in 1968, I had spent time outside Kenosha's factory gates wearing a miniskirt to pass out flyers to the laborers, asking them to vote for Les Aspin for Congress. My agreement to canvass for Les Aspin, to work the phones at his headquarters, was part of the bargain that got Marty to be in our shows. He would fill his role as a rare male in our plays, and we would help him with his work with Young Democrats. Les Aspin was the candidate for the times: he was a popular political science professor with a pretty blond wife with stylish, long, straight hair. Even his bumper stickers were hip, not the standard-issue red, white, and blue but a vivid spring green—a chartreuse that felt fresh and new and full of hope. We were politically vocal and spoke out against Richard Nixon and his shady ways, hoping against unsatisfied hope that Hubert Humphrey could defeat the war machine and bring us peace. Politics mattered. At The Prairie School, which Jeff, Marty, and Jim attended, they discussed current events and politics and the history of Vietnam. At my school, we learned about the Pilgrims and Manifest Destiny. Little did I know that my new boarding school was even less political.

Wayland Academy was in Beaver Dam, Wisconsin, a little town that welcomed folks on the way in with a giant billboard announcing itself as "Home of 14,000 Busy Beavers." Politically and geographically, it was closer to Horicon Marsh, a major stopping point for migratory geese, than it was to the political hotbed Madison. Madison, where students held sit-ins and where the student production of *Peter Pan* stayed true to the script but took a decidedly more political interpretation: the Lost Boys were stoners and played in the nude, the Indians were long-suffering, angry Native Americans (those were the days when Marlon Brando sent a pseudo Native American up to claim his Academy Award), and the pirates were the big bad police, who in those days were treated as pigs who put down the student protests. Yes, Beaver Dam was 42 miles from Madison by car, but 400 miles apart in spirit. The town bakery did sell fabulous apple cider donuts in the fall, though. Wayland was having its own version of a liberal uprising: just that year, girls no longer had to dress up for dinner: we could wear our regular school skirts to dine. Back in Kenosha, girls were winning the fight to be able to wear slacks—even jeans!—to school, and boys could wear their hair long. Hair wars were happening all over the country in those days, with parents suing school districts for sending their children home to get a haircut. Once the lawyers and the ACLU got involved, restrictions relaxed.

Wayland gave me perspective: While public junior high had seemed pointless and dreary, ninth grade at Wayland was only a little more inspired academically. The curriculum was rigorous and about a year ahead, but what was wonderful was the independence our class felt. The freshman class was small, and there were only eight of us boarding girls, so we had the first floor of the dormitory to ourselves. The floor parents were busy with an infant, and because they were across the building, they never hovered or interfered with us. We were our own tight and friendly little crew. And I had never been around rich kids before. There were upper-middle- class students there from town—the "townies"—but most of the boarding students were there either because their parents were captains of industry and didn't have time to parent between society fundraisers and business trips, or because their parents just didn't want a teenager around so they chose to leave their rearing to somebody else. That was my roommate's situation, and she cried every day for the first three months. It was dreary. Eventually we switched rooms so I could get relief and she could get a fresh supply of sympathy. I missed her tales of de-tasseling corn in the Iowa corn fields and her stories about her grossly-infected toe which she had slashed with her hoe when she was weeding corn while barefoot. I did not miss hearing that her parents did not want her, even though her father should know better as a psychology professor at Grinnell. My new roommate was a school legacy because her superstar older sister had graduated from Wayland, and she had big shoes to fill. Shelley Greenwood was a short little dynamo with long frizzy hair and boundless enthusiasm. She was the first person I ever knew to own a cassette player, and she had great taste in music. She turned me on to Laura Nyro, and I played show tunes for her. She was the first person I knew to own a hand-held hair dryer, and she came back from spring break looking fabulous with a professionally blown-dry haircut, all smooth and shiny. I brought back heavy glass bottles of Tab, in those days before plastic disposable bottles, and we stored them between the glass and screens of our tall dorm-room windows. One frigid night the bottles exploded and froze into a beautiful brown iceberg of shattered glass and saccharine.

Jeffrey wrote me long letters to cheer me on and keep me posted about theater. Those were the days of letter writing, in cursive script on colorful stationery. It was always fun to draw silly pictures or funny sayings on the envelopes. I would write letters as a reward to myself for getting my work done. I would write not only to Jeff but to Louie, Sue, and my family. I kept those letters and have them to this day. Deep thoughts, moral support, and clever observations. Pages, front and back. Long-distance calls were expensive, and costs varied by time of day and day of week: after 5:00

pm, the price went down, and after 10:00 pm, they went down further to the weekend rate. You would time your long conversations for the weekends or evenings. At home, I was not allowed to make long-distance calls, and the phone bills were policed to make sure I didn't. To make a call at Wayland, you would close yourself into the phone booth across from the mailboxes and drop in your coins or make a pricey collect call. If you would be receiving a call, you made arrangements in advance for what time they would call you and on which day, and you would wait by the phone. If a call came out of the blue, whoever was nearby would answer it and send somebody running to find you. Nobody had phones in their room or even on the upper floors of the dorm.

If the snail mail and lack of cheap phone access didn't isolate us, the school did a fine job on its own. Only one newspaper was delivered to campus. I had heard that a senior subscribed to *Time* magazine. After my recent political activism, I felt like I was exiled to an unreal rabbit hole. The older girls discussed their coming out parties, which back then had nothing to do with sexual preference but everything to do with pearl necklaces and formal attire. And speaking of parties, prom had an equally surreal feel. I do not know whose mother scored the decor from some charity ball, but I have never seen another high school do it up more beautifully. The gym was transformed with a giant tent within, and in that tent was an actual flowing stream, which you crossed over a cute wooden bridge. Live flowering trees were lit up and set all around. Fountains trickled, and a live band had everybody hopping. It was stunning.

I was accepted by my peers at Wayland—admired even. That was a first. I was no longer The Brain or Miss Organized. I was liked! What had changed? I had no idea. I was voted class secretary, a purely social acknowledgment, on the second week of school at a meeting I never attended. I went steady with Andy Aylward, whose family's enterprise you can still read on manhole covers all over the country. He had doleful brown eyes and a sweet disposition, unlike his elder brother who was rumored to bite the heads off rodents. He was lanky, with a shock of auburn curls. We never really bonded, but he was pleasant enough company and a nice kisser. He shivered in his tawny suede jacket, but he looked cool. I got through the winter of trudging around the campus by buying a vintage beaver fur coat from the Salvation Army. It was perfect, long and sensuous. With my hand-crocheted brimmed hat, I was warm and happy not to look like my peers in their short wool pea-coats.

Andy and I were in most classes together, and his agony in French was even worse than mine—he just couldn't get the accent. And Madame was a stickler for accents! She was from Belgium and spoke not a word in English to us—it was total immersion. The program was the Chilton Method, which used a book containing only pictures. We never looked at a written French word until the last month of school. We watched the filmstrip that accompanied the picture book, frame by frame, repetition after repetition, which was all repeated again in the required language lab periods, where we each sat in an individual carrel, listened to tapes, and spoke into a microphone. Madame would listen in from a booth at the front of the room, where she kept an eye on us and would occasionally interrupt to correct us individually. The tedium was beyond belief, but words started coming automatically. I did not realize just how much I had learned until the next year when I was back in a traditional foreign language curriculum in public school. In French II, I tried hard to catch a few winks by shading my face in my hand, elbow on the desk, pretending to study the book, but that damn teacher caught me every time. That traditional French II class was mostly review and vocabulary building, but it lacked the agony and ecstasy of the Chilton Method. I don't think that a one of us got out of that prep-school French class without crying in frustration at least once, in class or in private. Yet thirty-five years later, when I saw my boarding school roommate for the first time since then, we both broke into a broad, melodramatic recitation of the poem that we had to memorize for a French contest that spring—*Il pleure dans mon coeur come il pleut sur la ville. Quelle est cette langueur qui pénètre mon coeur?*—and we broke out laughing, in wonder that it stuck. But how could it not? We must have practiced it a hundred times.

I did not have to live without theater in Beaver Dam. The theater teacher took me up on my offer to bring in NuTheater to perform their latest production at the Academy, and it was opened to the public. I was proud, and I was also nostalgic, wishing I could go back home with them at the end of the evening. But the Academy produced *West Side Story* that spring, and I made callbacks for Anita, but an upperclassman got the role. I was in the chorus as a Spanish girl. It was pretty funny watching all us white prep school kids trying to play warring hoodlums. Can after can of spray-on hair black couldn't hide our Western European blandness. The dancing was a real workout, and with that and running track for PE that spring, I got down to my lowest weight ever. I looked and felt great.

But still, I wanted out.

I loved my independence there I loved being responsible for myself, having buddies around all the time, having a boyfriend, wearing what I wanted—within the school guidelines, of course. We still had to wear skirts to class and to dinner. I loved my art class and could really feel my skill growing under the persistent coaching from Mrs. Bev Dohmann. Art class was a haven where our small class gathered around the big table in what used to be a locker room off the gym, with its big block-glass windows softening the natural light. We had great slabs of wood onto which we taped our art and then filed them into vertical slots in the wall until the next day's class. Gallons of tempera paints lined another wall. We learned to mix them like champs as Mrs. Dohman was not into buying fancy colors: we did our own blending. We worked in pastels and charcoal, too. I still have pictures from that class hanging on the walls of my home. It was a productive year for my art.

We took our meals in a light-filled dining hall packed with round tables. Breakfast and lunch were cafeteria style, served up with the help of students who were on work study. Dinners were family style, with a teacher or house parent at each table. The boys had to wear their ties and jackets and pull the chairs out for the girls. We were assigned a different table each week to mix up the conversations. We learned to "offer to the right and pass to the left." You did not eat until each person had food. Chicken was served at least three times each week, and you could not pick it up with your fingers. I wonder how many surgeons got their early start in that cafeteria: you had to be deft with a fork and knife to cut all the morsels from those bony birds without your fingers. But once a month, the girls pigged out in the dorm basement. It was called the Y, and there was nothing at all about those evenings that remotely resembled the YWCA organization, but all our manners went out the window and we gorged on spaghetti, always spaghetti. It was a craven kind of fun to get away from the tablecloths and polite conversation.

In May, I let them know that I was not returning. I was itching to return to the real world and my activism. My parents did not mind saving the money that would have paid for tuition. My friends there were baffled and tried to talk me out of it. I didn't know how to explain, so when anybody asked why I was leaving, and many did, I said that the pancakes were always cold. They were. But my peers there had no idea what kind of life I had come from. In Beaver Dam, we were in an isolated bubble at boarding school. At home, life had been about politics and striving, drama and edgy conversations. Nothing at the Academy mattered. It was comfy and classy, but it was not real. It was not real life. I wanted the real thing.

Public Again

But I was oh, so scared to go back to public school. I was afraid that the black gloom would return, that my hatred for the inanity would send me over the edge again. If I could have more independence, more say in what I did in high school there, maybe it would be all right. My big sister, four years older than I, had just graduated and really liked the high school principal. They were friendly, a closeness forged of the many times that she was in mischief in school. She got me a meeting with him, and I was charmed. He was friendly, not at all distant and impersonal like other school leaders. He had black hair and dazzling, sparkling blue eyes which I doodled in my notes that day. He could see no reason why I couldn't arrange a modified schedule, independent studies, and more art and drama classes than sophomores usually took. I transferred in, full of hope.

And that summer he got promoted to superintendent of schools. The new principal said that he did not know what I had arranged with the former principal, but that I would take the regular schedule. And my unhappiness cranked up again. The English class was studying many of the same books that I had studied the year before at the Academy. I was able to arrange to do independent research about the playwright Edward Albee. I had directed a one-act by him, *The Sandbox,* back in junior high and wanted to learn more. I was allowed to spend the times that the class worked on *Julius Caesar,* which I had studied at the academy, to do my research in the resource center—as long as I did the *Caesar*-related project and took the unit final. The project was engaging enough—we had to cut out and paste pictures that related to the themes from a dozen quotations from the play—but I did poorly on the test. I had not re-read the play before the test, and many of the questions demanded an intimate knowledge of the details. The teacher was unhappy, and I was dismayed at the test's focus on memorizing minutiae rather than focusing on the big picture. And when I turned in my personal research paper, the teacher's mustache twitched with animated disappointed. Where were my transitions? The structure was not parallel. I had many errors. Hadn't anyone ever taught me to write? No, nobody had. I usually got As on my papers either because they were better than those of my peers or because they had original thought behind them. And that is when I began to learn to write. The next year, my writing began to develop when I took creative writing with Fern Hoeft and hung out in the newspaper office, although I refused to take journalism class. She was an excellent editor and only let one mistake slip by, and that was to teach me a lesson in a way that paid me back for my lousy attitude.

I liked the journalism office. It was cozy, with several long tables pushed together and not much room around it. It was a tiny zone of respite lodged between the enormous, noisy cafeteria and the smaller, noisy, sloppy commons area. This was where smart, witty kids hung out. I could volunteer to make myself useful, which gave me access to this exclusive room. I could type over 100 words per minute, so I would pound out rewrites on the special paper, with carbons. I could cut out articles after they were returned from the typesetter, and somebody else would take the rubber cement and lay out the pieces. Back then, cut-and-paste was literally cutting and pasting, and laying out was literally laying pieces out on the paper. The galley had to be taken to a printer to be printed, so all that work and expensive outsourcing meant that the fancy, important newspaper came out only once a month. There was a rough, weekly edition that was mimeographed, and more of my writing made it in there. That is where Letters to the Editor were published, or silly cartoons, or more timely news about sports and clubs. The newspaper office was just below the yearbook office, where similar manual labor was needed to produce the big, expensive hardbound volumes. I was enlisted to write photo captions and headlines. I loved writing headlines for articles, loved the combination of word-craft and math. Capital letters were worth two or three points, and wide letters were more points than an *i* or an *l*. If the article's column allowed you sixteen points, or if the article was laid out over three columns for fifty points, it was an art to catch the reader's eye with a full use of the space and a witty synopsis of the article. We did not expand the print or justify it like we do now with word processing.

Tremper High School was huge and impersonal. My graduating class had 750 students, and the school over 2,000. When I hear about high schools of 5,000 and more today, my heart clenches. The school was overcrowded, suffering from the Baby Boom. Hallways were stuffed, and crossing from one side of the hallway to the other during the four minutes between classes was like crossing an interstate during rush hour or trying to get out of a rip tide: you don't swim against it, rather you ride it out until you can paddle diagonally and then walk back down the shore. If you bent over to get a drink from the fountain, you would be rear-ended and possibly chip a tooth. If you had to get from the gym to the art class on the opposite side of the complex, you better be the first one out the door and not need to stop at your locker. You planned your locker visits carefully because you could not get to it after every class. Nobody carried a backpack in those days, and your arms wrapped around the binders, folders, and heavy textbooks clutched to your midsection. The only time anybody went outside was for PE or to sneak out for a smoke. The parking lot was patrolled during the day for class-skippers. If you left campus, you needed a pass. Sneaking away was a thrill.

Math teachers and I did not speak the same language. I do not think in symbols; even acronyms throw me for a loop. At the Academy, I spent the first marking period scowling at the math teacher, sending disdain his way as he dragged us through pre-algebra, and my grade of C was a direct result of my expressed attitude. The following grading period, I did the same quality of work but decided to smile and to look interested. My grade went up to an A. At public school, I found geometry to be ridiculous. We spent a lot of time writing proofs, and mine did not pass muster. I really felt that the steps that I took proved whatever mathematical point I was supposed to prove, but the teacher felt that there was a different, better route and I never understood why it was better. I wished that he would stay in the world of coaching golf. The algebra II/trigonometry teacher, Mr. Bussard, was a large, grumpy man who purportedly bartended nights. That was my first-hour class, and he was not a warm presence in the morning. His teachings were baffling, and were it not for my friend Betsy and our long phone calls to explain the lessons to one another, I never would have learned enough to pass the class. His teaching method consisted of humiliating students. We would be summoned to the chalkboard to work a homework problem, and he would impatiently make fun of the tack that we would use to get to the answer, and then he would show us the right way.

One weary morning, Bussard was verbally humiliating a gentle boy who was at the board, struggling to work through a problem while the teacher berated his lack of insight. I could see the back of the boy's neck redden, and I felt his pain at this big bully.

Enough.

"Shut up," I said.

"What did you say?" Bussard turned to me, angry.

"I said shut up," I responded quietly, cowed by his anger. "He's trying, and you're being mean, not helping."

"Go to the office."

"Gladly." I picked up my things and proceeded to my counselor's office.

The counselor was not a Warren Leisemann. This counselor had a caseload of about 500 students, and his job was more about writing college recommendations and adjusting schedules. He was surprised to see me. I told him what happened, and that I felt justified. He said that I had to go back to class, and that I should apologize to the teacher for my rudeness.

"But what about *his* rudeness? He was torturing that boy!"

"But you are the student and you need to apologize."

"I'll think about it. But not today."

The next morning, dull and early, I met Bussard at the door to his class and apologized for saying shut up. He stood tall and droopy-eyed but did not look me in the face. He mumbled something, and the class continued as usual. I got the feeling that somebody on the staff talked to him, perhaps the counselor. His harassment of struggling students seemed to abate somewhat, and I made it out of the class alive, thanks to Betsy.

Betsy Schindler was the closest person I had to a best friend in high school. She was tall and preppy, from an upper-middle-class, sophisticated family of super-high achievers. Her father was a vice president of Snap-On Tools. They belonged to a country club. Their home was tastefully furnished, and she dressed in corduroys and crew neck sweaters. Betsy was the youngest in her family, with two older brothers. One would go on to be a doctor (my sister had gone steady with him) and the other a famous illustrator of children's books. She was gifted and creative, too, and we had known each other since junior high school. Our only class together was math, but she was a yearbook editor, and I helped her out. Together, we figured things out via long phone conversations and we had great laughs. She had nothing to do with my theater world, and I had nothing to do with her jock world of sports, but we were friends. She did not hate school and did not share my misery. She was a proud individual, unique and special. In our math class, she did all her calculating and rough notes on a Magic Slate—one of those toys that kids would play with, the kind with a clear plastic sheet over a black, waxed cardboard. You wrote on the clear overlay with a red, plastic stylus, and the pressure caused the clear plastic to temporarily embed in the black wax, revealing your writing on the plastic. When you were finished with your writing or drawing, you would lift the plastic sheet, and your writing would magically disappear except for its impression in the wax, mixed with the hundreds of other impressions you had laid. Nobody else used one. She was ahead of her time for not killing trees unnecessarily. And yes, we all used plastic slide rules, as calculators were not portable, inexpensive, or used in schools then.

Betsy was a student council representative, and she wanted to run for student council president. She would be great: she had tons of ideas for activities, and nobody worked as hard as she would to pull them off. She had political tact and offended no one. She was known for her brains and athletic talent. There was just one problem: she was a girl. Girls could be secretary or treasurer or, if she were incredibly popular, vice-president. But girls were no more likely to be voted president of Student Council than a woman was to be elected president of the United States. So I became her campaign manager.

To get Betsy elected would be groundbreaking, a real coup, a monumental first. How would we get the dull, unwashed masses to vote for a brain, somebody who was neither popular nor beautiful? She had no cute boyfriend whose shirttail she could ride. The legacy of her brothers meant nothing to the current student body. Once we knocked out the day's trig torture, we discussed strategy. What did students care about? We paced around her neighborhood, debating whether to blanket the school with clever, catchy posters with her brother's amazing art. If we appealed to what the kids wanted—impossible freedoms, something for nothing, popularity—we were doomed. But if we appealed to what the kids really could get, made them feel that those kids were worth her effort, that she would work for them, then we might have a chance. The posters were great, even if her brother, like any red-blooded brother, did charge her a hefty sum for his work. As her manager, I had to give an introductory speech in front of all 2500 students and faculty in the gym. I did not know that my knees could knock in fear, but they knocked away below my cute little flowered minidress that afternoon when I addressed the crowd. "Betsy is not the most popular student," I told them. "You do not see her riding in the homecoming convertible, but it was probably Betsy who decorated it. You may not see her dancing at the dance, but she is probably the person who hired the band and recruited folks to sell the refreshments. She is not captain of a winning football team, but she wins at tennis and swimming, making our school proud. If you vote for Betsy, you are voting for somebody who is working for you and wants to work even harder for you to make great things happen for our school. Betsy gets things done, for you." And Betsy won. The first female student body president. Maybe that was one of the many, many factors that earned her a spot at Stanford upon her graduation. I have never been prouder of a strategic team effort to accomplish the unprecedented.

In that enormous school, I never found another student who felt as negatively as I did about school. To them, I was a tedious gadfly. In speech class, while other students chose topics such as "The Value of Football" or "Why I Will Join the Marines", I kept crafting speeches about school reform. In order to research for those speeches, I was allowed entrance to the inner sanctum of the teacher's lounge where the books about education were kept in their professional library. When the school board invited the public to come speak at an open meeting to solicit suggestions for improving the school district, I was armed and spoke out. The board members seemed genuinely interested and asked good questions. The next day, I got a phone call from the assistant superintendent, Jim Scanlan, who invited me to be the student representative on that same committee I had addressed. The committee's purpose was to establish school district goals and objectives as part of the district's push for programming, planning, and budgeting: theoretically, the district would follow this committee's recommendations as they established budgeting priorities, putting money toward the highest priority goals. I loved those meetings and we took them very seriously. I helped to craft an excellent document, and my contributions meant something. I do not know whether the district did anything more than put that document on a shelf; I know mine sat proudly on my shelf for years, until I finally realized that committees are where you send outspoken types like me so that their energies and words can be channeled and controlled. At the same time, I felt like I had made a difference, but I doubt that anything changed.

High school was not a place where I thought that I could endure three years. (While other school districts grouped grades 9-12 for a four-year high school, Kenosha grouped grades 10-12 for a three-year high school.) I had returned to public school with a promise of program modifications that would keep my love of learning going, but that hope was dashed when the nice principal left and was replaced with an institution man. You know the type, whether it is in a school system or a corporation—the type of person who is comfortable following the rules without question, without a thought toward the reason behind the rules in the first place nor the heartfelt mission of the operation. Nonetheless, I asked for his help. Couldn't we speed things up so I could get out to the real world? Couldn't I find a way to stop jumping through other people's hoops so that I could learn what I wanted to learn? Outside school, I was learning practical skills and expressing myself artistically through my producing, directing, acting, and marketing of NuTheater. In school, I barely tolerated the tedious trivia that comprised most of my classes. I knew that there were exciting ways to learn, a better rhythm of life. I wanted out. How could I graduate early?

The principal did not know. Nobody had ever asked that before. There were no procedures or policies in place. The state required a certain number of credits, and if I could fulfill those, then the board could vote whether to accept the route that I found. There were no opportunities to take community college classes for dual credit. There were no AP classes, gifted programs, or anything else in place to whet my appetite to stay in school. I knew that dropping out would be a very bad thing and imagined myself working at the Piggly Wiggly. No, I would graduate with all my credits. The only option offered was to take correspondence courses. So that is what I did.

I enrolled in four semesters of correspondence courses through the University of Wisconsin. Of course, there were no online classes back then. While I completed junior English and American history through the mail, I took my senior credits in school. The sticking point for getting the necessary credits for graduation, though, was PE: the state mandated that students needed three years of PE in order to graduate. How would I fit three years into two? I offered a reasoned argument: the goal of that requirement was to maintain a level of physical activity while in school. So by taking PE each year that I was there, I was accomplishing the goal, and the number of years was irrelevant. They did not see it like that. Three years was three years. I suggested that perhaps I could earn the credits outside of school. There were no PE correspondence courses, and students could not earn credit for participating in sports outside of school; that sensible option was twenty years down the road. I suggested that perhaps I could commit to a PE independent study and log the requisite hours of activity through walking and biking. No, the state required PE classes. And thus my loathing of bureaucracies solidified into a lifelong hatred for institutional inflexibility. Their one compromise was to allow me to take junior and senior PE simultaneously. While other students dressed out the required three days a week, I would dress out five days a week; missing the requisite sixth day (three days per week for each of junior and senior PE) was their concession. I would have loved to have had a study hall in order to do my extra load of schoolwork, but they thought that spending all my free time in PE was the better choice.

I gamed the system whenever I could to get a break from those PE classes. A strategy that worked a half dozen times was to corner the assistant principal to discuss my educational philosophy and concerns. He was a sincere conversant and would grimace when I asked for a pass to go back to the PE class that I had missed because of our talk. Another strategy was to discover plantar warts on my feet when it was time for the PE swimming unit. I already was an ace swimmer, and preventing my painstakingly-straightened hair from frizzing around the pool was more than I wanted to manage. A couple times, the PE teacher let me go for a very long walk after I promised sincerely that the fresh air and exercise would do me more good than repeating what I had learned in the PE class the day before. But for the most part, I showed up to PE and gave it a try. And that year, I, the chunky little girl who could never do a pull-up in elementary school learned to climb that daunting rope to the top of the gym ceiling. I learned the rules of basketball, but like I did every year during the basketball unit, I jammed my fingers painfully blue with the hard, heavy ball. I learned the rules of volleyball, which for me was really one rule: get out of the way or get hurt. I learned to shoot a bow and arrow, pole vault, jump hurdles, ballroom dance, dismount from uneven bars, and inflate my street clothes in the pool to use as flotation devices. It was weird the month that I took PE with the boys' class, which was doing gymnastics. I would return to the girls' locker room with white handprints strategically placed on my little blue jumpsuit from where the boys spotted me doing my tricks. In the modern dance unit, I had to choreograph a routine to a song of my choice. It was Melanie's "Little Bit of Me", which was my personal anthem about taking this crazy step to accomplish an early graduation. The lyrics were: "Balanced on the mountain / with the people all around / who say that I've been up too long / and they want to bring me down. Now I don't mind the coming down / it's the way it's gotta be / but I hope I got left inside / just a little bit of me." I chose to work solo, and I was the last student to perform for the teachers. I remember feeling nervous and self-conscious, as I had put myself out there emotionally and physically.

Afterward, as the teacher was chatting with her student teacher, I asked how I did, or what I got, and she said that she would tell me tomorrow. No feedback. I felt vulnerable, insecure. What I had done was not like the routines of the other girls. Had they been talking about me? Was it so hard to say that I did well or that it was interesting, at the least?

The correspondence courses were grueling. Each semester-long course consisted of 16 lessons, each of which was the equivalent to a week's work and required from 12-16 pages in written responses to questions about the readings. I took four courses in order to earn the two credits needed to graduate. These were written in longhand, so I wrote at least 800 pages that year. They would get mailed off to the instructor, then returned about 7-10 days later with comments and the new assignment. There were midterms and finals, too. These were in addition to the creative writing, economics, American government, art, novel, and ancient history classes that I took. And, oh yes, chemistry and trig.

My parents made me quit NuTheater. I had become the president when Jeffrey went to college, but it was just too much. I sobbed and protested, which convinced them even more that I was spread too thin. Yes, I was, but I asked them to let me drop classes, not the theater—the theater meant something, was real. To them, the theater was a frivolous nuisance and distraction, it would not lead to any kind of career, and it had me hanging with hippie types. Theater was all about emoting, and they'd had enough of my teenage emoting. My highly dramatic plea did not help my case at all. The theater folded soon after. The group had plenty of actors and artists, but I was the organizer, the one who made sure that things got done.

Getting Through 1972

That school year was all about just getting through. I was no longer a grade monger, and I did not always do my best because some things, as I had learned in junior high school, did not deserve my best. I wrote so many research papers that in not-so-subtle protest, I chose to write a paper about yawning. I was surprised that I had to go back to 19th-century scientific publications to learn about it. I was pleased with myself that I wrote the most comprehensive paper ever written about everything there was to know about the yawn. We exchanged papers in class to give one another feedback, and Scott Meltzer read it and asked, but why do our eyes tear up when we yawn? That was one point that I did not cover! Such an obvious omission! I was quite humbled. How had I missed that?

Most nights I worked on homework until midnight, give or take an hour. My desk was a fancy white French Provincial corner piece with a glass top. A radio played WLS or WXYZ out of Chicago.

The deep voice announced, "SUNDAY at beautiful U.S. 30 dragstrip!"

Feminine voices sang, "What's the weather for the weekend gonna be? Will it be hot? cold? rain? snow? ooo—ooo—ooo—ooo."

"Chicken Man! He's everywhere, he's everywhere!"

I can still hear them.

I had nothing to drink, as we kids were not allowed food or drinks in our bedrooms. Over the desk was my bulletin board, the one place in my mother-decorated room where I could put my personal mark. I loved looking at the quotes and pictures, drawings and calendar. There was that snapshot of four classmates from the Academy, stretched across the busy street in front of the school, arms outstretched to block my car's exit on the last day of school. Jacque's drawing, a riff on the style of Manet and Matisse, was a bright felt-tip marker image of birds and floating and freedom that he said reminded him of me. There was the magazine photo of chimpanzees, with the Shakespeare quote from *Julius Caesar:* "The higher a monkey climbs, the more you see of its backside." There was the photo from Leica magazine that worked like a calming meditative mantra for me: it was of a green d'Anjou pear on a white windowsill, with the window screen behind it gentling the pink tree blossoms out of focus. To this day, I conjure that image to banish ugly sights.

As a reward to myself for my hard work, I would meet Jack for coffee when he was in town from college. We'd go to McDonald's and talk for an hour—or mostly I would talk and vent and kvetch and moan, and he would cheer me on, offer support, listen, and make suggestions. Who was Jack? Well, I married him, but that is another story. Let's get me out of high school.

At one bleak point midwinter of my last year of high school, I remember taking a break in the TV room downstairs. That was a cozy little wood-paneled room with a big upholstered recliner for my father, a smaller upholstered armchair for my mother, a loveseat for anybody else, a coffee table covered with stacks of magazines that only I ever opened, an end table with newspapers and my mother's ashtray, and the big console television, a piece of furniture itself. I was sitting on the floor, my homework before me on the coffee table, staring in the direction of the TV, weary beyond words, when out of the blue, my mother showed an awareness of me I did not know that she had. "Do you need a break?" she asked me. I was floored. I was not used to being noticed. I knew that they did not have a clue of what I was going through and could not begin to understand it. Mother was a high school dropout. I was the oddball of the family, the only child of the six who succeeded in school. Mother offered to send me to Florida for a week to stay with my big brother and his family who lived there. I could sleep on their couch, thaw out from the bleak Wisconsin winter, bring my work with me, and take a break. I took the trip, colored up my pale winter cheeks, and got a lot done. Then it was back home for the final stretch.

My outspoken yap got me in big trouble again that spring. I received a form letter inviting me to be inducted into the National Junior Honor Society. The group did nothing. My grades got me in, but I had been fighting against grade-mongering. My response was to write an opinion letter for the weekly school newspaper. It follows:

To the Editor:

On Wednesday evening of this week myself and several other students will receive the 'distinct honor' of being inducted into the National Honor Society.

"Selection was based on scholastic merit along with recognition of character, service, and leadership," said the letter sent to the parents of the nominees. What a laugh! Making Honor Roll is a matter of knowing how to play the Grade Game. All you have to do is stomach X number of hours in any class so you can repeat what the teacher tells you to know (unless it's a skill course), or at least make a good guess. Too often you're not rewarded for the amount of work you put into the class, or how much productive thinking you do as a result of the class.

I am accepting membership into the Society because it will look good in the records if I apply to work in any more retarded institutions who choose to view the Society's standards of scholastic merit as anything more than fine gamesmanship.

National Honor Society is rewarding the champions of a futile, destructive institution who are lucky (?) enough to know how to play its own game and win. But are they really survivors in an intellectual and moral sense?

Students did not respond to the letter, but teachers read it. I seemed to provoke a sleeping giant, and teachers gave me cold looks or averted their eyes. I received an interoffice mail from the superintendent of schools, the man who made me think I would be OK in public school. That was shocking—a student getting an envelope from the superintendent! In it was a copy of the newsletter and my opinion piece with his comments, written in red. My lead sentence had a glaring English error, which he noted: my wording "myself and several other students" should have named the others first, as in "Several other students and I." Mrs. Hoeft, who regularly prevented me from embarrassing myself in my writing, had intentionally left my carelessness untouched in order to let me hang out there to dry. I deserved it and was humbled. I had the attention at the highest level of the school district, and enough teachers were upset about my letter that they met as a group with the principal, who had me sit outside his office while they were meeting. Some wanted me barred from Honor Society since I clearly did not value it, while others defended my right to my opinion and asserted that I should get the designation since I had earned it. They filed out, and I filed in. The principal told me that I had made a lot of people unhappy, but that I would be inducted.

In 1971, Neil Postman and Charles Weingartner published *The Soft Revolution: A Student Handbook for Turning Schools Around*. I read it many times, trying to learn how to effect change. Clearly I had not taken to heart the chapter that explained why flag burning was a bad idea. While you may understand that a flag is a piece of colorful fabric, to others it may be a symbol of their core values that guide their direction, make them feel safe, gives them community, and justifies their sacrifices. If you burn a flag—and folks were prone to that demonstration in the '60s to protest the Vietnam War—you burn any sympathy that the onlookers may have had for your cause. I had just burned a flag, so to speak, when I burned the National Honor Society and the school's grading system.

I was never certain that I would graduate until very late that spring, when I could prove that I passed my correspondence courses, and the school board voted to accept the credits. I was officially a junior right up to graduation. I could not think beyond Getting Through the Year. While other seniors were deciding on colleges, I had not applied anywhere. If I were going to go to college, I did not want a place that would just make me jump through their hoops. I wanted a school where I could be responsible for what I learned. Goddard College in Vermont was a forerunner in freedom to learn, and it had all kinds of cool and flexible learning going on, but my parents would not consider it because it was a "hippie school." New College in Florida was famous for its flexibility, but when they found out that Jeffrey went there, and when he told me about the flakey students and the dominant drug culture there, that school was out of the question. I gave up looking. The counselor had no suggestions. But one day when I was in the English department resource center, a room managed by Mrs. Hammond, the mother of one of my theater friends, she asked where I was going to college. When I told her my disdain and frustration, she told me that she and her daughter were visiting St. Louis the next week to look at Webster College. They had a fabulous professional residential repertory theater that interested her daughter, but they also had an innovative education department. What's more, the college did not require a basic core curriculum like most colleges did. Did I wish to go with them? Maybe there was hope after all, so I joined Renee and her mother.

It was a short, 45-minute flight to St. Louis, but spring there was a good month ahead of Wisconsin, and the trees were full of blossoms and bright new green leaves. The little campus of brick and sandstone buildings had ivy-covered walls and plenty of giant, shading elms. The theater was stunning, and the cafeteria food was tasty. Like most college tours, they arranged for Renee and me to have brief chats with teachers in our fields of interest. My brief chat with Irv Rhodes turned into a 45-minute, animated discussion about what education could be if freed from bureaucracy. I was hooked. And when I visited the college's laboratory school and saw a great school in action, with interesting activities and engaged children, I found out that I could work there from day one. I applied and was accepted. My parents were fine with it because the view book was very traditional and spoke about the school's history as being a girl's school, founded by Loretto nuns, and the view book did not betray its freedom-to-learn philosophy and theater presence. While the school was nearly as liberal as Goddard and New College, it did not look it.

My PE teacher, with whom I had spent more time than any teacher in high school (however much I tried to get out of PE), offered me a job for that summer after graduation. She spent her summers working in Girl Scout residential camps with a friend of hers, Jay Kerrins, who was an education administrator in Illinois. This summer they were going to work for the Seattle scout camp, and would I like to be a camp counselor? What an excellent adventure! I accepted, bought my "greenies" replete with forest-green knee-high socks, held up with garters and red "flashers," ugly shorts, white camp shirt, and sturdy Clark's Wallabees, those crepe-soled, suede shoes popular with outdoorsy types. What else did I need, I asked her and her friend. After all, the only camping that I had ever done was in a travel trailer with my family. Sleeping bag? Got it. Big flashlight? Got it. Raincoat, because it rains a lot there? Got it. Ten-pound ball of twine? No, but I would get it. Turns out they were fooling about the last item. I was good for a laugh, but everybody came to me when they needed twine, and we used a *lot* of twine at camp!

But I did graduate. The week before graduation was a comedy: I attended senior banquet and had a shot at being voted funniest girl, but most folks looked at me with puzzlement as to why a junior was at the banquet. Many of us contracted food poisoning at that dinner, as evidenced by the droves of us trotting in and out of the award ceremony the next morning. I had heard that bananas helped to stop diarrhea, so I went to the office and asked if any of the secretaries had a banana. I gobbled it, but it did not help much. I wondered if I would get an award. I fantasized: Most Independent? The English Award? After all, I had done an impressive number of papers and that independent study. Overall contribution for my help in journalism and yearbook, the school closed-circuit TV show, and emceeing the water ballet show? Or stage crew? Imagine my surprise when I got only one award: Departmental Honors in PE. Ironic. Of course, my piss-off about National Honor Society did not put my name at the top of anybody's list.

The day of graduation, I liberated myself from high school in a symbolic way: I got a haircut, a wash-and-dry cut that set my curls free and required no straighteners, no giant curlers, no bonnet hair dryers, no embarrassment over summertime frizz. I was ecstatic! I showed it off at my graduation party. There was no alcohol, yet plenty of kids came. The swimming pool was open, and my folks laid out a lot of food. We played tag and touch football in the field next to my house, and I was proud to have so many kids show up, as I was not part of any of the party crowds at school. Rich Bernstein gave me a gift of a new toilet seat, and we got out a Magic Marker for everybody to sign it. He and I knew how appropriate a symbol it was for my feelings about school. I kept that toilet seat in my parents' attic for years, much to their dismay.

That next week, I and my ten-pound ball of twine, as well as my trusty Schwinn, were off to Seattle. I had not seen mountains before, and the westbound flight stretched a brilliant sunset for hours, ending eventually with a flaming set over the Cascades, still topped with snow. I was enchanted. I was not in Wisconsin anymore; I was entering a whole new world. It was still the cool, rainy season, and I was fascinated with how green everything was, and how fertile! The trees were enormous, and where they fell, another tree grew out of the fallen timber. I saw ferns of every kind. Hazelnut bushes, spruce trees—and it all smelled so good! And those banana slugs! Good grief, they were six inches long and really looked like banana peels. There were leopard slugs and slugs in different colors. It took a lot of decomposers to tackle all that green. Everything was soft and quiet underfoot, thanks to the deep layer of organic matter. The camp was on the Tolt River, a 45-minute drive over the hills, past the suburbs and a strawberry farm, tucked beside the sweet town of Carnation, "Home of the Contented Cow," where the Carnation dairy folks had an outpost of sorts. The river was rushing and noisy, a raucous, rocky, sweet-smelling drone note to the singing and laughter of the camp. We slept in canvas tents on wooden platforms and learned never to touch the canvas or drips would find their way in. Dry socks were at a premium; I had melted my uniform green nylon knee-highs trying to dry them over a campfire. The camp had a swimming beach and dock, and a separate boat house and dock where the rowboats and canoes were kept. It was on a private lake, Lake Langlois, whose imagery was clear in the camp's lilting camp song:

Oh, have you seen Lake Langlois
When the mists begin to rise?
Or have you seen the mountain's shadows
deepen in the sky?
You can sing around the campfire
making friendships new
and the spirit of Camp River Ranch
will belong to you.

You can hear the laughter ringing
and the little thread of song,
you can follow paths where footsteps
swing so merrily along,
you can climb the hill to the ridge
see the sunset's blazing hue,
and the spirit of Camp River Ranch
will belong to you.

We spent a week in training and cleaning the camp before the scouts arrived. We had a lot of songs to learn, because singing was how we finished breakfast, singing was how we warmed up to evening supper, and singing was how we kept our spirits up climbing all those steep hills you had to mount to get to the lake or to the horse stables. Singing is what we did around the campfire, and singing is how we tucked each tentful of girls into their sleeping bags each night. There were jolly songs, silly songs, and plaintive songs about peace and love. But mostly the training was about how to give the girls a great camp experience. We learned how to do reflective listening, how to soothe and distract the homesick, how to encourage girls to rise to the chores with a smile. We learned how to build social groups and teams, and we played team-building games that we then played with our girls. We learned how to support one another, surprise one another, and be excellent friends. Each counselor had a "tilly," a secret pal for whom you left fun notes and bought little treats. It was the best camaraderie. I was a newbie, and one of the youngest on staff as I would not turn 17 until July; most of the other gals were college students. So I was surprised when Jay called me in after she was determining which counselors would work together in units. We had all been instructed to list four names on a piece of paper, the names of other counselors with whom we would like to work. She told me that mine was the only name that showed up on every other gal's request paper. She was impressed, and my heart bloomed. I found a place where I was learning, where I could revel in nature, and where I mattered.

Jay placed me with Sue Brown, "Bandi," one of the oldest counselors at nearly 30 years old. She thought that with Sue's calming older influence and my youth, we would balance each other out. Well, Sue was older, more experienced with a hatchet to split kindling and with knots to keep the tents up, and way more skillful at bike repair, but I was the organized one. We were a fabulous team and complemented each other in every way. We laughed a hundred times a day and supported one another with positive attitudes. We were in charge of a specialized bike unit, in which a small group of the campers brought their bicycles with them so that we could take little trips into town. What the girls brought were pretty much rolling sculptures of junk that broke down every 500 feet, leaving Bandi to replace chains, patch tires, and reassemble pieces that had fallen off. Each stop meant that I would circle the troops to sing or to admire the flora until we were up and rolling again, only to have to stop in another 500 feet. We did eventually make it into Carnation for a picnic, a trip that was hair-raising as we crossed a one-lane bridge across the Tolt River, praying that the logging semis or dairy trucks would not try to squeeze by.

Camp was where I developed hypoglycemia, or low blood sugar. I was always go-go-going at such a pace, fueled by regular meals interspersed with sugary treats—banana boats, s'mores, hot sweet Kool-Aid, cakes—that when dinner came, I was dizzy and nearly passed out. It was like trying to drive very fast with no gas in the car. I was encouraged to eat regular small meals of protein to last me longer. Those were the days before trail bars and high-protein diets, and the closest thing to protein that I could take were those foul, tootsie-roll-like Space Food Sticks. Yuck! So I practiced calming myself during the high-energy meals, where we were required to sit with tables of seven campers and help them to make sociable conversation and use good manners. I am an introvert, a person who gets energy from being alone and is drained by groups of people, so forcing myself to stay calm and reserve my energy when being required to orchestrate dozens of wild children was a difficult but important job.

The camp accepted Title I children who came from the poorest of circumstances in Seattle, and this acceptance allowed the camp to receive food supplements from the government. I was in awe of the canned foods: instead of boring, block-printed generic labels with government notices, these cans had their contents screen-printed directly onto the silver cans in bold colors of magenta and blue. They were ornamented with an art-nou-veau style that was an artful surprise. Canned prunes and "meat" looked like they belonged on the shelf of a head shop. And the apples! Washington State, of course, is known for its apples, but who would have thought that the government-program apples would be the top, premium fruit? These apples were over a pound apiece, hefty bright-red delicious bombs as big as these little girls' heads. The look on a tiny camper's face when you handed her an apple for a snack, and her hands dipped with the weight, and she looked like I had just handed her a basketball: what was she supposed to do with all *that*? We learned to cut them up for the girls with our trusty Scout knives.

There were about five camp sessions that lasted 7-10 days apiece. Sometimes we got a break of a couple days between, and the counselors would scatter to homes and to the city to catch up on laundry or have an adventure. Those were glorious days! I fell in love with Pike Place Market, its shops and colors and ginormous crabs and fish being tossed around. I found a musty army-navy surplus store and bought a pair of green army pants to cut off for comfy camping shorts. We discovered a little shop where very cute young men were baking bread from scratch. We watched and flirted and asked a hundred questions. We bought a loaf for lunch, warm and chewy and flavorful. Inspired (and ready to flirt again), we returned and bought a bag of flour, then went back to the counselor's home where we worked together to make our first loaf of bread, a brick so heavy, so dense that we knew we could only get better at bread making. But with fresh creamery butter and homemade jam, there was nothing better. And Seattle is where I tasted my first pizza that was not like the standard fare in Kenosha. It was on University Hill, and the pizza had ham—and pineapple!—and real, fresh ripe tomatoes, not just sauce and cheese. Heavenly, with a taste that I use as a standard to judge all other pizzas since then. For the break on my birthday, the Fourth of July, we all came back from our scattered adventures to meet at Farrell's Ice Cream

Parlor, where they treated me to, and shared, an enormous sundae named the Woodland Park Zoo.

On one delightful trip, we crowded into Algi's old red Nash Rambler and trekked east to Puyallup, where we set up camp outside of town beside the river. We had just gotten paid, and I had a wallet full of cash. We drove the five miles or so from the river into the little town, and when we pulled up to its one stop sign, I remembered that I had set my wallet on the roof of the car when we left the campsite! We pulled around and saw my wallet lying in the intersection, not 100 feet from where my memory had kicked in. There it was, splayed open, bills floating away in the breeze. I scrambled to collect it, and non—none! of it was missing! The same guardian angels watched over me the next day when we found a popular spot on the river to swim, where daredevils rode the wild current over a 7-foot waterfall. I jumped in and held my breath as the torrent pulled me over the falls, into the eddies below, and held me under for 50 yards. Fantastic! I got out and did it again, and had a pal take a photo of me with my Instamatic. I chatted up a fellow who was in a clutch of people standing along the shore, arms folded. Why were they watching and not joining in? Somebody gets killed in these falls almost every weekend, he said. You're taking a real risk. My third and final rush over the falls was a bit more subdued as I tried to imagine how the victims died. Did they hit their heads taking the wrong route? Did they panic during the stretch where the pressure held you under?

There was a lot of water that summer. The camp itself was in the temperate rain forest, and rain it did, every day until mid-July. But rain doesn't stop kids from Seattle! They're used to it. They were just as happy to wear a poncho made of garbage bags, and we slipped plastic bags over their dry socks before they would tie on their soggy shoes. Few had rain boots, especially the Title I kids. We swam in the rain, rode horses in the rain, and boated in the rain. Cooking was a little tougher, but every unit had a cooking shed where cooking pots were safely tucked into a rough cabinet, and a fire pit enabled you to cook a meal with the wood that was stacked dry under the shelter. Washing dishes outside for 30 people was a hassle: we had to boil the water over the fire, and boil enough for soapy water, rinse water, and then have enough water for a bleach dip. There was so much mulch and mud around, you might be able to wash the plastic plates and cups clean, but keeping them that way on the picnic table to air dry was another challenge. And when eggs would get burned on to the frying pans, well, yuck. The worst was when we tried to make caramel apples over the fire, and the caramel hardened overnight in the pan. We had planned to wash the pots in the morning because the light of the Coleman lantern was insufficient. Soaking didn't touch that hard, burnt coating in the pan. We had to chisel and scrub and scrub some more.

That's the last time we made caramel apples. Sue and I were not the best outdoor cooks. I recall one of our first cookouts when we wrapped hot dogs in biscuit dough and wrapped those in aluminum foil to cook in the coals, with the idea that this arrangement made a hot dog in a bun. We had no idea how long to leave them in the coals, and when we took them out 20 minutes later, we pulled back the foil to find hard, black chunks that should have been soft, fluffy buns. These were hungry kids: what would we do? It was rainy and dark. I broke mine open to reveal a juicy hot dog that was still edible, and I tried to put a positive spin on it for the kids: we had just made planters! All they had to do was scoop out and eat the hot dog, and we would fill the black holsters tomorrow with dirt and seeds for them to take home. I was taken aback when upon bedtime tuck-in, three of the girls had stashed their burnt buns in their tents. I had to explain that I was kidding. You did *not* want to have food in your tent! The critters would move in, and move in they did that next week into one little girl's suitcase. When she pulled it from under her bed to get fresh clothes, some of them had been nibbled into a soft, cozy nest for a mama mouse and her dozen squirming babies. The camper was enchanted, but we moved the family to the woods, where the girls tried but could not find them the next day. I imagine that her mother would have had a stroke if she had found those mice in the suitcase when the girl got home.

Lake Langlois was stunning, surrounded by deep forest and hills crisscrossed with trails. The lake was bottomless, an old spring-fed glacier lake. I did not know about the springs until one little girl pointed out her observation that one of the puddles we circumvented each day on the path to the lake was, in fact, spring-fed. Its water cleared so quickly after we sullied it, she observed, that it showed, upon closer inspection, to have water seeping up from a spring below. Those cool lake waters were tempting, and during a break when the camp director and all the campers were gone, I challenged my fellow counselors to a skinny dip party late one afternoon. My camp name, by the way, was Rowdy, and not for nothing! We were frolicking in the waters by the swimming dock when we were startled by the appearance of a fire engine there in the forest! It pulled up to the boat dock, and a couple of strapping young men dipped a hose into the water and turned on the pumper to fill their tank with water! We giggled and hid in the water behind the dock for a very long time until the men and their fire engine pulled away. Our clothes were up on shore, and they would have had a clear view if we had made a run for it.

I found God at that camp. I learned what blissful, ecstatic oneness with nature was about: I *was* love and joy. The creeks and rivers and hills and trees all spoke to me. My depleted soul was whole again. More than whole—I was bursting with a love for life. So the thought of going to school in the fall, after the misery that was behind me, just did not feel right. I couldn't bear it. I called and told my parents that I wanted to put off college for a year, which was not a big concern for them because I was not yet even 18 years old, and having graduated a year early, I had time. And even though I was the fifth of six children, none of my siblings had lasted more than a year in college, so the bar was set pretty low. Webster agreed to defer my enrollment for a year. I was free! I did not want to leave when camp ended in August. I wanted the camaraderie and connection to nature to go on forever. So when a group of the camp staff suggested a road trip to San Francisco, I was in! We crammed into hotel rooms, claiming to be just four people, but eight of us would squeeze in to share the expense.

There were wall-to-wall sleeping bags. At one point, we moved into the dorm at San Francisco State, where one of our gang was a student. When we descended on Chinatown, we claimed a big round table, and two waiters claimed us. They banished the forks and insisted that they would teach us to use chopsticks, or we could not eat! They flirted and made us try new foods, and we all learned to use those chopsticks. We went to Golden Gate Park and flirted with more boys. We met a couple of guys in their twenties, and I bet them that I could get us into the aquarium for free. I grinned and sweet-talked our way in, which wasn't too hard because the aquarium was only open for another half hour. One of the cute guys was short and had a big mustache and a tasty Italian name. We arranged a date for the next night, and he would pick me up from the dorm. The girls gave me all kinds of grief and stole my clothes from the shower. I still have the photo that they took of me emerging from that pre-date shower, towel around me secured with a belt. When I look at that photo, I think about losing my virginity, because that is what I did that night.

My virginity was a big burden, and I was tired of lugging it around, defending it, making it into something bigger than it had to be. I was no longer a high school girl; I was a young woman and could enjoy life. And so I did, in Apostolo's bed. I told him later that I was glad not to be a virgin anymore, and he was thunderstruck—why hadn't I told him before? He would have made it more special. He said that he couldn't tell because I sure acted like I knew what I was doing. Well, I wasn't exactly innocent. I had been sexually active; I just had not gone "all the way." My Italian boyfriend of the summer before had taught me to give a great hand job and an even better blow job. (Oh, those Italian boys!)

And then I had to go home.

To say that there was a period of adjustment would be an understatement. There was no oxygen at home. It was quiet. Boring. I did not talk with my little brother, who was in his own high school orbit. The older siblings had moved away. My parents had nothing to say. I could not even sleep in my bed for a week because it felt like a coffin; instead, I slept on my bedroom floor.

But I saw my home like never before. It was not the blur passing by as it was in my overworked and overwrought days of high school: I was seated, still. Watchful. Our big kitchen table, which could seat eight, plus a high chair, filled the eating nook. One whole wall was windows that looked out on the garden, a heated bird bath, and two always-filled bird feeders. Sometimes a Have-a-Heart trap waited at the bottom of the bird feeders to catch the neighbor's predatory cats, but it would just as likely catch a hissing possum or nervous raccoon. Each day's leftover, stale slices of toast or pancakes were tossed under the feeders for the grackles and starlings, while the Hilarious-brand bird feeders attracted the more colorful birds. A Hilarious feeder is a little house standing on a pole. You fill it with birdseed, and the birds sit on a perch to eat the seed spilling out from the bottom of the walls of this house. Cleverly, the perch is weighted with a spring that you can adjust so that bigger birds, or too many birds, make the perch sink, thus closing off the access to the seeds. Sparrows would fight each other for position. Red and olive cardinals cooperated, with Mama on the ground nibbling the seeds that the vigorous Daddy would toss over the side. Blue jays chased off the meeker birds. Squirrels would climb the pole and sit on the perch, confused about where the seed had gone: hadn't those birds just been eating? But a smart squirrel, "Fat Alice." figured it out: she climbed to the top of the peaked feeder house and dropped head-first over the roof, clinging to the peak with her hind toes. She was able to hang there by her toes, stuffing her cheeks. We have photos of the squirrels having a ball with a stale fancy gingerbread house that I had made for my parents. Dried corn cobs dangled from chains for squirrels to climb down for an acrobatic feast, and sometimes my folks would put one of those cobs in a giant glass jug and amuse themselves by watching the squirrels roll it around the yard, tryingly to get into it. A suet feeder clung to one of the shading oaks, and woodpeckers of every size flew in for some high-calorie nourishment. Nuthatches hopped down the trunks headfirst. Black-capped chickadees flittered about, and mourning doves strutted on the ground or took tentative, splashy baths in the birdbath. Mist rose from that birdbath on those cold winter days, providing the only open water for miles when everything else was iced. Clutches of pheasants appeared now and then in the fall to walk in their shy, stately path across the yard. The high-bush cranberries down the garden path held their crimson berries all winter, but when their sugars fermented, the exotic cedar waxwings descended and cleaned them off and then flew erratically, intoxicated. Those leisurely breakfasts and coffee with my mother were pleasant and entertaining. It became clear to me that I had missed something: I had been so involved in school and theater and all kinds of activities that I had not taken time to see the world outside my window. Watching the seasons change was a satisfying restoration.

As a child, I had taken great pleasure in the natural wonders of my yard. We had four acres, and I spent a lot of time roaming around it, playing and exploring as a child. I had a secret magic fairy pond out back, formed in a depression where three oaks came together at their base. It filled with oak leaves, stinking with their rot, but the water there made me wonder about what used it for drink or bathing. The yard was filled with trees: shag-bark hickory, oaks, willows, pines, and tall spruces. You could climb inside one of those giant spruces and have a fort under its low and hiding branches. Another oak's branches hung low enough that we could jump up and grab that branch, pull it down, then lift our feet and be carried into the air, bouncing back down to earth again and again. Four tall, thin oaks came together in another spot and formed a "telephone booth" for our pretend play. Stumps from fallen trees served as stages or banquet tables. We even had a mini-orchard: two plum trees, six apple trees, and two pear trees. One of the apple trees had been grafted by my grandfather to grow four different kinds of apples. Its branches grew wide and low, perfect for climbing. We had several big crabapple trees, too, which would fill with glorious, fragrant pink blossoms. Once I climbed it with my watercolor paint set in hand and tried to capture its magic. The yard was surrounded by lilacs of every hue, and I would bring my teachers giant bouquets in the spring and big bunches of peonies, crawling with tiny ants, on other weeks. The longer spring light launched a grove of wildflowers under the still-bare bushes: clean white trout lilies with mottled, spiked leaves, and deep purple violets with sweet round leaves. All kinds of mushrooms grew in the yard, and Dad had a friend who knew how to identify which ones were edible. Dad would allow him to forage in exchange for a bag for us, and just my dad and I would eat them, my mother looking on skeptically, afraid for our lives. The giant puffball mushrooms were the most fascinating: big, firm white masses that we would slice and sauté in butter. If we missed picking those when edible, we had fun with them later by pricking them and releasing a cloud of brown spores. My best friend and I once found so many that we tried to invent make-up with the powder, but the results were not pretty.

We kids would find baby birds, raccoons, squirrels, and opossums, and my father indulged us with a chicken-wire cage to hold them until they regrettably, but inevitably, died. We tried to feed them what we thought that they should eat and even managed to keep the possum alive for a month, but the tiny bunnies that we found curled into shallow holes at the base of the hickory trees never stood a chance. My younger brother, Bruce, really enjoyed that little possum, and I laughed until I cried when I saw the critter cleaning himself in my brother's hair. Bruce thought that the possum was tickling him, but the possum found Bruce's big, fluffy blond "Afro" to be just right to slobber in, then rub himself in to clean his fur.

Bruce and I had another animal adventure one Sunday morning. The rule at the house was that my parents slept late on Sundays, which wasn't all that late, maybe 8:30. But Bruce and I were up earlier than that, and we were not allowed to wake them. Our routine was to scale the kitchen counters to retrieve the Nestle's Quick and Horlicks to make ourselves tall glasses of chocolate malted milk, using way more sweet powder than the recipe called for so that, having drunk the milk, we had an inch of delicious chocolate slurry on the bottom. One Sunday, we went down to our playroom in the basement and discovered a frantic squirrel that had come in through the fireplace there. We were delighted and terrified of being bitten, but we chased it around and hopped on top of the furniture or the pin-ball machines to escape its wrath, then threw blocks at it to convince it to go back out the way it came in.

So nature love was not new for me, but that summer in the rain forest reignited my forgotten passion. School had stolen it from me, which became one more reason that I resented school. Why couldn't school capitalize on the joy and wonder and education one could get from nature? Why must the campus be just a shorn open field with no restorative patches of trees and gardens? Research shows that being able to gaze out at the green world, especially for girls, reduces stress. More and more classrooms were being built without windows at all, lit by flickering, disturbing fluorescent bulbs. Beautiful old school buildings that had tall windows were being retrofitted with smaller windows in order to reduce radiant heat loss and keep conditioned air in. What windows there were would not open, thereby keeping burglars out and students in. Expensive heat stayed in, too. Natural wood furnishings disappeared in favor of sturdy, easy-to-clean plastic, cinderblock, and metal. The vicissitudes and vivacity the life—of nature was gone from school.

Although I love nature, Wisconsin winters were harsh. I took the bitter cold personally. The winds off Lake Michigan were not brisk; they were biting. The fallen snow quickly turned to black cinder-stained clumps along the roadsides. My feet were never ever warm. I had to wear so many layers of clothes that I felt trapped and out of touch with my body. I had not yet learned that wool was a better insulator than the usual cotton knee-highs that I wore, my perspiration causing their dampness to give me an ever-present chill. It took extra time to dress to go out, and it took extra time to strip down in the cold mudroom, finding places to stack boots and to hang scarves and coats to dry. I did not enjoy the out of doors in January when the thermometer dropped below zero. I could not ice skate, and when I tried, my toes always got frostbit. Winter was my nemesis. There were, though, fleeting pleasures in the winter. Our backyard had a slight slope, and when a layer of sleet froze atop a deep snow, the yard became a crisp brûlée that held up the toboggan and allowed for a swift descent down to the hedge line. I remember watching my father walk slowly and steadily behind the snowblower, a shower of white flying through the air into the bushes. I was always in awe of my mother who would take the snow shovel and tackle the sidewalk beside the house: she would go out in 10 degree weather wearing short sleeves, or a light cardigan at the most. She worked up her own heat, or else she must have been fighting hot flashes.

Mother's metabolism must have been unusual. She got her period when she was eight years old and told of the humiliation that the nuns at her strict Catholic school caused her, sending her to walk home, chafing and without a napkin, for her mother to deal with her mess. That was just one of her many complaints about the Catholic Church. And mother could not wear a watch that required a battery because every one of them would race ahead, never keeping accurate time. Mother didn't mind the winters, but the summers did her in. We did not have air conditioning, and summers in Wisconsin could easily get into the 90s for weeks at a time, and the humidity would melt you. In the summer, Mother would powder the cups of her bras before strapping in, a sight that dropped my niece's jaw when she saw her do this on a shared trip. Mother begged my father for a swimming pool, but he did not want one, so it was of no use. She asked my sister and me to ask him and told us that she knew if *we* really wanted it, he would not deny us. "Did your mother ask you to ask me?" He figured it out. So we got through those youthful summers with the enormous, 4-foot fan in the attic, whose intake vent was just outside my bedroom door upstairs. We left all the windows in the house open at night and turned on the fan to drone and whoosh, pulling the air from outside to breeze past us and up and out from the hotter upstairs bedrooms. All the leaded-glass windows were shaded with canvas awnings, and I delighted to be able to stand in the window, completely dry during a thunderstorm, and listen to the rhythm of the rain on the awnings.

I'd sleep without a sheet or blanket, and frequently stir to flip the pillow over to the cool side. I'd lie as still as possible to feel whatever breeze came through, thankful for the cross-ventilation provided by the three windows in our corner room. The bed was most pleasant on Tuesdays, the day that the beds were changed. With all those beds to tend, Mother survived by sending all the bedding to the laundry rather than washing it herself. They would get returned to us in a thick wrapped package, all crisp and fresh. Those Tuesday-night sleeps were delightful, but by Wednesday the cool creases had relaxed, and the warm softness returned. I tried to sleep out on a cushioned, redwood chaise on the back porch, a screened summer room at the back of the house, hoping I would be closer to the fresh air, but it was not much better.

Father did say that he would get us a pool on one condition: that my mother would stop smoking. Now that was an incentive! He knew it would be hard, but he had stopped cold turkey years ago, so he figured that she could, too. Sure, she had smoked longer—for maybe 35 years?—but if he could do it, so could she. But smoking *was* Mary Jane in the same way that a martini glass was Dean Martin and a cigar was George Burns. Mother had always had a cough for as long as I had known her, a strangling, wheezing cough, and it would get worse every year when her chronic bronchitis flared her emphysema. Her eyes would water and she would shake her head, then light up again. Salem menthols, in the green and white package. There were ashtrays all around the house, and her favorite was a miniature cast-iron skillet, with a convenient handle for toting around. She was careful not to blow it in our faces, and she drove with the car window cracked open, but who knows how much secondhand smoke we inhaled? So despite the fact that smoking was destroying her health and she had lost all her teeth, she just could not kick the habit. There were no antidepressants or Chantix or nicotine patches back then; you just had to gut it out. But mother did not want to endure another sultry summer without the joy of floating weightless in cool water, so she committed to quit.

We tried to stay out of her way, and she did cut back, but we would catch her taking long walks around the yard, hiding her smoke in the palm of her hand. She just couldn't kick it. And as construction started on the pool, Dad gave her grief and laid on the guilt. Then Mom got sick. She could not move. She had weird pains. So she checked into the Mayo Clinic. They ran every kind of test on her but did not find anything that they did not already know about her lungs or any other organ for that matter. She grew increasingly paralyzed. It was a scary, uncertain time. Then one day the team of doctors studying my mother sent in a psychiatrist, a big black man whom Mother described him as looking like Rosey Grier, a famous football player of the time. Nobody was going to pry into her brain, especially him, so she got up and checked out the next day, still barely moving, but home. Her racism and fear of "shrinks" turned away the one doctor who could probably have helped her. She got better over the weeks, but she resumed smoking, and Dad threw up his hands.

1972–1973, Filling the Gap

In one year, I managed to work at a camp in the temperate rainforest, take a road trip to San Francisco, lose my virginity, learn a 10-key calculator , gain 30 pounds, lose 30 pounds, work as a waitress in two local landmarks, explore the fjords and cities of Sweden and Norway, elope, and move 365 miles away.

I packed a lot into that year after I graduated early from high school—a lot more than stare at birds and watch the seasons change. Now we call it a gap year, but back then, we were just figuring things out. And girls didn't have the pressure to figure it all out. When my big brothers turned 18, my folks made it clear to them that they were expected to begin paying rent. That made them responsible and got them out of the house pretty quickly: there was no "failure to launch." I was still not 18, so I had time, but I wanted to get a job. That fall I became a waitress at Mar's Cheese Castle, a Wisconsin landmark just over the border from Illinois, a castle dedicated to luring northbound tourists off the interstate to marvel at hundreds of varieties of cheeses. I was paid a paltry waitress wage to not only wait on customers and do dishes by hand but to clean and cook as well. Mario, the little, big-talking boss, was a rip-off. But I learned to make their famous grilled cheese sandwiches, which contained four ounces of any cheese the customer desired. They were slathered with butter—a heart attack on a plate. They were served with a side of sweet and slimy German-style potato salad. Our homemade soup, Mario claimed, was homemade because we heated it ourselves, one mini-can at a time, in a special little hot pot in the back. Scattered around the counters were stations with coffee creamers shaped like a cow's head; when tipped, the cow would spit milk from its lips, which did not make sense but tickled the customers. I was a cheerful waitress, but my uniform was never clean, what with all the cooking and cleaning, and the fact that I could only balance multiple orders by piling them against my midsection.

But I missed the excitement and adventure of the summer before. I wrote lots of letters, mainly to two guys: Apostolo, from San Francisco, and Jack, who had supported me through high school and was now in Rome, Italy, for a study year abroad. Apostolo had told me come back and see him anytime, and that January I decided to take him up on that offer. I didn't tell him I was coming, though. I knew he would worry about my taking such a big move when I wasn't even 18 yet. I never thought about what trouble he could get into, harboring an underage girl. I saved my money and tips and bought a one-way ticket to San Francisco. I crafted a letter to my parents to explain that I was not running *away*—not trying to get away from them—but rather I was running *to life*. I felt so much more alive in the vibrant big city of San Francisco, and they should not worry, because I was staying with a friend and I would call them in a few days to let them know that I was OK.

Betsy agreed to drop me at the bus that would drive me to O'Hare. She was worried about me and gave me a tiny little red New Testament Bible. She was a Jesus freak, as we called fervent Christians of the time, but knew better than to try to convert me. In it, she inscribed: *I don't want to get mushy but I want ya to know that ya been a swell friend I'll always remember how you were always willing to help me. If you're ever down, try this—not for me but for you. Keep it with ya and keep your memories.* I've kept it with me. Her inscription is the only part that I have ever read.

When I landed in San Francisco, I wandered through the crowds to collect my luggage and to find a pay phone. The PA announced arrivals and departures and gates, and meet your party at the baggage claim, and call the operator. *Paging Lorrie Laken, call the nearest courtesy phone for a message.* Perhaps I misheard in the din of the airport. Were my parents looking for me? I called Apostolo, waking him. He did not sound overjoyed, but he would be there in about an hour.

He said that it was good to see me, but he seemed stunned and concerned. He had to go to work very early the next morning, as he was a postman. What were my plans? I said that I would look for a job. What did my parents think? I would find out when I called them, as I had just left them a note. Apostolo squirmed. I told him I thought they were trying to page me at the airport. "Wow," he said.

The visit was a bit grimmer than our first meeting. Quite a bit. I called my folks the next day, waiting until the long-distance rates dropped but not so late that it was past their bedtime. Yes, they were worried, and yes, they'd had me paged. They wanted me to come home and said they would hire a detective to find me. They reminded me I was only 17. I tried to reassure them: "Let me stay a few days, then I will come home."

So that is what I did. The trip didn't get any cheerier. I remember that he used twists of toilet tissue to clean out his ears each morning, and he left the twists by the sink. I remember making out on his living room floor, and a long trail of ants crossed by us. He cooked me a steak. I remember trying to look sexy in my favorite cream-colored, see-through, lacy sweater. But I was no longer the buff girl who had been climbing hills all summer: I had gained 30 pounds that fall. We exchanged one letter after I returned, and that was that.

My father did not talk to me much on the chilly drive home from the airport, but he was clearly uneasy and agitated. "Are you in trouble?" he asked.

"No. Just tired."

I wasn't sure what I would do next. But Jack was back.

Jack

The seriously horny girls of theater know that it does no good to flirt with your fellow actors; it's the stage crew boys who are straight. It was 1970, the summer I turned 15, just before I returned to public high school. NuTheater was staging a medley of previous shows to raise funds. We were at the Catholic High School, using their stage crew to set lights. One of their crew was also NuTheater's regular tech guy, Dave. He brought his friend Jack.

Jack was 6'2, with a big mop of thin chestnut-brown hair that curled along the edges. He was hairy everywhere, a big furry teddy bear, soft to the touch but not at all fat. He had very pale skin, freckles, glasses, and long sideburns. He was all torso, so long through the middle that his shirts were always coming untucked. He was loose-limbed and wore holey Converse tennis shoes and ripped blue jeans. Jack kept looking sideways at me, so we flirted. He asked me out to coffee, and I learned that he was leaving for college in Iowa in a few weeks.

We hit it off, but until he left for Iowa, we talked. And talked, and talked. And laughed. A lot. We opened up to each other. He laughed easily and smiled a great big smile. He smoked but was thoughtful about his smoke and ashes, preferring to smear the ashes into his jeans rather than leave them on a nice floor. Every break that he came back to town, we got together. We wrote letters every week, sometimes more than one.

I had enjoyed most of that summer with another boy: Bob Cesario (oh, those Italian boys!) That June, a couple months before I met Jack, I was shocked to get a phone call from Bob asking me if I wanted to go to a band concert with him. I'm not talking rock band, but a marching-style band, an activity that he was deeply involved with. Kenosha was a marching band town, and the music program ruled the extracurricular world of high school. If you were in marching band, you practically had to pledge your firstborn son. You practiced before school and after school. You had evening concerts. You had football games to play. You had competitions. You needed special permission from the band director to participate if you were cast in the school play, or if you had a sport or speech competition. They owned you. In the summers, traveling high school marching bands competed in the Battle of the Bands. You could hear the brass and drum sections for miles. It was stirring, and I rejected it all. They stole my actors. It was just too traditional, too march-step for me. Bands were about conformity and harmony, and I was not. Bob was a band geek.

Bob and I had met at a basement birthday party for theater pals. I did not remember much about him, but he remembered me. It seems that we had played a silly game: I volunteered to get under a blanket, and the kids sitting in a circle around me agreed on something I was wearing. I had to guess what they had chosen, and if I guessed incorrectly, I had to take off what I had guessed and slide it out from under the blanket. I guessed my watch, then my glasses, then my dress. Before I could guess my underwear, they saved me and told me that the correct answer was my smile. Bob was impressed with my adventurousness—and my smile—so that is why he asked me out.

We had fun that summer. We "watched submarine races" and played pool in my basement. Well, usually we reached back and rolled the balls noisily around the table to make it sound like we were playing pool, because my parents could hear through the ventilation shafts rising from the basement past their TV room outpost. If the balls stopped clacking into one another or the chatting stopped, one of my parents would noisily head down the basement steps, giving us time to zip up and reassemble our clothing. Bob was an awesome kisser and very horny, so we learned all kinds of ways to please one another. We did not go all the way.

Bob needed a job that summer, and that was the summer that the pool was being built in my yard. I arranged for him to get a job with that crew, and they got a kick out of the gawky teen who had clearly never done hard labor. They had Bob digging with a shovel, filling wheelbarrows and rolling them up the steep incline of the excavated pool bottom. He sweated and swore, and they laughed and piled on the hard work. Bob was nervous about injuring his hands, which would hinder his clarinet performance. Musicians take care of their tools, and the pool crew could not relate to his soft tools. But Bob stuck it out, made good money, and took all the ribbing good-naturedly when the crew figured out that we were an item.

In autumn 1971, both Bob and Jack transferred to college in Milwaukee. Jack had decided after freshman year that he did not like the isolation of Iowa, so he transferred to Marquette University in Milwaukee, and coincidentally, Bob transferred to the University of Wisconsin in Milwaukee. We were closer and able to spend even more time together. When Bob came back to town, he regaled me with his adventures with coeds, and I was not amused. I did not want to hear about him with other girls. While Bob was reveling in his college adventure, Jack and I were heating up. Two boyfriends were getting too much for me to juggle, and what I had with Jack was much deeper. I let Bob down on one of his weekend visits that fall and told him that I loved Jack. He said that he was sorry and kissed me goodbye when he dropped me off at the door that night. More than 30 years later, he told me all the details of that night and of how devastated he was. That surprised me, because I thought I was just one of his many playthings.

During my "jenior" year, Jack made it the 35 miles or so back to Kenosha from Milwaukee quite often. His old American Motors car was a junker. It would stop and stay stopped at lights. The heater would go out regularly. The wipers might or might not work. Junk was all over the floor, and it never got a bath. But it was his, and in it, we were free and alone. My curfew was midnight, and we stretched that curfew within an inch of its definition. We would roll up my driveway at midnight but sit in the car talking and kissing for an hour until my father would flash the exterior lights on the garage, a signal that he was out of patience.

"But I was home on time," I protested.

"From now on, curfew means you are *in the house* at midnight."

So I would come in and bring Jack. Dad had to review his definition of curfew as meaning "in by 12, and out by 12." The folks did not always wait up. If they didn't and I snuck in, I had to get past the clanging trio of

Swedish bells on the door that jangled when it opened. I knew just how to snake in my hand to grasp the clapper before opening the door and slide the door shut without their sounding. I knew that steps number 9 and 11 squeaked on the way up to the bedroom. They listened for me, and I listened for them when Jack and I settled on the loveseat to watch TV with the afghan shared over our laps, hiding our wandering hands. I knew that Mother would sneak down the steps halfway and peer past the railing and could see us if we got out of control, so I would listen for steps nine and eleven, or the reverberation of the cast-iron stair railing if she grasped it coming around the corner from her room. Sweet, harmless, desperate games—my parents trying to give me space, but not too much—and I reaching for every inch of that freedom.

It was also a rite of passage in my city on the lake to "watch the submarine races." Couples parked at any of a number of the darker parking lots along Lake Michigan to make out. Police patrolled regularly but not too regularly, and if you did not pay attention, you could be startled by a knock on the window and a bright light illuminating your adventures. You did not want to park in *too* isolated a spot, though, as you feared perverts and murderers who would take advantage of that isolation to do horrible things. There was safety in numbers, but you did not want those numbers parked *too* close. I wondered for years how couples ever got together if they did not live by a lake and have the excuse of watching the submarines, of which, of course, there were none in the lake—although long, slender objects did get quite wet. Jack, ever a gentleman, always carried a handkerchief.

It was not all lust and laughter. I was not the only one battling and despairing. Jack did not know what he wanted to do with his life. He suffered from what he called "RSI," or Rotten Self Image. He needed frequent shoring up, despite his many beautiful qualities. He was an adequate student but found no studies that lit him up. He would despair and cry, and I would be strong for him. I would despair and cry, and he would be strong for me. As long as we did not despair simultaneously, we were OK. We had to take turns.

When I graduated from high school, Jack bought me a bright orange backpack to use in my camping, and I was touched. I missed him that summer I was in Washington, but he knew that I had to get out and enjoy life and that I would be going away to college, so the relationship would likely grow apart. I called him when I decided not to go away to college. Damn, he said, if he knew I was going to be home, he would not have signed up for his study year abroad in Rome. He would be leaving for Rome the week I returned from camp. But we wrote even more while he was in Rome. It was love, but we were young and had things to do and places to go. And I was making plans to go to San Francisco. When he came home at Christmas, he announced that he was not going back to class in Rome—that he wanted to drop out of college, stay home, get a job, and figure things out. He didn't want to waste his parents' money. And just as he got back to the United States, I went to California. And when I got back from California, we realized just how much we wanted to be together. It just had not worked out before with his going to college and me heading west, and our paths crossing for only bursts of time.

"Do you love him?" Jack asked me about my postman.

"No."

"But you slept with him."

"But with him," I explained, "it was not about love, it was about fun. I was tired of hanging on to my virginity." Of course I knew that he was wondering why I hadn't had intercourse with him, so I explained. "I couldn't do it with you—I was in high school. I had to focus on getting out of there."

"Well, I played in Rome, too, but a gentleman doesn't kiss and tell."

That winter, Jack went to work at the Coca-Cola bottling factory in town. I took a waitress job downtown at Bob's Keno Koffee Pot, across from the harbor. Bob was a skinny, 50-something alcoholic who did all his own cooking, and his daily specials were popular. I worked the breakfast and lunch crowd. Roberta Flack sang "The First Time Ever I Saw Your Face" on the sound system, and I was transported, struck by its echo of the deep feelings that were growing in me for Jack. And the song was as dark as those winter days. I remember a regular customer, an obese, quiet man whose rump hung over the counter stool, who regularly ordered a cherry ice cream sundae for dessert. Tips were terrible and traffic was slow, the customers depressing. Bob was prone to angry outbursts, and he was livid that I could not flip an egg over easy without breaking the yolk. I told him that it was hopeless, but he kept insisting that it was part of my job. A few weeks into the gig, I broke another yolk and he blasted me, slamming pots and pans around, so I just untied my apron, grabbed my coat and purse, and walked out the door in the middle of my shift. It was a cold mile hike to my father's office downtown. I climbed the steps, let myself into his office, and sat down in its dim interior, the chairs grimed with the chemicals carried in by all his dirty employees. Father owned his own electroplating company, and dirty, smelly chemicals bought our family's groceries—and pool, and vacations. He looked up at me, amused.

"I had enough," I told him.

"OK, I'll take you home when I finish here."

It was about that time that my work was finishing on the school district Committee to Channel and Control Outspoken Critics, and I told Jim, its liaison, that I was looking for work. He invited me to come work at his office in the School District administration building, and thus began my first job in the public schools. One of my projects was to do the calculations for the salary tables to be used in the teacher salary negotiations, giving visuals to the permutations of the negotiations. Now this was back in the day before scientific calculators or desktop computers, so every cell of the table, more than one hundred on each of the dozen or so permutations, had to be calculated individually because the formula changed after so many years of service or for a given number of hours of allowable college credits. When Jim saw how agonizingly slow I was, he remarked that he was surprised that I did not know how to use a 10-key calculator by touch, so he showed me. He was a patient and cheerful teacher. I have never been the quickest at picking up moves, whether typing or dancing, but the tables provided me so much practice that I got very good at using a 10-key by touch. Even now, I prefer to keep a seven-inch calculator taking up valuable space on my desk rather than using the handy calculator on my phone or the laptop. The numbers just feel more right, and it is easy to manipulate the decimal place for accounting. But the fact that I was being entrusted with numbers that would impact hundreds of people's livelihoods—their paychecks—daunted me. I was a baby beginner and probably made mistakes. I hope somebody caught them!

My eagerness to please amused the administrators. One day the secretary stepped away, and I had to answer the phone. It was a mass of buttons and numbers and lines and options, none of which I had ever attempted. The caller wished to speak to Jim, but he was down the hall in a meeting. I was afraid that if I attempted to put the caller on hold, I would drop the call, so instead I clunked the phone down and ran down the hallway in my stocking feet to knock on the meeting room door. I sheepishly admitted that the caller was waiting, and that I could neither hold the caller nor transfer it. Jim suggested that I take a message. Why hadn't I thought of that?

My family was making plans to visit relatives in Scandinavia. My father's father, Truls, had come to America on a merchant marine ship from Norway, and my father's mother, Astrid, had come over from Sweden to care for Grandfather's children who had lost their mother when she was surrounded by a wild prairie fire, attempting to rescue one of her children who had gotten caught in it. My father, Thomas, was Astrid and Truls's first child together. So I grew up hearing a mix of Swedish and Norwegian expressions and not always realizing that they were not English until I used them with my friends, who only looked puzzled. *Garning,* we would be called when we were mischievous, or *nufeeken* when we were being nosy and trying to overhear my parents' private discussions. *Dombom* was our moniker if we behaved like an idiot, and it was also the name given to the Saint Bernard dogs that we kept for years. I was a chunky child, and my father and his brothers teased me about my *shucky enden.* So we were going to head to Sweden and Norway in May of that gap year, before the summer crowds, to visit our relatives. Father and Mother had been there several times before, twice alone and another time with my big sister and my father's uncles. On one trip, father came back with a Volvo, which he sold to my brother after a year. Most cars he kept two years before trading in for the newest model. He was always looking for a bargain, but he did like to indulge himself with very nice cars.

So when we weren't working at our stop-gap jobs, Jack and I hung out and kept each other warm as we tried to figure out what to do with our lives. We were sitting in my mother's parked car in downtown Kenosha one evening; perhaps we had been to a movie theater. We didn't want to go home or to eat, so we just sat there talking, his head in my lap, my hands in the feathery soft hair of his head. His legs were bent and tangled to fit across the car, and he looked up into my face with his soft brown eyes and asked, "So when are we getting married?" He felt it was inevitable, so he didn't propose—he skipped right to step two. And it seemed like the right thing to do. We had seen each other through so many changes and tribulations, and we wanted to go right on not just loving one another but helping one another.

"I don't know," I answered. "I'm going to Scandinavia for a month."

"You should definitely go."

"I'm going to college in the fall, I think."

"You should go. I'll go with you."

"And do what? Finish college?"

"No, I still don't know what I want from college. I'll get a job while you go to school."

That was the plan. When I told my parents the next day, Dad got quiet, and Mom cried.

"Are you in trouble? Do you have to get married?" Mom asked.

"Good grief, no!"

"When are you getting married?"

"We don't know. Before I go to college. After the trip."

"Will you have a wedding?"

"Don't know. If we do, a small one."

The next day I was sitting around the TV room, watching the news, when my father came in and handed me a shoelace. "Here," he grinned, "this is what you'll be living on when you get married."

"Haha. Funny. We can do it."

"You're his responsibility now. I don't have to pay for your college."

That surprised me. I thought parents were supposed to pay for their children's college, and he could more than afford it.

"If you want a wedding, I will give you $1,000 to spend as you like for it. But if you don't have a wedding, I will give you $2,000 cash." This was the first time in my life that money would control one of my major decisions.

"We'll take the money. We need a car. His won't make it to St. Louis."

We worked all that spring and early summer. I could not return to the job for the school district after the long absence from my trip, so my father hired me to learn bookkeeping from his longtime secretary, Bea Hocknell. She was a stickler for tidiness and accuracy. Working there gave me the flexibility to quit when it was time for me to head south. Jack and I were eager to get married and move in together, but we also needed to earn as much money as we could before the move. We decided that we would elope sometime before we moved to St. Louis, as the little one-bedroom apartment that we found a mile from college would be available in August. I would turn 18 on the 4th of July, and despite our engagement, I had a midnight curfew right up until that birthday. I could use my birthday money to pay for the move-in.

Funny, my father had to wait until *his* June birthday to have the money to elope with *my mother*. She had told him she was 18, but confessed on their honeymoon that she was only 16. Father was 24, and my mother's father threatened to have my father arrested under the Mann Act for transporting a minor over state lines for the purpose of sex; they had gotten married at a Justice of the Peace just over the border in Illinois. Things never did get better between my parents and her parents. They moved in next door to his folks, who doted on my father and loved being grandparents a few years later.

That winter, I moaned about the weight that I had gained after camp. No longer physically active from morning until night, I had gained 30 pounds. I had been bugging Jack to quit smoking. "Yeah, yeah, you're right," he would say. But then he struck me a deal: if I would lose those 30 pounds, then he would quit. So I lost it, or at least most of it, by counting calories and easing up on sweets. What helped me a lot was the soup of the day special at a restaurant within walking distance from work downtown. I enjoyed taking the little two-top table next to the kitchen each day and crumbling a couple packages of saltine crackers into my big bowl. Every day a different rich and savory soup, every day as good as the next. Warming, filling, and not too many calories. All that winter, I had lounged around in one-piece denim overalls, but it was time to get back into blue jeans. And Jack stopped smoking. Success!

Come summer, that $2,000 plus change bought us our first car out-right, a brand-new frog-green American Motors Gremlin, made in our home town. It was the bottom of the line, with roll-'em-yourself windows and vinyl seats, but it was reliable. It needed oil every few months, but it was ours. Our very own. Paid for.

And on July 19th, on a steamy day, Jack called me after his shift and said, "Today is the day." We got cleaned up, packed small bags, called our mutual friend Dave, who called his fiancée, Candi, and met at the Justice of the Peace office, and took them to dinner afterward. We headed to Lake Geneva, Wisconsin, a popular resort area, and were shocked to find the only room available was in a real dive right on the main drag. It was pricey, at the peak summertime rate. We would stay two nights and then head back to my parents' to encamp until it was time to go to St. Louis.

People tease about all the lusty activities of a honeymoon, but nobody ever told me how hard it would be to learn to sleep with another person, especially somebody as tall as Jack, who was a foot taller than me. Every toss and turn woke me. What would start as a sweet curl-up into his shoulder would become suffocating. He would throw his leg over me, pinning me into discomfort. He would roll over onto my arm, deadening the nerves. He snored long and loudly. The portable air conditioner unit was right over the head of the bead, roaring and choking and whining all night. The honeymoon was exhausting, and we were eager for the relative peace of my parents' house.

Mother held a small reception at the house shortly after. I was not into fancy and froufrou, so she thoughtfully ordered a cake decorated only with fresh flowers. We received a few useful things to help us start our home. We had no bridal registry or big wedding to stock the house, but we did get serving platters, a hand mixer, and a cutting board that I still have. My mother gave me all her S&H Green Stamps, as I had been the one to patiently glue into the books all of the stamps saved from her abundant grocery hauls. We drove to a redemption center, and I turned in the books for a stick vacuum. I bought Corelle dishes, Chicago Cutlery knives, and a set of Revere Ware copper-clad pans, which I use to this day. Mother hit the West Bend outlet and supplied me with enameled aluminum pots and baking pans. Aunt Rita bought and stocked a spacious sewing kit that I use to this day. My favorite purchase was for bed sheets. I shopped and shopped for the perfect, happy sheets: they did not match but were of complementary patterns in bright primary colors, with bunches of spring flowers on a background of blue polka dots, trimmed with soft white lace, and clutches of pears, apples, and plums on sheets edged in happy spring green. I still have those sheets, frayed at the edges, but they make me smile every single time I whip them open over the mattress as I make a bed.

We used the local St Louis newspaper to hunt for an inexpensive, used bed and tied it to the top of the Gremlin. We had been sleeping and playing in sleeping bags on the floor, so a bed would be a welcome addition.

I recall how hot and edgy I felt that shopping trip, and that evening I had to keep peeing, and blood was in my pee. I blamed Jack: he had done something to me in our vigorous, adventurous sex, I was sure of it: who else was to blame after sex? When you are in pain, you want to place blame. We found the nearest emergency room and sat uncomfortably for hours. At one point, the registrar handed me a Pyrex two-cup measuring cup, the kind you use for cooking, and instructed me to pee into it. I returned it to her with ribbons of blood that everybody in the packed waiting room could see when I carried it across the room. How degrading, and I hurt! Eventually a doctor saw me and handed me a prescription for antibiotics. *Honeymoon cystitis*, he declared. Not uncommon for a newlywed like you. Follow up with us in a week.

The new doctor a week later made me blush. He was movie-star handsome and his name—I kid you not—was Dr. Sunshine! He looked like he got plenty of sex and knew of which he spoke when he told me that I should be certain to pee after intercourse. It was embarrassing to have a guy tell me to pee. Why hadn't any woman in my family ever told me that? That useful tidbit was not in the book that my mother gave me to learn about sex: *Everything You Always Wanted to Know about Sex but Were Afraid to Ask.* As I said, my parents were not readers, so this book came on the recommendation of my sister-in-law. The book was a ground-breaking best-seller because of its...comprehensiveness. It went beyond mechanics and anatomy to adventurous fun. If Mother only knew what I knew! Mother was not well-informed, despite having borne six children. I once asked her how she kept from getting pregnant during her first two years of marriage, and she said that the doctor told her that her uterus was "tipped," so he untipped it and then she conceived. Hmm. And when I asked her how she made sure that my little brother Bruce was the last of the lot, she said that she just washed herself well after sex. No, she was not a trusted source of information.

It took months of experimentation, practice, and feedback, but eventually Jack and I came up with a sure-fire way to satisfy me. He was good.

Those were frugal days. Jack found a job downtown in the shipping department of a tie factory, and he was able to save gas money by catching the bus across the street from our place. I rode my bike or walked to the college. That freshman year, the college was out of work-study funds, so the college was not a job source. I had a few regular babysitting jobs, and the parents allowed Jack to come along because we were married. I also answered an ad on the school bulletin board for a housecleaner. I cut coupons, read the ads, and managed to feed us both for $10/week. I did not buy a loaf of bread the whole time I was in college but baked my own from scratch: tender white loaves, cinnamon swirl, and occasional loaves of whole wheat. I sometimes traded a loaf of bread so that I could read an assignment from a borrowed textbook; I could not afford to buy my books. We had soup for dinner once a week, and Jack ate inexpensive lunches: he liked cream cheese and jelly sandwiches. We were married during a recession: there were lines at the gas station for the overpriced gasoline, and there were shortages of gas. The price of beef rose dramatically, so folks like us stretched our ground beef with TVP—textured vegetable protein, or soy meal. We reconstituted dry milk rather than buying it fresh. Plenty of Americans were in the same pinch, so there were always articles to be read about "How to Live Cheap but Good." We made our own Christmas gifts of foods: crafted mustards, delicious toffees, and lots of cookies. We got carried away with anatomically correct gingerbread men. When Jack's mother accidentally got a few of those in her gift box, her expression changed from tickled delight at the decorated trees and stockings to a strangled speechlessness when she came across the tits and penises on the gingerbread people. That was not her box of cookies.

The second year was a little easier financially. I got a work-study job in the education department, and Jack's big brother set up his bed in our living room while he finished his graduate studies at St. Louis University. His rent and his dishwashing helped, and he was unobtrusive.

Webster College was the perfect match for me. I was tapped for a special freshman reading seminar with a handful of other high achievers, and we discussed provocative books like *The Last Temptation of Christ* and my favorite from that class, *Magister Ludi* by Hermann Hesse. I took a class in glass blowing, which was actually more like glass bending. We took rods of glass and twisted and shaped them over a gas flame, making little animals and ornaments. The foundations of education classes, comparable to a combination of educational psychology and child observation, were called "Learning Process" classes. On the first day of my first college class, the education department chair introduced the class, which was taught by the whole team of teachers from the department. He was a dynamic, handsome man, bouncing on his feet as he wrote his name on the board, and bouncing around again to grin his big grin at each of us in the class. He was enthusiastic, with a thick mustache, twinkling eyes, and a bald head fringed with salt-and-pepper hair. He wore a sport coat and a tie. I raised my hand after he had introduced the other teachers.

"How do you pronounce *your* name?" I asked, because he had written it on the chalkboard without saying it.

He smiled broadly at me. "I'm glad you asked! It's not easy for a lot of people." It was spelled B-o-u-c-h-a-r-d. "It's pronounced Boo-SHARD, but where I come from in Maine, they say Boo-shaw. Now team up with somebody you do not know, and take two minutes each to talk about yourselves and why you are here."

A big girl with soft brown hair and enormous doe eyes was conveniently near, so we introduced ourselves. Her name was Joni Jay, and she, too, had graduated at 16. She was from the area but lived in the dorm because she wanted the college experience; it also got her away from her five siblings (like mine!) of which she was the oldest. It helped that she got a scholarship. We were both there because we thought school could be better than either of us had experienced. Ours was an instant bond.

So on that first day of college, in my first education class, I was given instructions that led me to meet my best friend for life, introduced by the man who would end my marriage to Jack.

College Daze

My relationship with Dick Bouchard during my freshman year of college was one of simple professional admiration. I called upon him for help to secure resources for my studies toward my individualized degree in the psychology and education of gifted children. He remembered my name incorrectly as Tracy, and we smiled when we saw each other in that small wing of the college administration building where the education offices were located. His office was the corner office, second floor, with tall windows that opened over the parking lot where his cute little silver Capri sports coupe had its own designated parking space. Beyond that, you could see the library past the stately elms, a library shared with Eden Seminary across the road. We spoke energetically from time to time about what I was learning. I quickly became a sophomore, having taken the CLEP (College Level Examination Program) exams and tested out of 12 credit hours of core classes.

That second year of college was something else. I now qualified for work study, so I was not as desperate to patch together babysitting and housecleaning jobs in order to buy groceries. I worked in the education office, scheduled around my classes and usually in the evenings. The master's program was open to teachers who were actively teaching at the time, so classes began about 4:30 in the afternoon, when the teachers could get there from all over the St. Louis area. I would keep the office open until 8:00 or 9:00 pm when the last classes ended, remaining there to take emergency calls, unjam the photocopy machine, and do the odd office jobs left for me by the day staff. There were no computers, just a couple of enormous Selectric typewriters, their metal globes embossed with letters jigging noisily inside, stamping out notices and documents. If they had no work for me, I could type my class papers while on duty, and typing them there was preferable because the Selectrics were faster and produced nicer-looking papers than my little electric typewriter back at the apartment. I got to know the teachers well, and to know them even better at our weekly Tuesday night parties in my advisor's office down the hall.

Margaret Niederer was my advisor, a woman who truly understood what good education should look like. She had done her studies at Bank Street College in New York, famous for its innovative, progressive schooling for children. That year was my practicum year, and she worked with a cohort of about eight of us girls, teaching us methods classes and making us journal at length about our observations and reflections of all that we were experiencing with kids and the curriculum. We got together each Friday for long meetings to discuss our assigned readings and to draw a connection between what we read and what was happening in our respective schools.

That fall, I was truly lucky to get a paid teaching assistant gig every morning, which I was able to use as part of my practicum. The money helped, but the learning was amazing. I was in University City at Delmar Harvard Elementary, working with a mixed fourth- and fifth-grade class in adjoining basement rooms. Dr. Patrick Dugan was my cooperating teacher, and we were a great team. The match had been arranged with the education office: Patrick had taught for Dick Bouchard when Dick was the principal at Spoede School in a neighboring school district, and Dick had cherry-picked me for that job. Pat Dugan was tall, with dark curly hair and big, soft lips that were usually parted or smiling. He was round-shouldered from leaning down to look students in the eye or to work with them individually. He was not afraid to touch or hug the students—or me. He thought deeply about his practice and could be counted on for long, soft-spoken philosophical discussion with me, with the children, and especially with the school's principal, another kind and thoughtful man.

The students were an excitingly diverse lot. Half the students came from the immediate neighborhood, from poor apartments and project

housing, and the other half came from across Delmar, from the neighborhoods surrounding Washington University and housing its elite faculty.
In my class, we had the son of the country's current poet laureate as well
as the son of the executive director of the St. Louis Symphony; we also
had students who smelled bad from wearing the same dirty clothes every
day. We had surly students and gifted students and students who needed
extra help. I keep up with one of those gifted students even to this day,
thanks to Facebook, and I look in on Patrick on many of my visits back
to St. Louis to visit Richard's sons. Patrick let me try anything with those
kids, and he helped me to understand what worked, what didn't, and
why or why not. We baked bread from scratch, and I motivated students
to learn spelling words with a reward of a picnic in the country where we
gobbled up fire-roasted hotdogs on a sunny, chilly day. Each month, the
class trooped down the block to the Dairy Queen where Patrick treated
everybody to an ice cream treat, its size determined by the child's reading
accomplishment that month. That class was where a student showed me
what good teaching looks like when he smilingly and patiently tried to
teach me to throw a football in a spiral. That was the class where I learned
that keeping an angry child in from recess when she wants to go out could
end with her literally clawing her way past me, leaving me with a bright
bloody scar on my hand.

On October 1st, Rabbit Rabbit Day (the first day of every month is Rabbit Rabbit Day), rather than meeting in Margaret's cramped office at the school for our weekly cohort meeting, we were invited to a potluck picnic at Margaret's house a couple miles away. It was a perfect autumn day, with a bright, azure sky and yellow leaves falling like happy confetti. We sat on a giant quilt on her grassy lawn, absorbing the warm sun on the cool day. When the sun started to dip and the chill set on us, we moved into her living room to finish our conversations. Dick had been invited to drop by, and he did. He suggested that we do a "strength bombardment." One of Dick's specialties was affective education, which nowadays is referred to as social-emotional learning. As with anything else in education, everything old is new again, just with a different name so some publish-or-perish-threatened professor can knock out a book. With a strength bombardment, the idea is to practice giving genuine compliments and accept them gracefully. We sat in a circle on the floor, and each of us took a turn sitting in its center, while the rest of us took turns with our observations, such as: "You bring so much enthusiasm to your work," or "I appreciate the helpful suggestions that you made about math," or "You have the kind of quiet patience that I wish that I had with my students." Each of us felt uncomfortable in the center, but each of us left the center warmed with praise, yet humbled. It was powerful. I went last. To me, Dick added that he had been watching me and saw how I gave of myself generously to my classmates, and even the fact that I wanted to go last proved it. The group disassembled and moved back into casual conversation groups, but Dick and I were not finished.

Did I cry? Is that why his hug lingered? His voice rumbled out of his chest, just below where my ear lingered on the shoulder of his sportscoat. "You're beautiful. You're special," he murmured, and kissed me. The other students seemed to be trying to look away. I could not turn away, could not resist. His embrace heated up. He smiled and looked into my eyes. "We should...." His voice trailed off and he kissed me again.

"What?" I asked in a whisper, dazed and bewildered. He led me into the next room for privacy, and we stood there, making out, he kissing my lips hard, his hands reaching into my jeans, and mine down his pants. I was perspiring, breathing heavily. He fingered me, and I held on to him. Minutes went by. Five? Fifteen? "They're going to wonder about us," I whispered hoarsely. He gave me a final hug, then held me by the shoulders at arm's length and looked at me, shaking his head.

"I love you," he said, kissed me, and left me there in that room as he said his goodbyes and I collected myself, willing the strength back into my legs. I felt as if I were standing in the wake of a 747. Powerful.

The weekend passed, and the memory of that momentous encounter rocked me, made me dizzy. What was *that*? I wondered. I felt it, but it was beyond belief. How could he love me? And how could I feel that way toward him? Surely he loved all his students; he was well-known for his generous hugs and friendliness with women. It must have just been the wine and the power of the strength bombardment. It was just a moment. I was, after all, married, as was he. I loved my husband. He had children. And he was a dean, a professor, and I was a student—only 19 years old! This could not be. It should not be. And yet it was too powerful to ignore.

I worked in his office, so it was not going to be easy to let it go. I asked for a word with him that Monday, and he closed his office door, sat behind his desk, and smiled. I smiled back, "That was something."

"Yes, it was. Were you OK?" he asked. "Did Margaret say anything?"

"No, but they looked at me funny. I didn't stay long after that."

"Mm-hmm," he rumbled, and his smile curled up the ends of his thick mustache.

"You said something to me. You couldn't mean it, could you? We were just carried away, right?"

"What did I say?" he asked, as we both tiptoed around the particulars.

"You—haha—said you loved me," I stammered with disbelief. "You didn't mean it like *that*, did you?" I tried to say it in a way that would give him an out, a chance to back out gracefully. He had to know that just because he had his finger in my very wet, very responsive nook below my belt did not mean that he had to say he loved me. He did not have to confuse lust for love.

"I did," he nodded, his eyes fixed on mine. "I don't say things I don't mean."

"Ah," I blushed, wishing I could smell him again. "What are we going to do?"

"We don't have to do anything," he said.

I was relieved—but not really. "Good," I said, our eyes still fixed on one another. "I shouldn't. I'm married. I love my husband."

"Yes. So am I," he added, and our smiling and nodding continued, our eyes in radar lock, my blush deepening.

"I should get back to work," I stood up, and so did he, and strode around the corner of his desk to me, and he took me in his arms. Then he kissed me, like that first time, wrapping me tightly in his arms. He stopped and pushed me backward, looking me in the eyes, shaking his head in wonderment. He smiled and let go. I stepped backward, my knees weak. I was feeling very hot and wished I could open his window to the cool evening air. I stood at the door to his office, trying to gather my wits so that I could turn the handle and leave. Finally, with a quick look back, I took a deep breath, twisted the handle, and returned to the desk in the office where I did my work. He emerged a short while later, wearing his coat, ready to go home. We exchanged smiles.

"Good night," he said meaningfully, and was gone.

Huh, I thought to myself. Huh. Words could not shape themselves around my thoughts or feelings. Huh. This could get dangerous. I could only concentrate on my work in very short bursts before my mind would slip over the edge into the kiss, the hug, the touch, the smell of him. And that night, as on most others, I made love to Jack, made *real love*, married love, lasting love. I confirmed my feelings for him, reveled in his long, furry body, his growing talent as a lover. I had no reason to reject him. I was not rejecting him. I wanted him, perhaps that night with a bit more desperation than usual, having gotten all lathered up by Dick.

And so for about a month, Dick and I tried to mostly talk, safely, across the desk from one another, a few times each week, his door open to those working in the office, to JoAnn across the hall. JoAnn saw all and knew all but said nothing. We got to know one another. We shared our histories and learned of our families. He was from Maine, from East Millinocket in the middle of the state, a paper mill town. He had worked in those mills in the summers and during school holidays, struggling to support his family of three boys. He loved the woods and hills there, and had been a beloved school principal, had played in the town band. He coached basketball and attended the Catholic church regularly, where he had been an altar boy. He had served in World War II in the Army Air Force, as a belly gunner in a B-17 over Europe. When he left to move to St. Louis, where he had been recruited to be the principal of Spoede School, the entire town threw him a going-away party. And when he had done so well as a principal in St. Louis, Webster College recruited him to teach and then to run the teacher-education program. We tried, like I said, but still there were hugs and kisses to sneak in. It was clear that we both wanted more, but we resisted. But the resistance did not get any easier.

It was a snowy day in late November, and folks in the college office were in a cheery mood, heading out to home and family to prepare for Thanksgiving. My own parents were driving the six hours from Wisconsin to have Thanksgiving with Jack and me. I lingered behind as people were leaving, and when they had gone, Dick and I stepped into his office and closed the door. The late afternoon light, dimmed by the falling snow, made all the world seem soft and comfortable, even the black shag carpet of his office, where we fell, embracing. Then all that waiting, all that pent-up chemistry, burst, and we grappled and groped, breathing heavily, reaching for slipperiness to mix with hardness. We unclasped one another's belts, dropped our pants, and he leaned me over his desk and took me. He pulled my sweater up to grab my breast, then papers clung to the perspiration on my breast as I rested my chest on his desk, succumbing to his thrusts, assimilating the energy given off by his release. We descended to the rug again, awkwardly, with our pants still tangled about our ankles. He tucked me under his arm, and we wrapped around one another, smiling.

All that year we found ways to play with one another in his office behind the closed door, and eventually at his house for "nooners." He might stop to pick up a little lunch for us, and a favorite was knishes from the Jewish delicatessen on the edge of his upper-middle-class neighborhood of sprawling ranch homes. I would crouch down in the front seat as he pulled into his driveway and come up once the car was in the garage and the door shut so that his observant neighbor would not see me. His bed would have still been unmade from the night before, and I would use his towel after showering so as not to create more laundry to arouse suspicion. After our visits, he would drop me a block or so from the college, and I would walk back to class. When spring arrived, we took the long drive to Lake Carlyle where he docked his sailboat, and we played on the water. The long, narrow bench below deck was uncomfortable, the air stuffy and heavy with the smell of old lake water in the bilge. Once we played on deck, and he slipped and fell back on the tiller, breaking it jaggedly off, making the trip back to port slow motoring. We had sunburn in intimate places to hide, but that wasn't as telling as the time that we each were scratching like crazy after an encounter in the woods, both of us suffering from chigger bites. The teensy critters burrowed where pants were belted and underwear elastic clung to skin. I brought in a bottle of clear nail polish to the office and daubed it all over his red spots to suffocate the little bastards. People may have been talking about us, but nobody confronted either of us.

We wrote passionate, angsty, sensuous notes to each other. Because I worked evenings in his office, I could leave him notes in his desk drawer and find his notes slipped under a pencil box. I kept all his notes, dozens of them, two years' worth of notes, all chronicling our joys and challenges. Some were on strips of paper torn from notebooks, some filled whole pages, and a few were on cocktail napkins. Here are a few of his notes to me.

> I am in my private space—a little insulating bubble I carry around with me, thinking and playing in my mind with you. Kidding you about the many faces and expressions of a smile. Listening to your soft furry voice—brightening my life when I hear you whisper my name. I'm wondering where yesterday went and why it is today so soon. Yesterday was a silly, satiating day....Have I Rip Van Winkled my days and nights away

through a winter and a spring? ... Pinch me! Wake me up! Tell me I have only missed a few hours with you and that I can look forward to all the beautiful "Be Here Now Rabbit Rabbit days" following in the winter and spring. Don't let summer come too soon....

———

I'm looking around now hoping to see you today—bouncing along in your pixie-like way. How I love your bounce, your spring in your shoes. The way you look hiking across campus like a Joan of Arc ready for full battle or like a determined lover ready for complete submission, I get high and excited inside watching you bounce into action. Am I going to catch a glimpse of you today? Yesterday was so long ago.

———

I'm feeling kind of down right now—nothing serious—just the rigors of a cold settling in my throat and chest. One bit of medicine I can use is to get one good look at you, to get one good hug from you, to get one good fuck from you. Any and all of the above would be greatly appreciated and treasured. I didn't want to get out of bed this morning—thought that a good day's rest would do me good. Thought of calling my secretary and asking her to cancel my day for me. But the strength of inner motivation and love has put me on my feet looking for you to bounce into my life again. I feel much better now just for thinking about it....

Love you today more than yesterday,

but not as much as tomorrow."

———

Had a beautiful dream last night. You were there standing legs apart, hands held high, dressed in a white linen long dress. Standing and embracing the glorious sunset, the orange and pink showing through your dress. Butterflies were all around you blending their colorful wings with the sky. The sun was a huge golden ball resting on the horizon and you were singing Christmas carols in French. After you soaked up the sun and all the colors of the sky, you turned to me and ran with all your might into my arms. I immediately felt charged with radiant energy and as I spun around I felt my body and soul transcend to another life, another world. What a beautiful high! I promised myself when I awoke from the dream that I would conjure up that dream again and drink it all in.

———

"Miss you muchly today, of course, but I know you are beside me whispering into my ear sweet and sensual thoughts. Wish I could spend some time with you this Christmas, but this is not possible at this time. Will it ever be possible? Yes!!!

I was alive with sex and loving. I had Jack in the evenings and weekends, and we were doing well. I had Dick on scattered days. I was able to keep these two men separate and love each one deeply and fully. I knew that this double life was not the way it was supposed to be: you are not supposed to have two loves, not at once. I did not wonder about life after college or having a marriage to Dick because I was already married. I presumed that it would end eventually, that we would tire of one another, or that his midlife crisis, last-fling episode would get worked out of his system, and we would be over. Maybe I was just experiencing my own version of wild college days, having a heady affair with a professor. "Be here now" was my philosophy, and I even owned a book by that title.

That summer, after my second year of college, I worked at another Girl Scout summer camp run by the same woman who ran the camp in Washington. This camp was at 8500 feet, just down the road from Pike's Peak in Colorado. Jack came along to work, too, which was so much better than the summer before, when I had worked at the camp while he stayed in St. Louis. And although he was there for me, I knew that Dick was visiting Colorado and was just down the road. My yearning for him was distracting, but the pull was as strong as gravity. I had invited him to bring the family by for a visit, but he did not, thank goodness. I don't know what I might have done, but I am sure that it would have been reckless.

When Dick spoke of his wife, Lois, he spoke of a woman completely dependent on him. She built her world around him. Once, somebody had asked Lois if there were a fire, and she had to decide whether to save her children or her husband, which would she chose? She said that she could not decide. Dick saw that as evidence that she was too wrapped up in him, because what mother would not immediately say that she would save her children first? He had persuaded her to get her teacher certification, and she taught kindergarten. But he saw me as much more exciting, more independent, and that made him feel free and strong and stimulated, while with her, he was looking at a quiet retirement, with her reading books and not adding much life to their party. But I liked Lois, the few times that we had chatted. And he spoke about his star pupil to her, about how I was working my way through college, both in his office and doing babysitting and housecleaning. She asked him to ask me if I would like another cleaning job, cleaning their house. He reported this to me, appalled at the irony and wickedness of me cleaning his house where I had played in his bed. "You'll tell her I'm grateful for the offer, but I have a lot on my plate right now," I told him. Occasionally she would come by his office, once wearing the giant squash blossom necklace he'd given her, its chunks of turquoise crafted into complex silver figures, its expensive size overwhelming her tiny frame. She was always cheerful, with a full head of brown wavy hair, and big brown eyes with deep, dark circles below. She was a nice lady, and I was not jealous of her. I had what I had. That was enough.

It was the next year, as I was getting ready to graduate, that tension built, both between Dick and me and between Jack and me. I didn't know what to do. I tried to pick apart my relationship with Jack, but he fought for us, and we worked it out. I tried to get blasé about Dick, but we couldn't keep our hands off each other. I couldn't talk to just anybody, and certainly not to my family, but I could talk to Joni. Her apartment was halfway between the college and my apartment, so I frequently stopped and visited her, climbing the dim stairwell to her place above the storefront. She would listen, I would cry, she would make me tea, and one time I tried to eat an entire carton of Breyer's Butter Brickle ice cream. Ice cream, after all, is the go-to food of the heartsick. The year before had been amazing, enjoying the love of two men and loving them. But now it was time to get real. I would graduate in May, I had to find a job, and I had to decide. Neither man was the sharing type, and I felt the need to give myself completely. If only polyamory had been out in the open back then. I found myself drifting to Dick, choosing Dick. But that was foolish. It made no sense. He had a good wife, and I had a good husband. We would hurt our families. What would the college think of him? Neither of us wanted to hurt anybody, but we thought of divorce with dread. I sensed that we were out of control and that bad things would happen, as I wrote in the following poem that year:

This beautiful new building is on fire.
All the brick and asbestos and sprinkler systems,
No codes nor engineer's skills could prevent it.
No concerned neighbors could be of any help.

Freely the fire rages,
Structures and strictures melting
and crashing down,
The familiar complex reduced to the basic elements.

In the fertile rubble or the ravaged soul
waits a phoenix.

So on April 1st—another Rabbit Rabbit Day—a month before graduation, Dick and I went out to lunch together. We spoke calmly about my imminent graduation and agreed that it made sense to end things then and give me time to take care of all my end-of-college assignment; I had packed in an overload of courses that last semester when I saw that doing so would get me certified at both the elementary and secondary levels. The break up would allow me to focus on getting a job. We each sighed and nodded and were sad. We were glad for what we'd had but knew it had to be done. We drove calmly away from the restaurant, and he dropped me a block from the college, as was our custom so that we would not be seen together. I had work to do in the library, but as my logical, responsible, task-master part of my self sent me trudging across that spring-green lawn to the library, my heart clawed its way out of the closet where I had tucked it. It bashed down the door and knocked me sobbing to the ground under one of the massive oaks. I had never wept like that—great, wracking sobs of grief and loss. I cried and keened and curled into a ball.

Somehow, some time later, I hauled myself up, my face bloated and red, my eyes aching, my head hurting, my throat tight. I trudged into the library and up to my favorite spot upstairs where I snagged a comfy reading chair by the big windows looking across the street to the college, to Dick's office, to where he parked his car. The library's architecture evoked a forest, with beautiful natural redwood grids covering the lights, and the ceilings were supported by columns that branched out like those of a tree, with the wood pattern of the concrete forms clearly visible. It was peaceful. The white noise of the ventilating system washed over my weary, sad self, and I closed my eyes, nearly dozing, trying to recoup the strength to finish my homework and take back a monogamous marriage to Jack. Maybe ten minutes passed. When I opened my eyes, Dick was there, sitting across from me, watching me, and he smiled. How had he found me? He would have had to search all over the library to find that nook. He didn't go to the library.

"I can't do it," he said, shrugging, then leaned intently toward me. "I don't know where you are going, or what we are going to do, but I won't live without you." He smiled broadly and his eyes were bright and wet. "I don't know how this is going to work. Today is April Fool's Day, and I was the biggest fool of all for thinking that I could end this. Things are going to get ugly, and people will get hurt, but I want to spend the rest of my life with you. I won't say good-bye to you. The rest of our life begins now."

And so it did. And he was right: people did get hurt, and things did get ugly.

I told Jack that April. I told him that I never stopped loving him, that it didn't happen because of him, but it just happened. I told him I had tried to end it but couldn't. I wanted a divorce. "No, this isn't over," Jack argued. "You love him? How long has this been going on?" I could see that his mind was whirling. He grew pale. He sat on the floor, his knees bent, trying to make sense of it.

"I can't have you both anymore It's not fair," I said.

"You can't decide what's fair for me. I don't want to give you up."

"I'm sorry."

"I think I should move out." He whirled around, got up and grabbed some clothes, stuffed them in a bag, and left, walking past his brother Tom, who was living in our living room.

"What's going on?" Tom asked, looking up from his homework.

I was too hollow to answer. I started to cry, and retreated to the bedroom. He spoke with Jack and found out, but Tom needed a few days to move out. That was awkward. As I was puttering in the kitchen that week, he had the radio playing. A song came on and the singer crooned, "*When I fall in love, it will be forever.*" Tom looked at me as I passed, and snidely interjected, "Guess that's not *your* song."

Later that week, Jack and I spoke more calmly. I would not change my mind, I let him know. But I was afraid to tell my parents. I knew they would be angry for what I had done, especially that I was mixed up with a married man, breaking up his family. They were so happy: I was graduating in May, their first child to graduate from college! They already had plans to come for the ceremony. Wait until after they leave, Jack suggested. Don't ruin it for them. But you moved out, they'll see that we are splitting, I moaned. Somehow, we came up with the idea that he would move back in for the time that my parents were in town for graduation and that after they left, I would break the news to them. So it was an awkward graduation, and I have a photograph taken of Dick, in his black gown and doctoral hood, standing in the sunshine, shaking hands with my parents, standing across from me, so proud of their daughter's accomplishment and departmental honors, while Jack stood between us, watching that exchange.

My parents liked Jack, and he and my mother were buddies. But what hurt them most was when they found out that I knew about our breakup before graduation, and had lied to them by not disclosing what was really going on. Jack wrote my parents a letter and asked them not to be angry with me, that he was letting me go and wanted me to be happy. Jack wrote me a long letter too, full of despair but wishing me well, and he told me that no matter what, he would always love me, and that I could always go to him. I took him at his word.

Loving Richard

Dick was a charismatic man who radiated love and acceptance. He saw the beauty in everybody, and students grew in his presence. He commanded auditorium crowds as easily as he did shy preschoolers or angry parents. He did not condescend to those who faced challenges of learning, physical, or mental disabilities but instead found it easy to connect to them; he would go out of his way to chat with them. Dick spoke of not just accepting others but of enhancing others. He was a spokesperson for the personal growth movement of The 60s (which we know includes the early 70s, but "he 60s" is how we refer to that era). He was passionate and exuded boundless, contagious energy. He was free with his hugs and touches. Many adored him. So when he bowled me over with his love, how could I resist?

Under his leadership, Webster was at the forefront of progressive education. Traditional teacher preparation had teachers working in classrooms at the end of the four years of undergraduate work, but Dick saw that students were in classrooms from the first week of school. The college had its own lab school, and its teachers also taught graduates and undergraduates. He was an idealist with a practical background but who thrived on innovation. As a result, his master's program for working teachers was an enormous success for the university. He stood for everything I believed to be good and possible in education.

But what was it like to be loved by him as his wife, not his acolyte? He was unfailingly kind and supportive. He was open to adventure, adored traveling, and had no fear of taking on big, new projects, whether building his own house with his own hands, as he did back in Maine; starting a summer camp in the Ozarks, as he did with his sons in Missouri; or speaking to national convention crowds, as he did on his speaking tours—or marrying a woman decades younger than himself. He had two speeds: fast and off. He had an inner GPS, never got lost, and was fascinated with maps: he would pore over them before, during, and after trips. He was strong and loved to do hard, physical work. I can see him on the riding mower at Rainard, his shirt off, his handkerchief (men of his generation *always* carried a handkerchief) tied at the four corners and sitting pirate-style on his sweaty pate. He was part Penobscot Indian, so he would quickly turn a deep walnut color by early summer. Even at my tannest, I looked like porcelain next to him. I loved that contrast.

He was a good listener but a better lecturer than a conversationalist. I was frustrated that he did not ask questions of me, so I told him that it felt like he did not care to know me. To him, questioning a person was intrusive, while to me, the curiosity felt like making a caring connection. He felt that if somebody had something that they wanted the other person to know, then they should go ahead and share that. So imagine my shock when at the age of 86 he asked me one day, "How are you doing? What's going on with you?" That was the first time he had ever asked. Dementia can lead to some pleasant changes along with the sad.

After Webster, Dick dropped that nickname and its pejorative connotations and resumed his given name, Richard, so that is how I will refer to him now.

The only times he would get angry with me was when I was mean or dismissive in my bouts of frustration. He hated to be criticized, which explains why he seldom criticized others. But as he aged and his physical pains grew, his patience with naughty or lazy children grew thin, and he could lose his temper with students. He always had a short fuse and could explode with a loud rant and pounding of fists or banging of pans—but then the storm passed quickly out of his system, and he was back to his patient, loving self. Our Rainard students accepted these outbursts, but I had to learn to fight—not physically, but to meet his yelling with volume of my own. Until I learned how, I was shook to the core when he would have an episode. I had never experienced anything like what he did. My parents did not fight; they used the silent treatment. The quiet tension could go on for weeks, then Dad might whisk Mom away to the Caribbean or do something nice that I never witnessed, and all would be smiles again. If it ever got to the point with my parents that they were to yell, I could be certain it was the end of the family and life as I knew it. Richard's fits, then, felt catastrophic and devastating to me, but to him, they were simply relief valves. If I ever got wound up to the point where I yelled, it would take me hours or days to calm back down; I was slow to boil and slow to cool off. So I decided to learn how to yell back, which certainly took Richard by surprise. As a result, I didn't have to hear the tirades as often, I could release my tension too, and we could get down to a solution without me being completely intimidated. We became more equal, and I became more understanding.

Oh, but he loved me. He was always bragging about me to others, regaling them with lists of my qualities and accomplishments. I felt self-conscious and embarrassed that others had to endure his gushing, certain that they could see it was all exaggeration and hyperbole. But when somebody whom you love and admire sees the good in you, how can you help but want to live up to it, to believe that you can?

Creation Process

When my theater friend Jeffrey got to New College, he experienced an explosion of creativity. He became fascinated with Kabuki and with Bun-Raku shadow puppetry, and he created a Bun-Raku production of "Mother Courage." He wrote to me:

> I'm clogged. There are vats of pictures and ideas and sounds and colors in my head, and I can't let them out. I have to sit tight. I'm ....in the middle of a big creativity spurt, and I'm not allowed to be. ...I have a fully-developed CCC [Caucasian Chalk Circle] inside me, and I'm having labor pains, goddamit. And I've got a *Toy Cart*, and *A Man's a Man*. And they're all coming at once, and I can't control them any more—I'm going to start regurgitating all my masks and dances and colors and shapes indiscriminately all over my life.

I knew just how he felt. Once the labor starts and the long gestation is over, there is no turning back: you must create. The pulse quickens, the breath comes in short pants, and the nervous energy must be channeled into creation or you will drive everybody around you bananas. As Jeffrey continued in that letter: "I throw things and laugh uncontrollably; my arm twitches constantly, I get headaches...." That is how it was for me when I invented Rainard, as each day I retreated to my black notebook to pour it all out on paper. I would stare out the window in deep concentration, then the words would rush out, filling the theme paper with the beauty I wished to put in the world. There was one particular record album, and on it, one special piece that I would play when I was all charged up: it was as if I needed to get in harmony with something outside myself, some other part of the universe, as what I was creating was something bigger than me. Creativity has been described as a cycle of retrieving within and reaching out, and the music bound the reaching and retrieval together.

The song was Keith Jarrett's "Köln Concert Number Five" on his album *Facing You*. I had first heard it on a rare and beautiful evening in an even rarer and beautiful place. It was during Richard's and my second summer together, when we headed west from St. Louis to visit Colorado and the West Coast. We then traveled across the top of the country, then turned and went through Kenosha to visit my family. The summer before, we had done the East Coast and visited his family first before turning left and coming down through Canada to visit my family.

We took off each time with a tiny, two-man backpacking tent, a pretty thing in sky blue and yellow, and two sleeping bags that we zipped together into one cozy sack. With a small cooler and a Coleman stove, a little rag rug to put at the door of our tent, and two folding camp chairs, we were an efficient camping pair. Richard was an outdoorsman, too, having spent his childhood freely roaming the forests and hills of central Maine, and later having been part owner of a ranch in the Ozark foothills. But that summer we camped in Lake City, Colorado, chuckling at the thieving chipmunks who managed to carry the rind of an entire cantaloupe high up into the spindly, long-legged pines that struggled to survive at that elevation - 8700 feet at the campground. The tiny town was rumored to have an oasis of gustatory pleasure for us, too, tucked into a restored mining-town building.

It was the perfect aesthetic evening, with just-caught mountain trout, local greens, and fresh huckleberry dessert. I was enveloped in the warm glow of my wine and enchanted by the music in the quiet little restaurant, with piano riffs and rhythms playing over the perfect sound system, taking me away. "Waiter, what *is* this *music? I love it!*" And that was how I found Keith Jarrett. The song to me is about anticipation sated and work begun with optimism. It is about creative energy, and Jarrett's audible moans as he plays make the music as human as my own breathing. That is the music I would play when I sat down to create Rainard. That is the music I returned to twenty years later to create the high school.

The creative process is about fits and starts, and when the result is right, even if it is not something you have ever seen before, you know it is right and good. It is as though a tuning fork has struck, and the note of your creation is aligned in every vibration with the mathematical rightness of the pitch. It's not about research and experiments to support a hypothesis or prove your perspective; it's about truth and beauty.

It's a heady process, creating something big, and one of the side effects of exciting my mind is a somatized, generalized energization. I have energy to burn, and all my senses are wide open; I practically glow. And that makes me susceptible to sex. Maybe Virginia Hunter was right about libido after all.

Richard benefited from the brunt of my passion. Ravishing him shed the excess energy like a dog shaking off after a hosing. Ideas stimulated all of me, especially ideas about things I cared passionately about. When I was an undergraduate and he was the chair of the education department, my energy for my work in education got spent in his arms and hands, and wrapped in his legs. And now, as a thirty-year-old, I was in my prime — so the literature said. I did what I could to wear us both out.

That November 1985, as I was putting it all together, I knew that I needed to catch up on what I had missed in my five-year hiatus from education. I found a part-time job in a school working with preschoolers, an age that I'd never worked with before, because I knew that I would start Rainard with the youngest children and grow them into the kinds of students that traditional schooling simply would not produce. I read like crazy, and I went to the annual convention of the Texas Association for Gifted and Talented in San Antonio. I could not afford the pricey convention hotel, as all those educators could who were there on the dime of their school districts or colleges, so I had arranged to stay with the relative of one of Richard's coworkers in one of the beautiful old Victorian mansions in the King William District. I was anticipating a lovely bed and breakfast, but it turns out that I had paid to displace their six-year-old daughter. I slept amongst a sea of pink Strawberry Shortcakes, Care Bears, and dollies. I felt like an intruder, but they made a few bucks off me. They did not offer to feed me, but I was able to enjoy the president's reception at the lovely hotel, with a free glass of wine and a buffet of hot and cold hors d'oeuvres. As I looked over the stuffed jalapeños, the dark man on the other side of the buffet popped one in his mouth and told me, "Oh, these are terrific! You've got to try one." We chatted on and found a place in the crowded room to tuck into our little plates piled with what was surely going to have to suffice as my dinner. Art Sierra was his name, and he was a cheerful, interesting conversationalist. He, too, was a teacher and the parent of two gifted children. He was a local and had grown up just a few doors down in the King William district. We left the reception and we walked along the stone sidewalks that wound through the Riverwalk. We listened to the haunting percussion music from the garbage can man who played under one of the cool stone arches that bridged the river. Lighted party pontoons drifted by, and mariachi music echoed over the water. Fueled by the energizing ideas from that day's convention sessions, the wine, and the romantic Riverwalk setting, sparks were flying between us, and it was time to ignite them. We found a room in one of the many hotels there on the Riverwalk, as neither of us had a private place to where we could go. The room was pricey, but he paid it, and we got our money's worth that night. He was kind and gorgeous, and we spoke the same language.

I had not really cheated on Richard before in our eight years of marriage and had never gone on the prowl. I had not been on the prowl that night, either, but I was very receptive to the connection. For some time, I had felt like there was something amiss between Richard and me. I had lost 63 pounds after our daughter was born in the hopes that he would find me exciting again. It did not change anything. That night on the Riverwalk, Art and I exchanged phone numbers, and as we walked away, I found myself absent-mindedly humming a little made-up tune—a happy melody about filling a hole that I had not known needed filling.

At first, we got together nearly once a month, meeting at Grumpy's hotel, a halfway point between San Antonio and Houston; we'd split the cost. On several visits when I had some important writing to create for work, I would bring my writing materials and revel in the relief of a romp with him between writing sprints. Sex and writing just seemed to go together so well. Once we arranged to spend a night together in the Lost Pines of Texas, in a cozy log-and-limestone cabin built years ago by the Civilian Conservation Corps during the Great Depression. Another time, Richard and our daughter went away camping, and Art spent the night in my bed. That visit, he brought a porn video of nothing but cum shots, which he loved but I found ironically dry. For eight years, we saw each other, although the times between grew to months or even a year. He liked to hear about Rainard's growth and struggles, as he had been there to hear about it before it even opened. I liked to hear about the accomplishments of his growing, overachieving son and daughter, and we laughed when he talked about trying to fix his little girl's long, unruly hair with elastics and barrettes when her mother was out of town. One time he brought me a gift of six boxes of red felt-tip Flair pens for the school. Most other visits, he would bring a little trinket for me: a piece of costume jewelry, a flower, a unicorn magnet, some home-baked cookies, a bottle of sweet German Blue Nun Rhine wine to share. The only time that I ever saw him upset was when we visited a tiny local cemetery down the road from the motel. "Damn it, I knew it!" he said. He showed me how the cemetery was divided in two: one side for whites, the other side for the Hispanic surnames. He was angry at the prejudices that Texans had against his people.

The visits grew longer and longer between. At our last visit, he said that he couldn't do it anymore, that he felt too guilty. He would always be my friend and wished me well. I was angry and perseverated on the disappointment for years, my befuddlement torturing me as I shampooed my hair or paused between keeping the books at the school. What had happened? Why did it take so long for him to decide to cut it off? It isn't as if he and I had ever talked about a future together, as we both loved our spouses. He had gotten me through some very tough years. We just enjoyed one another, so had he stopped enjoying me? I didn't know. When he was on a trip to Washington, DC about ten years later, he and his wife stopped by to see the high school where I was working then. We all had a very civilized lunch together, and he talked about how the last year had been rough because he had battled prostate cancer. He looked much older. I did not miss him, but I was grateful that he had been my friend long ago. I could no longer feel the anger at his dismissal years before.

I did not look to fill the hole that was left when hope of reconnecting with Art died. I did not want to jeopardize my marriage or my reputation. After all, teachers—and especially principals—are expected to be moral exemplars. It helped that he lived 180 miles away and traveled in different circles. So Richard and I rode our marriage like a tide. There were long, frustrating stretches when I wanted to kill him, and equally long, joyful stretches when I was glad that I had waited out the ebb tide to enjoy our peace and affection during neap tides. While I may have had a couple one-nighters during out-of-town trips, I did not have another long-term relationship after Art for a good, long time.

While my creation process was whetted by sex, it was sex that resulted in my very best creation ever: Emily, Richard's and my daughter, born when I was 24 and he was 53. I wanted to do everything right with the conception: I had read that 24 was the optimum age for a woman to give birth. I worked in a public school then, and I did not want to harm the fetus, so I got a German measles vaccine and waited three months, the exact number of months recommended, after the vaccine before allowing myself to conceive. I stopped taking the birth control pills months before, too, so their hormones wouldn't mess with mine. However, I was skeptical about whether I would actually conceive because Richard had contracted a severe case of mumps as an adult, after his youngest son from his first marriage was born, so his fertility was an unknown as the infection could have rendered him sterile. But I was not taking any chances. Surprisingly, I conceived immediately and timed the birth for the end of the school year like a good teacher should. We were delighted. And ever cautious, I did not tell the world until the first three months had passed, which was just before Christmas. I told my students, who took an active interest. Richard and I scheduled a big open house for his college colleagues and family at our home. And a week later, at my check-up, there was no heartbeat. The baby had died. I could not breathe at the news. The doctor said that sometimes this happened, and that we would wait to see if it passed. If it did not, then he would schedule a D&C after the holidays. So I spent Christmas carrying around a dead baby, struggling to find a way to respond to the congratulations without making everybody as uncomfortable as I was.

I was teaching fourth grade in public school then to a sweet bunch of kids. They were excited about my pregnancy. I taught their reproductive system lessons that year, and they knew how babies were made. I had to tell them something. We owe children honesty, and tap-dancing around tough topics just opens the space for fear to grow. I sat them down and told them that sometimes this happens, that it is the way that the body makes sure that during that amazing growth process, if something isn't working right, the growth shuts down, the woman has a miscarriage, and the body prepares to try again. I let them know that it happens in one out of eight pregnancies, statistics say, and that like anything else related to sex, people are shy to talk about it. The kids were cool about it, and we just picked up from there and had a great second semester.

The principal, however, was unhappy and called me into his office. He only spoke to me when he heard something negative, which was not often. Once a teacher tattled on me when, in the presumed safety of the teacher's lounge, I had vented that I would like to rip out one of my disruptive student's livers and feed it to the crows. I assured the principal that I would never actually do that. This visit, he was upset that I had discussed my miscarriage with the children. He said that my decision was inappropriate and that parents had contacted him to say that their child was upset and asking uncomfortable questions.

"Did you want me to pretend that I was still pregnant all the rest of the year? Or did you think that it would all just leave their memory?" He did not have an answer. And weren't children allowed to be sad?

I truly loathed that man, Chuck Hoppe. He was a smiling, older, coach-type principal. He visited my classroom once in the three years I taught there. He showed up ten minutes before lunch—not a great time to visit, yet he decided that he would give a twenty-minute lesson during the end of my math class—about the wonders of the globe. He seemed to think that he was being inspirational, but he only inspired a flurry of desperate looks from the children, to me, then to the clock, then to me, as their allotted time for the tightly scheduled lunch line was slipping away. But he kept a tidy school, tidy like his spiky gray buzz cut, so tidy that there was only one piece of playground equipment to get in the way of the wide-open field or expanse of asphalt. It kept things tidy, as I said, but it is not as if he ever had the playground plowed. In the winter, we could go weeks without play time outside because he did not want the children tracking snow puddles into the school. Children had to move tidily through the hallways, without talking or whispering, keeping the lines straight between the linoleum seams. He kept costs down, too, by not turning on the heat until the teachers arrived. It was radiant heat from pipes under the floor, so if you wanted to come in early to work, you would be in a 50-degree room until all the children arrived and their quick bodies added to the radiant warmth of the room.

One of his neat swoops sent me right over the edge. I loved to develop comprehensive units that integrated all the disciplines. I developed a unit about tulips. At the time, I was working on my master of arts in teaching, with a special emphasis on media/arts. As part of that coursework, I developed a slide show of the botany of tulips and bulb flowers, adapted from a comprehensive feature in *National Geographic* magazine. Nowadays, that would just be a matter of combining a PowerPoint, scanning, and cut-and-paste, but back then, it would take hours to photograph the magazine pictures using a special fixed-mount camera with careful lighting. Then the film had to go to a processing center that could make slides. We studied the geography of the Netherlands and read all about how to grow bulbs. We compared bulbs to seeds and learned the distinction between annuals and perennials. The students raised money to buy a huge collection of bulbs, taking time to choose carefully and thoughtfully. They marveled how such a knotty, oniony-looking thing could grow into such bright, parrot-proud shapes. They loved the book *The First Tulips in Holland*, illustrated by none other than S. D. Schindler, the big brother of my high school best friend. They waited patiently all winter after we planted the bulbs in a plot in front of the school sign, and we celebrated when they rose up in the spring and brightened the plain school entry. And the next week, Chuck ordered them mowed down, despite the fact that they were not finished blooming, because, he said, they were starting to fade.

He was not a sensitive man. This was even more evident the spring after my miscarriage. It was an afternoon in the late spring, at the end of the marking term. I was teaching and was startled by a warm, liquid rush between my legs that was definitely not urine. I felt woozy and declared that we were having a spontaneous SSR time—sustained silent reading—because I needed to go check on something in the office. Students dutifully took out their recreational reading books and settled into quiet, and I headed down the hall to the staff bathroom to find that I was completely soaked with blood, and more was coming. This was not a menses, as I had just discovered the month before that I was pregnant again. Fortunately, I had been wearing black slacks, so nothing showed. I walked into the office and said that I had to leave, and could somebody take my class. There was no privacy in the office. The secretaries quietly and grimly bustled around to make arrangements for my students while I made several phone calls. I tried to call Richard at the college but could not reach him. I called my doctor, who told me to come right in. I knew not to drive myself. I called my sister-in-law, and she picked me up in her truck. Each bounce jolted me and made me more uncomfortable. She waited with me at the doctor's office. He examined me, extracted an apple-sized clot, and examined it carefully.

"I find no tissue in here. That's good news, but it's too soon to tell if you have lost the baby, so I would like to run some tests. Let's put you in the hospital."

I spent a night there and called the principal to tell him that I would not be in until Monday. He offered no soft words but only asked when my report cards would be in. Those were the last things on my mind. They were due Friday.

"I can have them in on Monday," I said, dreading all that pressing down on those 75 3-part NCR report card forms to hand write comments and check multiple boxes on each. I did not want to think about them at all.

"They're due Friday," he reminded me.

"I am in the hospital and I may have miscarried, but I can get them in Monday."

"If that's the way it must be," he said, and hung up. No condolences, no offer to extend me another day or to help explain a slight delay to parents.

I was back in the hospital where I'd had the sad D&C that January. When I was recovering back then, I was annoyed at first at having to share a room with another young woman during my time of grief. Her husband and little girl were visiting her, and after they left that evening, we chatted. She had just had a D&C that day, too, for the same thing—what they called "an incomplete abortion." Those words made it sound like we had tried to take coat hangers to our uteruses, but that's what doctors called miscarriages. Even back when my mother was going through child-bearing, she had suffered a miscarriage between babies three and four, and on her medical record, it recorded six live births and one abortion. She wrinkled her face in indignation and nearly spat when she saw that. But my room-mate and I shared our mutual sorrow and wished each other well when we departed the next day. Now I was back in the hospital, on an IV, and they drew blood for the special hormone test that had to be sent away to Kentucky to be analyzed to see if I was still pregnant. They would have the results in a week to ten days. I would have to wait patiently to see. The tests came back and reported that my hormone level was borderline, indefinite. So every two weeks for the next couple months, I was to come in and bring a first-pee-of-the-morning urine sample. However, my appointments were scheduled for after school. And the pee had to be refrigerated. These were the days before home pregnancy tests were perfected and made more sensitive. At least they no longer had to kill a rabbit with an injection of mother's urine. So I would dutifully bring in my sample jar, wrapped in a baggie and a paper towel, stapled into a brown paper bag, and jammed into the staff refrigerator with the hopes that we had no lunch-bag thieves. And once again, we would find out if I was still pregnant. Those were long, uncertain months of waiting and tension. At last we were past the 90-day mark, and beyond. On the last day of school, I sported a maternity T-shirt with an arrow pointing down to my midsection, with the message *Under Construction.* The children lit up. We had gotten through the year, and our shared sadness of months earlier was now shared delight. The staff pitched in for six months' diaper service—which I never saw, never even got the name of the company. I did not intend to return in the fall, and the principal and I never had a conversation about that fact. I was not asked to turn in any paperwork. I was glad to get away from him, and glad to get away from all that was intractable about the school system.

I finished my master's degree that summer, fearful that the strong chemicals used to clean the silkscreens of my serigraphy class would damage the fetus. I loved my ceramics class, and that is where I got the inspiration to hyphenate the baby's middle name. It dawned on me that none of my siblings' seven children had been given a name that hailed from my mother's side of the family, but four of them had names from my father's side. That did not seem fair. A classmate suggested two names, so Emily had the appendage *Astrid-Augustine. Astrid* was the name of my father's mother, and *Augustine* was my mother's maiden name. Despite my bulging belly, I still worried what would emerge after the terrors of the spring. I'd had at least four long ultrasounds, and there were no visible calls for concern, but ultrasounds were not as clear or as easy back then. You had to have a special appointment at the hospital, and you had to have a completely, painfully full bladder for the sound waves to bounce off. I learned the hard way, after drinking three quick cans of soda and sitting uncomfortably for an hour, that carbonated beverages interfered with the reading. It also did not help that the movie *Aliens* had just come out, and the image of those horrible creatures bursting from the bellies of the unwitting space crew gave me nightmares of my own baby emerging violent, horrifyingly ugly, and very, very angry.

Richard had already been a father three times before in his first marriage. His first wife's pregnancies were all calm and normal, and their first son was born nine months after the wedding day. He had to be driven to the hospital in the nearest major town, a harrowing fast drive over logging roads with the baby in a laundry basket in the back seat, as he needed a transfusion because of the incompatible Rh factor. Other than that, Richard had not been a pregnancy partner with his wife. He had not been present in the hospital room when they were delivered, so having our child was a new experience for him. We went to Lamaze classes together and practiced my breathing so that he could coach me through the labor and delivery. He would be there.

I worked right up until the birth. People spoke of a burst of energy just before the baby came—nature's way of helping you to get everything done, all your ducks in a row. I was just exhausted, so the onset of labor was a surprise. I had offered to babysit my 7-year old nephew and 9-year old niece that evening, but as I was serving their dinner, my water broke. They were so excited! We managed to track down somebody else to watch them, and I had to have Richard paged at the college to come home so we could go to the hospital, which was not optional because my water had broken. Richard was exhausted, too, and kept complaining about his cold, which made me angry: he was acting like a big baby, trying to get attention for his pitiful little cold when my insides were roaring and my back was breaking. He'd weakly push on my lower back during my long back labor. I went through three shifts of doctors and nurses, each one having a look up my bottom, until so many had been there I felt as if there might have been only three people left in all of St. Louis who had not seen my cervix. I was hooked up to monitors, and they screwed a little instrument into Emily's head. The nurses said that the monitors indicated that the labor was not all that strong, but I begged to differ. Finally, somebody twitched the little internal sensor, and the monitor needles jumped. Oh, you were telling the truth, they said. Ya think?

I was getting impatient. I had been up all night. I was grateful when they gave me something to help me sleep. I had no idea how helpful a series of three-minute naps could be in between bouts of strong labor pains. I would doze off, awaken to pains, stare at a spot on the wall, breathe as I had been taught, give gentle effleurage to my enormous, roiling belly, then doze off again, to repeat in three minutes. When at last the anesthetist had me curl onto my side for the epidural, I wanted to run off and marry him: nobody had ever made me feel that good. I loved him. He was a god. I was so grateful! And at 1:16 in the afternoon, after seventeen hours of labor, Emily Astrid-Augustine was born, all pink and perfect, with a high Apgar and no signs of damage from having nearly been miscarried, no deformed limbs from art class chemicals, no arrhythmic heart from all my stress in those uncertain months. There were marks from the forceps that drew her reluctantly into this world, and with the delicate, star-shaped soft spot of her fontanel, it brought to mind that sweet Cat Stevens song about the special child who was born "with the moon and star on his head." I hummed it to myself, accompanied by the cooing of the pigeons on the windowsill outside my room, as snow fell softly. Later that night, another woman joined me in my room who had just given birth. Emily's healthy birth was the first miracle that day, but that woman was the second: she was the same woman with whom I had shared a room in that hospital months ago, mourning our miscarriages. She had given birth to a healthy baby that day, too!

My mother flew in from Wisconsin and was busting with delight. Mother was born to be a grandmother: it was why she was put on the earth. While her six children had challenged her and stretched her patience to snapping, her grandchildren had her smiles and patience. She was a doting, spoiling grandmother. She and Richard stopped for a few drinks before coming up to the hospital to check on us, and they were gleeful. Mother beamed, "His first wife may have given him sons, but it took *my daughter* to give him a little girl!" She cleaned my house and cooked me yummy foods, including a memorable baked scalloped potatoes and ham.

At last, she and I had something we could bond over. This had not always been the case. While I loved her, it was my father with whom I enjoyed stimulating conversation when I was growing up. It was he whose hobbies interested me, and whose accomplishments I admired. In my political, rebellious teens, Mother seemed like an uneducated, prejudiced, narrow-minded housewife. But now my mother had the heart and experience to get me through my own new and unfamiliar path as a mother. The space that had been so wide between us grew small when I married, and it no longer existed now that I was a mother. The day, six years before, that I rode away to elope with Jack, she stood in the driveway and cried. "Why so sad?" I asked her. "I've never understood you!" she sobbed. We understood one another now.

And I understood her, eventually, reluctantly, when she could not stop smoking, despite two operations for lung cancer. Try as she might to stop, we would find her slipping out into the yard, admiring the garden with a Salem cupped in her hand behind her back. Cigarettes did for her exactly what the old ads said they would back in the 40s. We had found an old newspaper in the detritus left behind in the basement by the previous owner of my brother's new house. It had a cigarette ad: *Ladies, are your nerves bothering you? Feeling stressed? Enjoy the cool comfort of our menthol cigarettes.* The ladies who smoked in the ads—in the newspapers, on billboards, in magazines, and on television commercials—were sleek, glamorous, elegant, and fun-loving. Nobody coughed. You could not smell the stink on their clothes. Their windows were clean of the cloudy skim from indoor smoke. Their clothes and upholstery had no tell tale holes from errant ashes. Smoking had actually been encouraged as a restorative back in my mother's youth, when she had started. So as I grew into a woman, coming of age in the time of "women's lib," I no longer saw my mother as stupidly self-destructive. Her strangled cough no longer sounded like she was trying to kill herself to get away from us. I did not see her weakness; I saw her smoking as her survival tool. Those cigarettes were her respite when her six kids and husband drove her crazy, when the pressures of endless housework, cooking, and chauffeuring around willful, ungrateful, adventurous children got to be too much. Those cigarettes got her through her days before I was born, when my father was actively alcoholic and sometimes irresponsible. Smoking got her through the estrangement with her own parents and their deaths. They got her through those days when she felt trapped and undervalued, when she spoke of her desire to claim her worth, which in her mind would be evident if somebody hired her, perhaps as a clerk in the grocery store. But my father would not have a wife of his working outside the home. How would it appear? Like he could not provide? Didn't she have enough to do at home? What could she see herself doing, without a degree or even a high school diploma, with no skills, he asked. And the smoke filled her after my brother was killed, when a piece of herself was killed, and she forever blamed herself for not figuring out how to prevent him from the dangerous dance with alcohol that her own husband had passed on.

Roger

Some people say that grief that is kept inside festers and grows cancers. If that is so, it was the case with my mother. When my brother Roger was killed, and people would express their sadness and condolences, she spent her energies to comfort them and to keep her own brave face. She was proud and would not let herself be embarrassed by letting others see her fall apart and cry. She never got over Roger's death.

Roger was the most charming of her six children, a grinning, roguish, playful fellow with glasses, unruly, curly, dark blond hair, and long, thick eyelashes. If you looked at my father's handsome high-school photo, you saw Roger, and you could see why he and mother had a special bond. He was close to the siblings closest to him: Janet, three years his junior, and Keith, two years his senior. He would tease Janet mercilessly, and she would borrow his sweaters. He and Keith would have adventures, and Keith could be counted on to rescue Roger when he would get into fights. But with me, he seemed to know what I needed. He was eight years older than me, but the few times I remember him paying me any attention, he was spot-on. I was a very chubby little girl and self-conscious about it. I was convinced that nobody would ever love me. Kids teased me: "Lorrie Laken, full of bacon." Other little girls were picked up and tossed around, but I was playfully chucked on my round cheeks. I can still recall that Roger picked me up once and dangled me by my knees. He was strong and stocky, and that lift made me feel like, I, too, was a girl, and that there was hope for me. I squealed in delight. And he gave me a birthday present one year, something my other brothers never did. Roger gave me a two-pound box of chocolates! I hid them and hoarded them, and thankfully, I did not eat them all because when the chocolate "bloomed" in the heat of my closet that July, I mistook that white haze—a harmless separation of the fats in the chocolate—for mildew and tossed most of it away. But Roger and Keith got into so much mischief, my parents thought it best to get assistance to keep them out of trouble, so they were both sent off to Northwestern Military Academy on Lake Geneva, about an hour from home. They were forced to handwrite letters home every week to let the family know how they were doing. I remember boring Sunday visits every few months and watching them in their dress parade from across the school field. They wore kilts and played bagpipes, as part of their tuition was paid by a scholarship conditional upon their learning to play those pipes. Keith was disciplined there for shaving his own head, but Roger had the audacity to steal the headmaster's speedboat to cross the lake to pick up some local girls, and then he accidentally sank the boat.

On one of their summer breaks, my parents hired a housekeeper and took a long trip to Scandinavia to visit my father's relatives. The house-keeper had no control over the boys, and they would have beer parties in the basement after she retired to bed early every night. One muggy night, Roger, who of course had been drinking, borrowed Mother's Oldsmobile Vista Cruiser station wagon and took the turn by our house too sharply, crashing through the next-door neighbor's fence and into the living room of her house. Nobody was injured, but mother told the story of how on that same night in Sweden, she sat bolt-upright in bed in a dead fright (time difference notwithstanding); that was the kind of bond that she and Roger shared.

He was a cracker-jack marksman, and he and Keith competed in shooting competitions. That marksmanship may have helped Roger to survive Vietnam. He could have been deferred, having suffered some hand injury that left its mobility in question, but he said something to piss off the recruitment officer, so Roger was in the army and off to the war. My folks visited him when he trained in Oklahoma, and my father and Roger took off on a motorcycle to chase bison. Like most Vietnam vets, when Roger returned from the war, he would not talk about it. He was changed—messed up. He had done some very hard drugs in the army and contracted hepatitis, so we all had to get painful shots in the rump. He listened to angry music on his record player.

Janet hung out with him sometimes, and it was he who helped her score some LSD. Janet invited a girlfriend over to spend the night, and they dropped acid together, with my parents in the next room. I had been happily displaced to the back porch to sleep on a lounge chair. I remember being drowsily aware very early that morning of somebody hovering over me. Janet and her friend were whispering, "Wow, look at all the *colors* in her hair, they're so *beautiful.*" I fell back into sleep, to be awakened by blood-curdling, horrific screams. "I'M SHRINKING!! I'M SHRINKING!" I ran up the stairs to my bedroom, where Janet was sitting calmly, dazed, on the bed, and her friend was standing in its middle, stark naked, breasts bouncing, eyes wild, panting. My parents were at the door, father red-faced, asking Janet to get her a robe or something. I was sent away from the mad scene, trying to eavesdrop as they made phone calls for the friend to be retrieved, and to track down Roger to threaten him to within an inch of his life. Dad had said he would kill anybody who gave his kids drugs—and now it was his own son. They checked Janet into the psychiatric ward of the hospital, a move for which she never forgave them. She stayed a few weeks, and for years after that, I found her changed, with a look in her eyes as if she were not all there.

Roger was Mother's third child, and as she described him, he was in a big rush all his life. He was in such a rush to be born that she only got her slacks down around her ankles at the hospital before he burst out of her. And he left the world quickly, too, at the age of 33, a father of two, ages 3 and 5. It was them he was protecting that night he tried to stop the drag racers who plagued the quiet street in front of his house. He wanted them to slow down in the neighborhood where his children played. And when he stepped into the street to force them to slow down, the boys who had been drinking and driving did not see him in time, and they hit Roger. He flew 30 feet and was killed instantly when his body slammed into a fire hydrant. The driver spoke of seeing a strange figure clad in rags jump in front of his car. In fact, Roger was wearing his "skins," a primitive suit he had made when he was on a black-powder hunting event in Lead, Colorado, a retreat he had enjoyed several times. He had worn that leather outfit to an impromptu poker game at the neighbor's house, thinking that they were going to dress wild, too. He'd had quite a bit to drink, and the coroner ruled that he was inebriated when the drinking driver hit him. The driver served no time and paid no penalty. My parents went to that court hearing and were forever dismayed at the unfair verdict. But because Roger had been drinking, the driver was not charged with manslaughter.

And so my mother's cancer grew. It's not that she didn't try to quit smoking, and she actually did for a while when the doctors told her that if she did not quit, then she would not see her beloved grandchildren that

Christmas because the cigarettes would kill her by then. There was no more powerful motivator—not a swimming pool, not cash. But she couldn't help it, and she gave in to them again. My daughter Emily had the lucky benefit of almost three years of Mother's spoiling, with presents and visits between surgeries and chemotherapies. She and father were on a road trip, driving from Janet's in Phoenix to my home in Houston, when I got a call from my father saying that they wouldn't make it; they had to fly home right away. He had awakened in the night to Mother beside him making strange strangling sounds, and she was panicked. They flew back to Wisconsin, and I got the call from Dr. Mike, a friend of my brothers, who told me that the cancer had metastasized to her brain, and that very soon she would be completely incapacitated. She grew bloated with edema and forgetful She wore a bad wig, and she lost her voice completely. On my last visit north that winter to visit her, I sat beside her on the sofa, holding hands—no, *gripping,* her hand—feeling the desperate love between us, completely silent, knowing that it was our last before I had to return to Texas.

Father took care of her at home the best he could, but eventually he had to admit defeat and checked her into a nursing home. Mother said that she never, ever wanted to be stuck in a nursing home. He checked her in on a Thursday, and she died on Sunday. Hospice was not the norm then, but it would have been a real help and blessing if it had been. Mother also made him promise not to allow her body to be shown and not to have a funeral. She was self-conscious of her looks and did not want all those people to get maudlin. We argued with her that people wanted to pay their respects and to share their grief, but she would have none of it. Her stubbornness was even more exasperating considering the fact that she never forgave Roger's wife for having him cremated immediately before she could see his battered body, before she could say that final goodbye. She knew how important that goodbye was, yet she would not give it to others. And so the obituary in the Kenosha News informed people that there would be no funeral and that only the close family would gather. My brothers and sister and father, and our spouses and our children, gathered in the big family living room where we had celebrated every Christmas. We sat on the same hard, upholstered chairs that were reserved for only formal occasions and special gatherings, on the same organ bench where my sister and I had played tunes that pleased my mother. Her ashes were elsewhere, waiting for interment beside Roger. Father said nothing. I choked my way through reading a piece about her. Friends and neighbors dropped by or called, wondering how to grieve, how to help. People loved my mother. She was plain and humble, with an easy laugh. When she could show a kindness or share her generosity, she would. She had just turned 60.

1985–2004, Rainard

It was crazy: that is certain. The few others I have met who started a school had a following amongst their friends or in the education community. They had money of their own or a well-to-do spouse. They had the support of a public school charter, or a foundation and grant money. They had property in a church or in their own homes. There was a demand for what they had to offer.

I had none of the above. I had been in Houston for only three years, working in retail, pulling a small salary. I'd been out of any classroom for five years and therefore had no local connections in education. We were poor from Richard's bouts of unemployment and our moves from Missouri to Colorado to Texas. What I did have was a do-or-die attitude. I had spent my youth railing against lousy education. I had burned out and said that I was out of education for good. Despite that, I had kept boxes of education books and materials and lugged them around the country. Richard had written on those cardboard boxes with Magic Marker "FOR THE SOMEDAY SCHOOL." I had just turned 30. Now was the time to stop dithering around. It was time to see if my vision could really work. I felt that I had no right to criticize if I couldn't make it happen. Richard said that I could not keep calling it "The Someday School," so I invented Rainard as a blend of Rainy, his nickname for my Lorraine name, and "ard" as part of Richard and Bouchard. It sounded dignified. I did not want a cliché name like "Acorns to Oaks" or something cutesy like "Wee Scholars" or pretentious with "Academy" in the name. I did, however, insist on the word *gifted* in the title. And I was very particular that it was for gifted *learners,* not gifted *students,* because *students* would have implied that our focus was on advanced academics for high achievers. Instead, I knew that these exceptional folks may not be achieving well in school, either because of disinterest or disability. I intended to engage them in interesting, even inspiring learning. I knew how to adapt to work from their strengths rather than focusing on their deficits.

Everything to start a school had to fall into place simultaneously, which was impossible because each step relied on another. Securing a location required money. A loan required collateral, and all we owned were cars and life insurance. Securing 501(c)(3) status required a financial plan, which required projected enrollment, which could only be wishful thinking at that point. Folks would not enroll until they saw the site, which could not be secured without money. Folks wanted to know the vision: well, that I could do. I created marketing materials and press releases, but they could not be released until I found ... a location. Eventually, I secured $5,000 from the banker husband of a colleague. We located a daycare center that had gone out of business. While I could not afford to take over the building, I bought its contents for $500 and all its playground equipment for another $500. Another $500 went to move and set up the equipment.

I picked the brains of two other women who had started private schools in Houston. One woman had started a school for gifted children that had been cited as required reading in gifted education classes. She mortgaged a new building to the hilt, and she went bankrupt the year after I opened. The other lady described how she found her location by grabbing a beer and driving around potential neighborhoods on a Sunday. That's what I was doing—but without the beer. She secured a few portable buildings and grew from there until she could afford to build. I drove around hunting for a place that had a lot of nature and space to play outside, as I knew first-hand that time outside in nature is imperative for mental and physical health. While others were converting spaces in the strip shopping centers that Houston developers had overbuilt, I wanted outdoor environment more natural than six inches of pea gravel over a hot parking lot.

I found Rainard across a busy MKT railroad track and down a dead-end road just west of the Houston city limits. It had been a family's country home, back when that was country. The long ranch house had a covered brick porch that extended the full length of the building. Inside were a 1950s kitchen, a great room with a vaulted ceiling, a fireplace, and plenty of wide, leaded windows. Down the hall was a half-bath with an antique toilet flushed by a pull-chain on a wall-mounted water tank. One small bedroom had a cork floor, twin beds with wagon wheel headboards, and cowboy curtains. It had its own bathroom. Down a hallway was the second bedroom with windows on three sides and its own bathroom. The rooms had waxed oak floors and thick knotty-pine walls. It had heat and air conditioning, well water, and a septic system.

There was a built-in swimming pool, one of the first built in Houston. It had its own pool house with two bathrooms, a shower, and three changing stations, as well as the equipment and filters in the other half. There was even an underground, domed bomb shelter in the yard! Giant live oaks and a magnolia tree shaded the campus, and a bricked patio area was enclosed by redwood benches and a brick barbecue pit. The property was fenced and waiting for children. I negotiated a lease that would start at a reasonable rate and escalate with enrollment. I understood that the property would continue to be for sale, but I persuaded the landlord to move his "For Sale" billboard to the unrented eastern portion of his twelve acres. We rented four acres and shared a parking lot with the caretaker who lived across the property. Two large warehouses were on the other part of the property. The owner's family had been in the oil pipeline business, but the warehouses were now empty.

It was expensive to set up the school and bring it up to code with Harris County. I had to project enrollment five years ahead and expand the septic system to accommodate that many students. The contractor who did the work left an open septic tank and drain system for weeks after the school opened until he finally got around to meeting the inspector. I learned more about septic systems, perc tests, and drain fields than any other principal I knew. Every closed space needed its own smoke detector, fire extinguishers had to be clearly labeled, and battery-powered emergency exit lights were hung. I had to change out the faucets in the student bathrooms so that they wouldn't scald themselves by turning on only the hot water. I installed a high chain-link fence and gates around the pool. I had to secure phones and an answering machine, since we would not have a secretary. I had to get the lines from the propane tank inspected for leaks. I needed to learn how to conduct monthly well-water samples and drive them to Houston for testing. Richard took care of the four acres using the ancient, inadequate riding mower until it died. When we asked the landlord for a replacement, he was angry that we had been using it and suggested we get a goat. We could not afford a janitor for a few years, so Richard and I did the cleaning, he after his day job, which brought in the salary that allowed us to start the school, and I on the weekends.

The school was for students who were gifted—who were in the top 3-5% of the bell curve of intelligence tests. Few students had IQ tests that they could bring to our admissions meetings, so we did our own screening. Psychologists would charge $150-$250 for an IQ test, but we did our screening for $50, with the understanding that it was an identification screening, not the IQ test, and no written reports would be given. Richard, whose PhD was in educational psychology, pulled together a battery of short IQ tests and skill assessments that took 30-45 minutes to administer one-on-one. This was done on Saturdays and Sundays. I would talk about our program and learn about the student from the parent while Richard met with the student, and then he would give the results to the parent while I got to know the student. More often than not, the student passed. Richard had a true gift for putting kids at ease and getting to know them in a very short amount of time. It was not unusual for a parent to cry over the results because nobody had "gotten" their child like he had. Why did so many pass? Cynics would say that Richard was overly generous in order to increase enrollment. In truth, there were some students admitted about whom we had to remind ourselves that not all gifted children were high achievers, and even gifted students could have learning and behavior challenges. But in fact, most parents have a pretty good sense of their children. Before they ever came in for a screening, I would speak at length with the parents on the phone about their child and what our students were doing. No parent wants their child to be at the bottom of the heap, so many would screen themselves out if they thought that their student was not able to do what our other students were doing. Additionally, I strongly urged parents to come by and tour the school on a typical day so they could see for themselves what kinds of peers their child would have and observe our unusual program in practice. What they saw was unlike anything that they themselves had ever experienced. I frequently gave prospective families the phone number of a random enrolled parent so that they could ask frank questions. I did not want people to be unpleasantly surprised.

We opened that September with two students: my daughter, Emily, and a little boy named Marc. By the end of the year, I could brag that enrollment had grown 250%—to five students! I started by accepting 4-6 year olds, then added an age each year until we hit middle school age.

What were some of the many things that made Rainard different? For one thing, I intentionally grouped the students in mixed-age groups, not because that is how enrollment grew but for its many benefits. Having students at many levels requires the teacher to adjust expectations according to what each can do. In a traditional, single-grade class, the teacher has a narrow set of expectations for what is normal, what is poor performance, and what are advanced skills; students get labeled. But gifted students are renowned for asynchronous development, in which they can have highly advanced skills in some areas but not in others. A six-year-old, for example, could be reading at a seventh-grade level but not have the attention span for books of that length or the emotional maturity to deal with seventh-grade themes. Another six-year-old may just be learning to read but be craving advanced knowledge about dinosaurs or car repair. In small classes—no larger than 12 students—a teacher can focus on each student's development and individualize as needed.

A mixed-age class functions together as a family; in fact, the Brits call the mixed-age model family grouping. The older students model behavior and routines for the newer ones, and the younger students delight in learning the same things as older students. Parents of the youngest children in the class bragged that their children were learning with the older students, but the parents of the older students would fret that their children were being held back by being in class with immature babies. I helped them to understand that when new students were being taught skills that the older students had already been taught, that casual exposure was a valuable review, more palatable and efficient than direct review. *I'm not going to pay attention because I've already learned this,* a gifted student might resist if directly expected to sit through a review lesson. However, when given the opportunity to share what he already knows and to look smart and helpful, that same student easily accomplishes the material review.

Teachers were encouraged to "aim high" and not to worry if the youngest or newest students in a class did not master what the higher-level students caught. After all, repeat exposure makes each subsequent exposure "stickier."

Another value of mixed-age family grouping is that it expands time to learn. How? With a typical 3- or 4-year age spread, such as 4-6, 6-9, or 9-12, only about 1/3 of the class is new each year, which enables the class to hit the ground running in September without having to take a month to learn the rules and to write the typical "All About Me" projects.

Our curriculum was unique. We were aware of grade-level expectations in the state curriculum, but we did not design what we taught around them. Yet we made sure that if needed, students could transfer back into a traditional program without problem gaps. Our focus was on engaging topics and themes that centered around science and social studies, in particular, three annual themes. In "Spaceship Earth", our focus was on earth and space sciences as well as geography. During the "Uniquely Human" year, we studied life sciences and sociology, as well as early History. For the "Freedom" theme, we learned about modern history and government, physical science, inventions, and the many avenues of creative expression. Each level in the school—primary, elementary, and intermediate—had its own special topics and projects within those themes, so that "Spaceship Earth" looked different to the student when it was approached each time. Classes shared between levels, which reinforced prior learning and enabled teachers to share material that could help an older student with a gap or a younger student ready for more advanced material.

Math was one subject that was taught apart from the themes. While we incorporated thematic math applications whenever possible, we worked for continuous progress. Students would move between classes to take math at their individual levels. It was not unusual to have four different levels in a room. Students appreciated the multiple levels. Those who were advanced benefited from review when asked for help from younger mathematicians. One girl explained why she liked the system: "I had always felt terrified of long division, but seeing the older kids survive it made me feel comfortable."

We took full advantage of the learning opportunities in the vibrant Houston area. Field trips were an integral part of our program. We went everywhere that we could to bring our studies to life, and we averaged one field trip each month. We used parents and teachers to drive students on field trips, and occasionally we took public transportation. Every class saw at least two plays each year. We visited the public library so teachers could check out 50 books at a time to provide the depth that our students needed (remember, this was before the Internet). As students got older, we took them farther away. To make this financially doable, we camped as much as possible. To get students good at camping, we started with even the youngest students, who camped one night each spring in tents on the playground. Elementary students camped in one of the state parks just outside Houston. Intermediate students traveled farther, to San Antonio or other Texas areas. The plan was that by middle school, they could travel around the United States, and by high school, they could travel internationally.

It's been said that students today are nature deprived. Kids do need to get outside, not just to run around, burn off energy, and soak up vitamin D, but to absorb its lessons and its balm. Students had up to a half-hour recess in the morning and a half-hour at lunch. If kids needed another break, teachers had that discretion. We picked dewberries along the fence and made wreaths of Carolina Jessamine. We collected and dissected owl pellets from the warehouse. We watched ant lions dig traps for ants, and we marveled at the beauty of velvet ants. I taught the students not to be afraid of the ubiquitous blue-black mud dauber wasps, who were not aggressive and only wanted eight-legged critters. I would say to the fearful child: *How many arms and legs do you have? Four? You're safe.* One break that I loved with the kids was taking them on "nature hikes." The school was on a dead-end gravel road that had fascinating ditches full of life on either side, a sometimes-pond, an overgrown scrap yard where berries grew, and a cattle guard over another ditch. What child could resist the power of plunking stones into the water? To cross that cattle guard was a rite of passage for little kids. Some were terrified of falling between the rails to imagined snakes below, so confident kids helped the timid across until they grew brave. We observed the seasons change. We wondered about litterers and cleaned up what they tossed. We watched the crawfish mountains grow and the dragonflies hunt insects. Nature was not a once-every-few-years field trip like in other schools: it was a daily, important experience.

One conviction that I had to give up pretty quickly was that school should be year-round, but with plenty of breaks. My original calendar never went more than six weeks without taking either a long weekend or a two-week break. That break gave me time to plan new units and do administrative work, and it gave families a time to take vacations without having to do so with the rest of the world at peak pricing. It eliminated the two-month break during which students lose knowledge and get out of the habit of being a student. Rainard tuition included a six-week summer program. However, families with other children in traditional schools found this problematical. I tried to point out how nice it was that our students could have their parents' attention as an individual, but that was not as important to others as it was to me, the fifth of six children who seldom had my parents' attention to myself.

It became clear that the school had to bring in more money than our five students supplied, so I turned the summer program into an enrichment summer camp, "¡Summer Incitement!," and opened it to any motivated learner, not just identified gifted students. We marketed heavily to students and their teachers in gifted programs in the hopes that some would like what they saw and stick around for the school year. The summer program was a huge success and its income helped. I recruited teachers who were excited about a subject that they either just couldn't get enough of or had not had an opportunity to teach during the year. Some were certified teachers, and others were professionals in their field who thought it would be a nice break to teach kids. Unfortunately, if I had any student attitude or discipline problems in the summer, they were with the regular Rainard kids! What was happening was that their mothers would drop them off at the summer program, which they were required to attend, with words like, *Oh, I'm sorry you have to go to school today. Your sister and I will be baking cupcakes and playing at the pool.* So in subsequent years, I did not require attendance at all six weeks. Instead, students could choose which four of the six weeks to attend, and choice makes all the difference. Later, rather than raising tuition, I would simply include fewer and fewer weeks of the summer program as part of their tuition. The fact that our program was very flexible helped to make it successful but a challenge to organize. Students could come for as little as two hours a day for one week or as much as 9 hours a day for six weeks. They could stay from 11-1 for "Club Noon," with supervised outdoor play, swimming, picnicking, and a cool-off time inside before afternoon classes or going home. Some years, the program attracted as many as 200 students over the course of the summer, which was quite a change from our usual population of under 50 students.

Enrollment did not come close to my expectations, and because I had started out charging what I thought that private school tuition should cost, I was not making enough to pay the bills and pay me a livable wage. I was paid nothing the first year, $500 total in the second year, and at least a little something every month of the third year. I had to either raise tuition to cover costs or close the school. I gathered the parents to tell them of my predicament and announce that tuition in the coming year was increasing 40%. I understood that this was a hardship for many, but I needed to know by April 1st whether I had commitments to the new tuition from a set number of families in order to keep the doors open. I wanted to give them time to find places at other schools should closing become necessary. I was shocked that enough committed, and I announced that the doors would stay open. Later that week, two parents backed out, and I should have as well, but unlike them, I kept my word.

Publicity was everything and ongoing. Every person who came by the school could get the word out. Every student wore our logo and school colors when we left campus, and every summer student got a lively T-shirt that they liked to wear year-round. I networked at conferences and served on committees for local gifted education. I spoke to teacher groups, to journalists, and on public television talk shows. I wrote press releases when the summer program was announced, when we acquired new classrooms, when we hosted fundraisers, and when our students won awards. I learned to write 10-, 15-, 30- and 60-second radio public service announcements. I took classes in how to maximize direct mailing results. One year, I handled all the registration fees for a regional academic competition through a separate Rainard account, so all those folks had to write the school name on their checks. I passed out hundreds of business cards. The first logo that I designed was a dancing star, to communicate the playful joy of learning. Along a similar vein, one of our successful magazine advertisements showed a blackboard being erased with the words *Is your child's love of learning being wiped out?* In later years, we changed the logo to five stars dancing across a more serious font of the school name to make it look more like school that was worth the increased tuition.

Fundraising, too, was constant. We sold popsicles to pay for the school's pets—the gerbils, the guinea pig, the cat, the parakeet, the fish, and, for very brief spells, a dog and a hedgehog. Students washed cars and sold chocolate bars to pay for field trips. We held a spring carnival and capital campaigns. We served alcohol to grease their wallets. Our biggest fundraiser cost us $40,000 up front to clear $10,000 profit when we hired the illusionists Penn & Teller to perform. My favorite fundraiser was the annual Valentine's "From the Heart" auction. Every student, teacher, and family would put something into a silent auction for Rainard family members only. There was exciting variety and something for everybody. As examples, a child might donate an afternoon of playing video games or a week of doing the winner's classroom chores, while a parent might contribute hockey tickets, a bottle of wine, or a custom-made dress. I usually donated a big pan of homemade lasagna, fresh salad, and red wine ready to go home for dinner that night. The competitive bidding could get fierce. I had to learn to disguise my bids because people were afraid to bid against me!

Running the school, wearing all the hats at some point, teaching all the students at others, was exhausting. It was rare to have a weekend off. Every family had my home phone number so they could call me anytime with concerns. I let them know that if their child was crying about homework or spending more than an hour on it, something had been miscommunicated, so give me a call because we were not in the business of torturing children. I told them that I would prefer that they checked out rumors through me rather than raising alarms amongst the families by spreading concerns there. "Parking lot parents" sometimes did real damage. It was a year-round, 24-7 job.

There were certainly risks. My family could have lost everything. The board had directors' and officers' liability insurance, and the school had accident insurance for the students and staff, but the school did not have other insurance for the first ten years or so. Before we bought property insurance, we were lucky. All those parents and teachers drove students on field trips, and nobody had an accident. When we did finally get insurance, we had one claim after another. A tornado took off chunks of the roof, which got us a new one. A burglar ran off with all the school's electronics, which got us replacements. A fire ruined one of the portable buildings, so we got a new one. After that series of unfortunate events, we were forced to find a new insurer.

I am proud of all that we accomplished at Rainard. We gave a great education to many kids. I was able to put my passionate beliefs into reality. After the freedom and the power to make my dreams come true, it would be hard to find anything else with as great an impact. I did, however, look forward to lifting some of the weight off my shoulders.

2004: Bye, Bye Baby

It took years for me to leave Rainard. Throughout my 18 years running and growing Rainard School, I would hit at least one spell of despair each year when I wondered if it was all worth it. Joni and my family were used to my frustrated calls when I would toy with the idea of closing the school. It was a seven-day-a-week job, with plenty of nights thrown in. We had saved no money at all and frequently floated loans to the school using those convenient credit card checks that arrived unbidden in the mail. I played credit card roulette, shifting the balance from one to another, or opening a new card, all to game the interest rates, taking advantage of the offers for zero percent interest for six months. I kept a ledger of my credit card debt in order to keep track of all the dates for the transfer balances so that the interest would not come due. The school would get flush with cash in the late spring, when fall tuitions would come in because we offered a discount if it was paid in full in advance. In addition, the summer program brought in much-needed cash. In August, the school would pay me back and purchase all the supplies it needed to last the year, and we would return to an endless series of fundraisers to fill the gap and try to prevent having to sign away our life insurance or our car as collateral for another loan to float the school again until spring. Most of the time, the budget balanced, at least in terms of cash flow, but when it did not, it was harrowing. I am proud to say that the school took on no debt, except to me.

My board, a necessary component of a nonprofit organization, did nothing whatsoever to help with the finances. They were happy to speak at length about how one more student admitted would balance the budget, and two would enable us to buy what we needed. They suggested that all I had to do was to write a grant proposal because surely one of the city's many foundations would give us money. The board did not have any connections at any of the foundations, so their suggestions were worth the air that they floated away on. The board member who did the most was Clarence Sullivan, who came to us as a volunteer accountant from Texas Eastern, a downtown energy company that gave employees release time to help nonprofits. He taught me to keep the school's books and looked over the work of the office help I was later able to hire. It was a struggle to find any board members at all, especially since I did not want to have students' parents on the board to avoid the conflict of interest. I tried to shield the parents from the ongoing financial struggles of the school, because given a whiff of shakiness, I knew that many would abandon ship. So the Board members that I did have—Clarence, Harold, and JoAnn Scott, who I found when she was the head of the committee for children with the local Mensa organization, were Board members for life, despite the bylaws that specified term limits or excessive absences that might have dropped them from the board. And they did stay for life. JoAnn got sick and could no longer attend, and Harold died of pancreatic cancer. Shortly after I left the school, poor Clarence died in the downtown Greyhound bus station, waiting for the bus that would take him to help somebody else who needed his generous assistance with their books. The folks in the bus station thought that he was just a homeless man sleeping on the bench, until somebody finally realized that he was not breathing. It was his heart. Of course.

For years and years, I put my family's security on the line for the life of the school, so I could pay my employees and keep the trust of my students' families. It felt good to be able to not only provide a superior education for the students but to provide a decent job and income for my staff; I took the stewardship of the school, including its people and resources, very seriously. But as my husband neared 80 years old, I knew it was time for me to make enough money on my own without his needing to work at the school. I had eased him into part-time work at the school, which he accepted kicking and screaming. So I began to look for employment elsewhere. I wanted to put my years of experience in gifted education and in administration to good use somewhere where they could pay me better and provide greater security. It was a long, slow look, as there are very few private schools for gifted students. I had no desire to go into a public system and deal with all their limitations, overly large classes, and bureaucracy. It was a disadvantage that my administrative experience was over such a very small school—fewer than fifty students when I left—but the breadth of my duties and the length of my service compensated. In 2000, I earned a doctorate in curriculum and instruction for gifted students. I was ripe for the picking by the right picker.

The Roeper School near Detroit, Michigan, brought me in to interview for its head of school opening in the fall of 2003. The interviewers did not ask me to be a finalist, but their rejection came with a delightful surprise because they said that they really liked me, and would I consider applying for a different position in the school, that of Lower School director? Apply I did, was offered the position, and accepted to start in the summer of 2004, the same time as their new head.

To leave Rainard behind was the best thing for me and my family, certainly, but it was really the best for the school, too. The school was my baby, and it was 18 years old, a time when babies and their mamas need to separate, and babies need to grow up and go out in the world and stand on their own two feet. The school had to find a way to survive without "mom and dad." Roeper made the offer late in the spring, about April, so that gave very little time for the Rainard troops to find my replacement. We formed a search committee and clarified what the school needed in terms of leadership. We added our first parent board member, David Steakley, a man retired in his 40s from Accenture, wealthy and with several students in the school. He had the time, the money, the business acumen, and the vested interest. He took charge of the board. At the meeting in which I turned the metaphorical gavel over to him, the Board voted on the future composition of the board. Richard and I felt that it was important for the head of school to be a voting member of the board, but the other three members of the board did not. They wanted to be able to control the new head of school (a title I use interchangeably with director) and to be able to discuss the running of the school candidly. I was gravely disappointed and offended. What had they ever not been able to say with me there? Nor were Richard and I made honorary board members, or ex officio, or anything that would allow us a say in the future direction of the school. My baby dumped me. Ouch.

When my transition out of the school came that spring, it was a time that would demand even more change from the school: our landlord of 18 years sold the property. Our lease specified that with just 90 days' notice, the landlord could evict us. That was another financial reality that I found it wise not to share with parents until it became necessary. We had been lucky that the school was not on "the right side" of the freeway, but on the industrial and farmland side to the north, so we were pretty safe from having it sold out from under us. City utilities had not yet been extended there. But by 2003, the plans to expand Interstate 10, which ran in front of the school, were looking like they would really happen, and after years of a very slow economy, property along the freeway started selling. The school's property sold to a speculator/developer who visited us that first week after the sale to tell us that he was immediately doubling the rent, filling in the swimming pool, and cutting down all the tall shrubbery that separated us from the noisy freeway. Well, as Richard and I were no longer on the board, it was going to be somebody else's problem—a very big problem—to move the school. We were moving to Michigan.

Shafted

Our house sold easily, and I exchanged it for a dreamy place in the Michigan woods, with access to two private lakes and plenty of gardens for me to putter in. The house had four porches, a sitting room off the kitchen with glass walls and roof, floor-to-ceiling windows in the master bedroom, and abundant skylights so you always felt like you were in the garden, the woods, or under the starry sky. I loved that house and all its quirks. The previous owner was artsy and had added aesthetic touches that sang to me. In one of the kitchen skylights was painted Mother Theresa's quote: *You can do no great deeds, but only small deeds with great love.* The living room and entryway had a bookshelf lining the entire perimeter, giving me adequate space for my large book collection and tchotchkes. There were two outbuildings: a smaller one for the lawn equipment, and a larger one for bigger storage, which I had visions of turning into my art studio one day. Sure, it had no basement or air conditioning, but it was gorgeous. We made enough of a profit on our Houston home to put down a big chunk of money.

Roeper was a well-established school with a great national reputation in gifted education. The Lower School, which I directed, was on the main, 12-acre campus that had begun as George and Annemarie's home. Now their former home was the administration building, preschool, and cafeteria on the top of the tree-shaded hill. Nestled in the woods behind that building were two other modern classroom buildings and several others that housed the science rooms and the music building. At the opposite end of the campus was a cluster of various-sized domes, where my office was housed, as well as the lower elementary classes and the PE/multipurpose room. Between these buildings lay the newest, modern, two-story classroom building where the 2nd-3rd grades, foreign language classes, computer lab, and art studios were housed. Behind it all were woods and a bubbling creek. A big, open play field was in the works to become a community building to be shared by the Lower School and the Upper School, with a competition-sized gym and space enough to house graduation and other whole-school meetings. The Upper School was five miles down the road, in an old public school building. The head of school kept an office on both campuses, and I would drive back and forth for meetings that would change locations from week to week. And they loved to have meetings! I was overwhelmed at the beginning of the year when we got out our HP iPAQs and planned out the entire year's worth of regularly scheduled meetings. There were administrative team meetings, facilities meetings, marketing meetings, Roeper Review meetings, and individual meetings with the head. There were division director lunches, diversity committee meetings, grade-level meetings (actually, grades were called stages there), search committee meetings, and many, many other meetings. Those meetings then generated even more meetings; nothing was ever done swiftly there because the school practiced consensus decision making. Everybody weighed in. At Rainard, if we saw something that needed to be done or that we wished to try, it could happen the next day. At Roeper, things were discussed *ad nauseum,* and things happened very slowly until everybody, especially the diversity committee, weighed in.

That first summer, I was charged with hiring five teachers or aides. However, I had to have teachers on the selection committee, and they were all on vacation. I was required have at least one member of the diversity committee look at every resume and weigh in on every meeting—and they were all on vacation. It took endless calls and arrangements to bring people together. The stack of applications easily stood three feet high on the floor of my office, evidence of the glut of new teachers on the market for the very few openings in Michigan's depressed economy. Each teaching applicant came in to give a demonstration lesson with a handful of real Roeper students, who were bribed to come in with a promise of popsicles. The parents were eager to bring the children because it meant that they could get first words of gossip about the new hires. I found these demonstration lessons to be the absolute best way to see if an applicant could walk the talk. They were told the age range of the children and were told to teach anything at all in a 30-minute lesson. I told the applicant that I expected the lesson to possibly fail, but what mattered to me was how the applicant fared in the debriefing after the lesson: what did she learn from the demonstration lesson: What had she observed of the students? Where did the lesson go wrong, and why? What worked, and why? If the applicant could not demonstrate an awareness of the individual differences of each learner and how to adjust for those, then the candidate would proceed no further. If the candidate thought that it was all about making the kids smile with a simple craft involving marshmallows and gumdrops but could not extract any deeper thinking or inspired creativity from the children, then she was history. The committee would then discuss the candidates, and we would come to a conclusion about who we wanted to hire, and we would recommend that candidate to the head of school, who would have a conversation with the candidate.

The diversity committee was a thorn in my side. Whether a candidate of color was qualified or not, the committee insisted that we bring her in because of the school's commitment to increasing diversity. It was a very white school, with only a handful of black students, but the Lower School coordinator, Carolyn, and the new head of school, Randall, were black. Because the Detroit area was far blacker than the school's population, there was an urgency to make the school better reflect the local demographic and to undo years of prejudice.

In my second summer, we needed to hire a teacher assistant who had the ability to move into a lead teaching position in a year or two. It was a directive of the board of directors that we be prepared for the imminent attrition of our rapidly aging teaching staff. The committee saw that ability as a prime qualifying characteristic, which meant that the candidate should have teaching certification; the search committee reiterated its hope to find a diverse candidate. Historically, the low-paid assistants did not move up into a lead teacher position, and if they did, it was after five or more years so they would be well-versed in the particular cultural nuances of the school. The search committee, with its requisite representative from the diversity committee, interviewed five candidates, and one was a woman of color. The committee narrowed the candidates down to three and said that it was a shame that the woman of color was not better qualified, but Cathy, who would be her lead teacher, said that she was just too tired to have to train somebody new to education. The committee said that they would be happy with whichever candidate Cathy chose. Cathy did have another teacher sit in on those final interviews. Cathy made her choice, with the blessing of the search committee, and Randall, as the head of school, approved the hire. And the candidate we hired did add to the diversity of our staff: she was an "out" lesbian who co-mothered one of the school's students.

When the hiring came up for formal ratification by the board of directors, one board member was upset that we did not find enough qualified candidates who were people of color. Another member asked about the statement in my report that "the hiring committee hired," wondering if that was, in fact, who did the hiring. I knew where he was leading with the question. He was trying to take the heat off me and put it back to where the buck stopped: with Randall. I did not want to throw Randall under the bus and always worked to accept responsibility for my decisions. No, I stammered, it was Randall who did the hiring.

But Carolyn was angry. I explained the committee's steps and reasoning, but that did not assuage her. She called for a meeting with Randall and me later that September and said only that she wished to talk about some of her ideas for diversity. The meeting turned into a very long litany of all the ways that I had misinformed everybody about the process and how I had missed the opportunity to hire an excellent woman of color. A bell went off in my head with the realization that Carolyn may have offered more assurance to the candidate than she should have, yet Carolyn had not seen the demonstration lesson nor those of the other, better candidates. The black candidate's course preparation and her lesson showed that she did not have what it took to be a successful Roeper teacher. I argued that she was not well qualified, and that we should hire the best qualified candidate. It was clear that Carolyn knew the woman and had spoken to her on several occasions, but not as part of the search committee or with any other staff members. She must have had a hard time saving face when that candidate was not one of the final three chosen. After I listened politely and patiently while she got her frustration off her chest, she asked if I had anything to say. I told her that she had called me a liar, and she said that she did not, only that what I told was not the truth. Randall only sat quietly and listened. It was her word against mine. She was the beloved old woman of the Lower School—and a woman of color. It was two against one. This was one of the first issues that led to my early release from my contract.

The Lower School director position was challenging but in some ways easy. The Lower School ran like a well-oiled machine, so there was little need for me to straighten things out or organize any glaring messes left behind by my long-serving predecessor. Rather, what the staff was begging for was support. They wanted to be observed and to be known. I can understand why my predecessor did not spend as much time in their classes as the teachers wished: with all those meetings, she would have been hard-pressed to make the time. So when I made my daily rounds, popping in briefly, staying to delight in the students' writing and art work, marveling at the displays, chatting with the students, word spread among the staff like wildfire: Rainy was here! Those quick visits meant an inordinate amount to them. Even so, the one greatest issue that needed fixing was the rift between stage two and stage three.

The Lower School was divided into four Stages: Stage I were the 3-4 year-olds, admitted to the school without any IQ testing but observed at an invited play session. They had a wonderful, playful program led by two very artful teachers. To advance be admitted to Stage II, a child must receive outside testing and be given an IQ score of 130 or above. The school was loath to turn away students who had been in Stage I, whether they tested as gifted or not. Stage II students were the equivalent of K-1st grade students, housed down in the Domes with my office. Stage III students were the equivalent of grades 2-3, housed in the big, bright new building in the center of campus. Stage IV students were grades 4-5, and housed in modern buildings tucked into the woods at the back of the campus. Stage II instructors taught reading as they observed the students showing readiness. There were workbooks but no homework. There was an abundance of excellent children's literature but no basal readers. It was a holistic approach to reading. Phonics skills were taught, but reading lessons did not take up the majority of the day as they do in most primary classrooms. Stage II, like the rest of the school, did a wealth of highly engaging projects, and the reading and writing were integrated into those projects. Students had plenty of small-group time with the two adults in each classroom. Reading was happening, but there was a lack of clear communication of how that reading happened. The teachers had been there for so long, doing what they did for such a long time, that for them, it seemed as difficult to explain how they were teaching reading as it would be for you or I to explain the details of how we drive a car. Stage III complained that Stage II did not teach reading, and that when students came to Stage III, there was a lot of catching up and instruction to do. These students were gifted, said the Stage III teachers, so they ought to have been able to learn reading by the time they were seven years old. Stage II teachers argued that when a student is ready, that student will put all that foundation work together rapidly, integrating all the development that had been done in the environmental-language immersion approach, then progress through the reading skills at a wondrous pace. Stage III teachers acceded that yes, this sometimes happened, but what was more often the case, in their experience, was that students needed much remedial reading instruction to get up to grade level. Parents were aware of this negative perspective on reading in Stage II and would take sides with teachers, sometimes in defiance of their child's teacher, sometimes in deference, but involved in the rift as well. Thus the rift had festered for years, and with the teachers housed in separate facilities, they made little progress in building trust and appreciation between the levels.

Charged with fixing something that had been awry for years before I arrived, I tackled it boldly. Communication, it seemed to me, was the key. If Stage II could do a better job of communicating how they were teaching reading, Stage III would be appeased. And parents, too, would be happier, because as they met with me in my interviews and on-boarding, they asked for more communication. The parent organization published a beautiful newsletter a few times a year, full of photos and stories of events of the past quarter and asking for involvement with the upcoming fundraiser, but the timely news of what was happening in the classroom was left to individual classrooms, and those communications were varied and spotty, more intermittent than regular. At Rainard, we published a weekly newsletter in which each teacher summarized the events of the past week and what was to come, including homework, field trips, and ideas for how the parents could interact with their children with topical discussion points. It would be posted online and printed out for those who preferred or needed a hard copy. I edited the newsletter and added my own irregular column of philosophy and observations. It was clear to me that this type of communication would benefit the faculty and parents alike.

The other stages jumped aboard with their weekly news, but Stage II resisted, grew angry, and got frustrated. Stage II had some of the oldest teachers, women who had not kept up with computers and resented having to climb the learning curve of word processing or even sending an email. They were vocal about their view of computers in the classroom as a bad thing that blocked the warm, human interactions between students and teacher. These teachers had been children of the '60s and now were fighting the dehumanizing technologization of what they saw as a sacred bond. They treasured their personal communications with parents and did not believe that any of those parents were critical or worried about their child's education. They felt that if only Stage III teachers would spend time in Stage II, they would stop being so critical. That, and they had no idea how to explain how they were teaching reading. They could not elucidate what they were doing any more than they could explain the paths that their synapses took when processing a thought. So I spoke with each of them at length about what they were doing, trying to help them to put it into words. They got a bit better, but instead of rising to the challenge, they delegated the writing of the weekly news updates to their younger assistants. They continued their bitterness about my forcing them to communicate in a way in which they were uncomfortable, and they were convinced that I did not understand, despite the fact that I had taught reading the very same way for many years at Rainard.

The head of school had two daughters in Stage II. They were delightful girls who, as luck would have it, were placed in the most disgruntled teachers' classrooms. Those teachers were fabulous with the children, but they communicated their frustration with me to the wife of the head; the girls' mother was a frequent visitor who charmed the teachers. She seldom stopped in to see me as she passed my office on the way to visit her daughters' teachers. She made no effort to connect with me or to communicate any concerns that the teachers raised to her. She saved that venting for her husband, who was fed a steady diet of concern about the changes that I was imposing on these respected, old-guard teachers. Meanwhile, the other Stages were giddy with the positive changes that they saw happening and pleased with all the positive attention that they felt from me.

Another conflict occurred when the head's secretary planned to leave her position. Having been there for years and knowing all the ins and outs of the head's duties, she had agreed to stay on to ease the new head's transition. When it came time to replace her, Randall interviewed candidates for her replacement. He did not use a search committee, as was required of all other positions in the school. The Lower School coordinator, Carolyn, applied for that position, and I encouraged him to hire her. He had frequently sung her praises and insisted that she and I find a way to support one another. I respectfully suggested that if he was convinced she was that good and knowledgeable, she would be invaluable to him. He showed irritation at this suggestion and hired somebody else. I was irritated that he could choose his secretary but I could not. I did not have a secretary, despite being responsible for more than forty staff members and nearly 300 students. Yes, Carolyn coordinated many things and was a sounding board for staff. And Sue handled all the paperwork, files, phone calls, and Band-Aids, and was also a sounding board for staff. But neither of them reported to me nor felt any obligation to refer to me the teachers who would land in their offices with concerns. Nothing in their job descriptions insisted that we work together. If I asked for something, they could choose to supply it or not, or say that they were busy doing their jobs. They did not want any additional duties. I did not have anybody watching my back, as a good secretary or office manager should, and like I'd had at Rainard.

There were other irritations between Randall and me. The first occurred during the first month of school. One particular single mother was throwing a wrench into the smooth workings of Stage I. She would not follow the directive to walk her child up the long, steep hill each morning to deliver him to class; instead, she would send her four-year-old up the hill alone. He was a disruptive, aggressive student. She was consistently late picking him up. She argued with the teachers. She and her son were clearly not fitting in, and after many conversations with her and the teachers, I told her that she was obviously unhappy, her son was having problems, the teachers were concerned, and perhaps another school would better suit her needs. She left the school and the teachers were relieved. But Randall wasn't. "I am the head of school!" he angrily informed me. "If a family is to leave, that is *my* decision! You made it without me!" I wasn't trying to go around him; I just saw my job as Lower School director as being head of the Lower School—its principal, charged with dealing with its staff and students. "From what I understand, I would have likely made the same decision, but it was *my* decision to make," he said.

"What decisions *do* I make as the Lower School director?" I asked sincerely. "How can I take care of things that get in the way of your being able to focus on the big picture of the school? I am experienced with these matters, so you don't have to do all of them. You can delegate to me."

"They are *all* my decisions. The buck stops here."

Well, that made it clear to me. So when another disruptive student situation in Stage I reared its ugly head, rather than asking the family to leave, I kept Randall informed as we bent over backward to make it work.

We even allowed the boy's nanny to stay with him in class all day in order to prevent his disruptions, a presence that the teacher found intrusive and uncomfortable because she interacted with other students yet was not on the staff. If it had been a parent, she would have felt differently, but this was a foreign-born nanny. The little boy had been adopted by a very high-profile parent, a litigious lawyer who handled controversial criminal cases. He was famously outspoken and argumentative, and he was overtly condescending and dismissive to his meekened wife. The little boy had serious issues, including aggressive impulsivity. Out of the blue, he would push other children down or hit them. One day, he went from sitting quietly on his teacher's lap to delivering her a brutal right hook to her jaw, leaving her injured and upset. When I got up the hill to take care of the situation, the little boy was in the comfy admissions office, being sweetly spoken to by that administrator, who was soothing him and letting him know that everything would be all right. He was smiling and swinging his legs. I got the facts of the situation and approached him as his principal. "You hit your teacher. That was a bad thing to do. You must never, ever hit somebody here again. You will never, ever hit your teacher again. Do you understand?" My tone was stern and slow. I did not raise my voice. He needed to feel that he had done wrong. He had not shown remorse. He was getting positive attention for being a brute! He looked away and nodded his head. The admissions lady looked on, aghast. How could I be so rough on the boy? While I had not raised my voice, to her, I was downright mean and bullying to him. She was the administration's biggest gossip, and she quickly spread the word that I had yelled mercilessly at the boy.

His mother was called to retrieve him. He would not be allowed back without a meeting with his parents to discuss the matter. Randall wanted all of us to sit down: me, the famous father, the cowed mother, and the injured teacher. We wanted them to know that it was our professional opinion that the boy needed outside, professional help. The meeting was uncomfortable and ran long. Randall did his best to talk around the hard facts, to try to sugarcoat them with concern for the best interests of the boy.

The lawyer did his best to dominate the conversation, to say that we were making a mountain out of a molehill, that boys would be boys, that the school was failing him, that we had a duty to complete our obligation to educate him, that he could not understand why we thought this was such a serious problem. Randall and the lawyer talked around the problem, the lawyer bullying and dominating, for more than two stressful hours, around and around. I'd had those kind of fiery conversations with upset parents before, when I had to break the news to them about their child's behavior and insist that they get professional help or leave the school. We would keep those meetings brief and to the point, offering whatever hope or referrals that we could. Otherwise, the parent would verbally and angrily stumble around in confusion and blame and frustration, wearing everybody down. Finally, the meeting was summarized that the boy would not return to the school until it could be shown that he was ready to benefit from what the school could provide. In my mind, that could have happened 90 minutes earlier with a lot less strain on everybody.

What the previous administration did have the foresight to provide was a transition person assigned just to me. Julie had her feet in both worlds: she was a teacher, and she was the teacher representative on the board of directors. She had been on the search committee that hired me, and she had flown to Texas to look at my school in action. She was a huge supporter, and she met with me regularly to let me know how people were feeling and to help me to navigate the politics of the place. But she was in Stage III, and her closest colleagues were not in Stage II.

As in all schools, more drama was headed our way, but I knew to keep Randall informed and involved, as he wished. He could have just made me the heavy and scapegoat for some of these issues, but he did not. So when Stage III begged me to closely watch their fellow teacher Jill, I did, and concurred that she was the weak link in their team. She had not managed to fit in with them, and they saw her as different and more "public school." Nobody wanted to teach beside her, and her classroom was alone on the second floor while the other three were downstairs. There was nothing glaringly wrong or offensive about her, but none of the other team members liked her. Randall observed her, as did I. I tried to build bridges between Jill and the other teachers, but they were adamant that she had to go, so Randall let her know that her contract would not be renewed for the coming year. At the end of school luncheon for the teachers, she had her say and told the staff that she felt she had been treated unfairly. She had dignity, and the other teachers shifted uncomfortably in their seats. When Jill left, two of the teachers surreptitiously burned a smudge stick in her classroom to purge it of its negative energy.

Another drama that involved both the Lower School and Upper School campus involved a beloved high school teacher who was married to an excellent, lovely Lower School Stage III teaching assistant. The two had been having marital difficulty, and the woman had struck up with a friend of the family who also happened to be the father of a student in Stage III. The teachers separated, and the estranged husband was going off his nut. He was found breaking into one of his high school students' houses, drunk and trying to talk to her and confide in her—except it wasn't her house at all but a stranger's. He threatened to hurt his estranged wife and behaved so erratically that he was suspended from teaching. Randall hired an off-duty policeman to sit in the school parking lot to watch for the maddened husband and to protect the teacher on our campus. At a directors' meeting with Randall that week, he rubbed his forehead in frustration and said that if she would only learn to keep her legs together, this wouldn't happen. I was shocked but said nothing about it to anybody. But the male directors must have said something to him, because the next day, Randall called me to apologize for his insensitive comment. I did not think that was necessary, because I know how people can say dumb things when they are under pressure.

The biggest brouhaha occurred in October of my second school year. The school had deferred repairing the roofs of the Stage IV classrooms for some years and was finally getting around to the repair. The workers covered the incomplete work with a tarp over the weekend, and when a heavy rain occurred at that time, the entire roof collapsed into the classrooms. Classes had to be quickly rescheduled to meet elsewhere on the campus. Nobody was injured, only inconvenienced. School went on. I spent the day working out logistics and answering emails from parents. They reacted very strongly to the roof collapse. The parents were frightened at what they saw was a near-miss: What if their children had been there when the roof collapsed? How could the school be so irresponsible? Why were the repairs being done during the school year instead of in the summer? Dozens of emails poured in to Randall and to me, and many parents phoned or stopped to talk. We addressed all of them quickly and professionally, even the parent whose name—I kid you not—was Berserck. And that parent did go berserk, shooting us several lengthy, flaming, insulting, vulgar missives, way over the top. Randall and I were slammed hard. But it was an unfortunate accident, and we did the best that we could to make things work for the good of the students. In fact, the school put even more money into refurbishing the building, making it better than originally intended.

And then my sense of humor brought the roof down on *my* head.

I'll never remember who sent me the funny picture in the email, the one that has gone around thousands of times. It shows an office desk with a little sign: "To submit your complaint, pull pin and toss." The sign is affixed to a hand grenade. I laughed because it hit home for me, having just been badly battered by terrible, outraged insults and complaints from angry parents. So I put it in the weekly newsletter with the caption: "For your complaints to the administration."

And then *everything* exploded. Not right away when the newsletter came out. It was a lengthy newsletter of about a dozen pages each Wednesday, and my small article about the classroom refurbishment, along with the meme, was tucked somewhere in the middle. Not everybody took time to read it thoroughly, preferring to flip only to the pages related to their own children's classes. Many folks laughed and brushed past the grenade illustration, but it offended some folks—a lot. Randall called me on Thursday and told me that he was "hopping mad." One of the teachers had been crying in his office, upset that I would joke about violence at a time when violence was scaring people. She stood every weekend on a corner in town with a placard announcing that it was time for peace and to end our wars in the Middle East. Parents had contacted him upset with the cartoon, too. What in the world was I thinking? Did I think it was a good idea? He demanded that I distribute a retraction that the school's legal counsel had prepared. Dozens of emails responded to the retraction, stating that they felt that no apology was needed, that the folks who were upset were overreacting and had no sense of humor. People supported me and thanked me for the apology. I mentioned those letters to Randall at our next meeting, which made him angry. But why, I asked him, was it OK to focus on the negative responses without also considering that there were positive ones, too? Wasn't it fair to look at the whole picture? But to him, my argument only proved that I could not handle a sticky situation well nor could I own up to a mistake.

I asked if we could discuss the matter further. He said that he was busy Friday, all weekend, and Monday, and that since we had no school on Tuesday, we would have to wait until Wednesday meet, after another scheduled meeting with a parent and teacher to work out a concern. So things festered until Wednesday. After that meeting, he asked me to wait because he needed to get a cup of coffee. Instead, he returned with the school's resident legal counsel. He sat down and said that the school had decided not to renew my contract for the coming year, and that I would not be finishing out the year. I was there on a two-year contract, which I had negotiated before the move when they had offered me only a one-year contract. I knew that the first year would be about learning and adjusting, and that the second year was when a new person tends to hit their stride. The contract said that I could be dismissed "for cause," but "cause" had never been defined. I was stunned.

"Why?" I flushed deep red, willing my adrenaline to keep me steady and to learn, not fight or fly.

"Well, because of conflicts like that. The grenade situation was a big mistake. The Jill thing. The situation with the lawyer's little boy."

"Except for the grenade, all those decisions were yours. I followed your orders and involved you at every step. And with the grenade, I delivered a sincere apology."

"These were your situations, and they left us exposed. And the hiring in Stage II was a problem. You might want time to think about this, and we will meet Friday to discuss the wording of your resignation letter to the community, and whether the letter would be jointly from the two of us."

"I see. Can we talk about this again?" I asked. "Because I do not believe that this is something that cannot be worked out." I was both numb and alive with electricity. He said no, it was decided, and that he did not have to give me any more reasons. He felt that my leaving before the end of my contract was a benefit to me because it would allow me to pursue other school administration positions, as those searches take place in the fall. "I don't think that this needs to happen," I said. "To lose a director at this time of year is not good for a school. I feel good about the work that we are doing as a staff in the Lower School."

I left his office and passed the Upper School director, on my way out and told him that I had just been let go. Gregg was quiet. I proceeded on my customary morning rounds around campus, thinking how much I would miss this place, wondering how to make the best of what was left of my time there, reeling with the uncertainty of Randall's closing, upset that he was blaming me for every conflict in the school. It was the same feeling I'd had in a work dream that I'd had a few months before, the one in which I was frustrated, trying to climb a steep, sandy cliff but continuously slipping back, gaining no ground. I passed Julie's class and saw that she was alone, so I stopped in for a reality check. She had told me the month before that she felt that her job as transition person was over because I had transitioned well and she was no longer needed. "How do you think I am doing for the school?" I asked her.

"Some people are upset with you, but I have scheduled a meeting with Randall to let him know that he isn't getting the whole picture." She had asked for the meeting on Monday, but he couldn't see her until Thursday. I then told her that he had fired me. She was shocked. She was supposed to be in the loop regarding me, but she'd had no idea. And it was not something that had been discussed with the board, of which she was a member and the staff representative. I asked her to keep it confidential, that I needed to figure out what to do, and asked her help. I was continuing my rounds, not saying a word to anybody else, when Randall called me on the school cell phone.

"I told you that I thought you should think about things," he said. "Instead you are going around talking to people."

"I'm not stirring things up. I told Julie because she was my transition person.

I am just making my rounds."

"As was our problem," Randall said, "I did not communicate to you that while I suggested that you might want to take the day, I failed to make it clear that you were to leave campus."

"No, I'm fine. I have a lot of work to do."

"I am telling you to leave. The more you talk to people, the less we will have to negotiate in your favor with the severance."

"Right now?"

"Yes."

This was crazy. I wanted to have a real conversation with Randall, to work things out. Couldn't we get a mediator from the board? Never once had I done anything but support the man and speak well of him. Perhaps I had been wrong to do that. He was a baby beginner head, having previously been only a division director at an exclusive boys' middle school outside Washington, D. C. He did not have the thick skin needed to make tough decisions because he wanted to be liked—the self-preservation flaw of administrators and politicians. His *modus operandi* was to listen and use charm, good looks, and platitudes to persuade people to see things his way, to follow his lead. Leaders like him want everybody to feel good, and when there were conflicts, he could not deal with the fact that the rejected family, the rejected teacher, the frightened parent, the teacher upset with change all brought their unhappy feelings and fears to his door. Not everybody will be happy. He seemed to think that because the biggest dramas of the year happened in the Lower School—which comprised half the school—I was to blame. Getting rid of me would get rid of all those uncomfortable situations for him. Despite the fact that he had a masters in education from Harvard, he was in over his head. Was he intimidated by me, too? He admitted that he tried to read the article about my doctoral dissertation research and found that he could not understand it. He was clearly more comfortable with the other two directors who were men and led the middle and upper schools, which were his areas of experience. Elementary school, especially a private one, with its entitled parents and exceptional students, was something very drama-filled and unsettling for him.

The next day, I asked if we could talk before this got out of hand to work things out. I let him know that his "lawyering up" did not allow us to speak freely with one another. I felt that we could work it out. So we met again, and it was clear that his decision was final. Instead of the lawyer, he brought in the business manager to witness. He was not about to talk to me as a person, and he was not about to work things out.

What was incredibly ironic about the way I was forced to leave the school was that all other positions in the school were covered by a written due process before a person was let go. When we were in the process of letting Jill go, she was allowed a hearing at which she could be accompanied by her choice of a faculty person to represent her interests. The intent to let her go had to be in writing, and there was a process involving multiple people. In my case, Randall had not involved anybody else in the decision to let me go. He had the absolute power, and he was taking it. And because the board of directors, who had the final say in hiring and releasing of employees, would not be meeting again until the end of the month, he had weeks to craft my release before he would be held accountable for his decision and process before the board. Even more ironic was that the school's decision to hire me had taken months and involved formal input from every constituency, and every person had a say. My interview took two full days. I flew in on an afternoon, and a half dozen teachers took me to dinner. Those dinners are not casual affairs but are interviews in which you are being scrutinized and asked questions every minute. The very next morning, I was to meet with Stage II for breakfast, give a short talk, then answer their questions. This was followed by a meeting with the specials teachers, who had their own issues to discuss after my talk. Then it was a mid-morning snack with Stage III and lunch with Stage I. I met with Stage IV after lunch. Later I would meet with the other directors. I had dinner with board members then gave a 20 minute presentation to parents and answered their questions. The next day I met with a representative group of students, followed by the admissions and marketing staff. I spent another hour with the woman I was replacing then met with the teaching assistants. I had a final interview with the search committee. After every meeting, each participant completed a form about their impressions of me. The meeting ended with a conversation with the outgoing head of school, who sat with his arms crossed and said that they would be in touch once they had—wait for it—another meeting to review all the input. Members of the search committee then flew to Texas to interview constituents of my school there.

But when it came time to release me, only one person made the decision.

Teachers and parents were not given a say in my review and release. But a group of teachers, most of whom had been on the committee that voted to hire me, were livid when they heard what had happened. They asked for a meeting with Randall, and he delayed it until the end of the following week. I was told that there were a lot of tears, and one of the teachers shouted and slammed the door in anger. Another teacher reported that Randall had a deer-in-the-headlights look on his face when he heard that only those few teachers who had his ear were disgruntled, that their issues were ones that had preceded my arrival, and that they felt that I had made progress with those old issues. They had not come to him earlier because they were happy and did not know that he was displeased. He nonetheless told them that his decision had been made and would not be rescinded.

I called the new president of the board, a woman who had just taken office two months earlier. She said that she did not want to interfere with Randall's decision and suggested I see a lawyer. I met with the former president of the board, a wise and respected fellow who had tamed that crotchety bunch for years and had just retired from his role with much love and fanfare. He said that he had not known anything about Randall's decision and did not wish to get involved. He advised that the more time passed between when Randall and I could talk, the harder it would be for him to save face and do a "take back." But Randall had completely closed off that opportunity to work things out. And so it was up to me to hire a lawyer.

I called my big brother Keith for advice.

Keith had been a business manager for a long time. He had been an entrepreneur and a plant manager as well as the head of research &

development. He had defended his company and won in wrongful termination suits. He had an MBA from Washington University, and he knew how things worked.

"Because you are 50 years old, you are in a protected class, so they have to be careful," he told me. "Nobody is hiring people over 50, so they just cost you 15 years of your working life. You need to ask for your salary x 15 years and for your health insurance coverage, and they need to pay off your house. They just ended your career. You need to hire the best employment lawyer in the state, and you must be prepared to take it to court." His advice seemed melodramatic, but it was more accurate than I ever thought possible. I called around for a lawyer and found out that in Detroit, the lawyers were there for the employers, not the employees. Nobody thought I had a case, especially after the grenade comic, which the school's lawyer could call a violent threat to the school. One lawyer did agree to negotiate the severance, and it cost me one-third of anything that she was able to get above what their original offer was.

When my delightful next-door neighbor heard the news, she knocked on my door and handed me a package of Kool-Aid.

"They say when life gives you lemons, make lemonade," she smiled sympathetically.

That neighborhood was the nicest bunch of people I've ever lived around. In the winter, when they saw Richard out with a shovel, they would rush over themselves to clean our driveway. They always said hello and invited us to gatherings. They threw us a going-away party and had a picture taken that they put it in a matted frame that they all signed.

I put that beautiful house on the market in October, and it got no action. It took us 16 months to sell that house, and I lost $45,000 in the sale. The agents advised against putting it up for rent, as the Detroit market was glutted with rentals. I should not have listened to them. I changed agents after a year. The house kept costing me money. A mouse had died inside a wall, and the stench lingered for months and scared off prospective buyers until I paid big bucks to have a hole cut in the wall, the mouse exhumed, and the wall repaired. The house was spotless when I left, with nothing in it, but the agent insisted that it be cleaned after a year, and that cost me $250. For an empty house!

The absolute worst, most insulting part of the severance agreement, in my mind, was their clause that I was never to apply for any other position with the school or its related programs. Even if Randall moved on, I could not come back. And I was not to put anything disparaging about them in writing. Is the truth disparaging? I asked for the same concession, and they agreed. Randall wrote me a positive recommendation, one in which I was able to add the list of my accomplishments for inclusion. The severance money meant that I did not have to rush into a job, but I tried my darndest to find something that would let us stay there. One day it dawned on me: I had been sitting around grousing that there I was in Michigan, with no job. But then I realized: I am in Michigan, and I don't have a job! I am free to explore! So explore we did. Richard and I drove north and visited Mackinac Island, Sleeping Bear Dunes, and Traverse City, a cute little town famous for their cherries and for Interlochen Arts Academy, the school I had wished to attend as a teenager. I dropped off my resume. And I got to fulfill my lifelong dream of seeing how breakfast cereal is made, stopping at Kellogg's in Battle Creek, where I posed with Tony the Tiger. (I've always been a factory tour junkie). It was a beautiful autumn to see Michigan, and I could see why my former teacher from Houston would wax rhapsodic about her home state.

She was still back at Rainard, and I had spoken and traded emails with Rainard's parent board member, David Steakley a few times. He inquired about school policies and reasons behind procedures, and he wanted to fact check when faced with conflicting stories about how things were done. They had found a new home for the school and completed the move that summer. They had even hired a big crane to move Fort Rain, the playground structure that Richard and the kids had conglomerated over three summers. I was insanely jealous that fall when he said that the board had agreed to consider expanding to high school the next year. I had always wanted the high school but had never gotten the money or a big enough enrollment to pull it off. So I wrote to David and told him that I was available and would love to talk with him further about his ideas for the high school. A conversation later, and it was agreed: I would start in December. Rainard would pay to move me down and house me for a month until we found a home. My job was to start the high school. I let them know that I did not want to run the whole school, and they said that they understood.

Pain

Why do we inflict pain on ourselves? Is it because the pain makes tangible the emotional pain we are feeling? Mother's smoking inflicted pain on herself. When my daughter Emily was a young teen, I found that she had been wounding herself, a self-mutilating act that I knew needed professional intervention. She was not using a knife but was using an eraser, rubbing over and over her leg or forearm until she got past the epidermis to the raw layers below. I was filled with a dread, and that dread abated after a few months of therapy for her and for us as a family. I, too, deliberately cause myself pain when I conjure up and mull over the wrongs done me. I can't leave it alone and let it heal. I keep replaying the events that led up to my dismissals, and I get angry with those people. But unlike the cutting, my mental perseveration over those wrongs does not create a physical pain that deflects my emotional pain.

The replay of a painful experience was not new to me. When I was about 12 years old, I went to my first sock hop gathering at the Y downtown. I did not really expect to dance, just hang out with my friend Pam and giggle about the boys. I'd had my first kiss that summer with a boy, Ambrose, and it was a highlight of my summer. She and I had met him and a friend and went down to the lake for a picnic. We had a package of hot dogs but no way to start a fire, and they had a hip-bottle of brandy, so we wickedly sipped the brandy and nibbled the salty, uncooked wieners.

It was all giggling and shy bravado, and Ambrose kissed me. I was on air for weeks, but we never really saw each other again until the Y. I walked past him on the busy sidewalk, and he stuck out his foot and intentionally tripped me—sent me flying and landing hard on my face, scratched and bleeding. And he laughed, like 12 year old boys so often do when trying to impress their buddies. That crude, mean behavior made no sense to me. I thought about it for months and still remember it nearly 50 years later.

Being let go by the headhunters was painful, but it helped me to feel better when five others from the firm left within months, all victims of the Houston downturn. I did not feel that my rejection was personal. But the worst dismissal was in Michigan. It was so blatantly wrong, so mis-handled, so damaging. I would think hateful things toward Randall. I was having a vivid, recurring fantasy that he and I were passing one another on escalators, with Randall going up and me about to head down. I would reach over and push him backward down the escalator, enjoying his painful fall. I wanted him to hurt as much as I did. But after each aggressive thought, I would be startled at my violence, because I am a pacifist, a nonfighter. I knew that punching him out would be wrong and would make me as bad a person as he was. I had to rise above it. So all that anger kept flopping around in me with nowhere to go. I could not forgive his unfairness and ignorance. I sought healing. Before I left Michigan, I took relief through a wonderful yoga class. I learned to breathe through the hard poses when my muscles would twitch and the perspiration rolled down my spine. I learned that you could do anything if you can just breathe into it.

I had a recurring visualization in my practice, and it functioned like a mantra. I would see a large, galvanized metal watering can flecked with a pattern of little snowflakes. I grasped the can by its handle. In this visualization, I had been gardening, and the watering can's interior was clotted with mulch and leaves and dirt. I took the garden hose with its sprayer attachment and sprayed that hard, cold water into the can, and I tipped the can so that the spray would drive out all the detritus, filling it with fresh, clear water with each of my inhales, purging it with each exhale.

I could hear the drumming spray against the metal can, feel the refreshing mist in the air as I drew in each breath, deep into my lower belly first before topping off my lungs, like filling the bottom of the watering can. I could feel myself in the garden, standing on the soft, organic earth, smelling green all around me, smelling old leaves recycling themselves into food for the new, green leaves.

Because the yoga helped me so much, when I got to Houston I rushed to the closest yoga place I could find, which was part of a chain of Dahm Yoga studios. It cost hundreds for an initial membership, but I knew how important it was to my well-being in that hard time. I had to wear the issued bulky white pajamas to class; they were way too big for me, made of heavy cotton canvas. This was not my Michigan yoga. This room had no art, no little buddha shrines, no incense, but it had a wall of mirrors and bright fluorescent lights. It was more like a martial arts studio than a yoga den. Each session, we gathered in a standing circle, legs spread, hands on our bellies, and pressed into our bellies with each percussive exhale. Counting aloud was mandatory, making audible the forcefulness with which we were to use our abdominals to push out each count. We would face one direction and count to 100, then turn 90 degrees and count another 100 push-outs, and continue around our own circle. We might then lie on our backs and do the same thing, counting to 500. There were no poses, no new-age talk about energy flowing through our bodies. I felt ridiculous but kept going because I had paid in advance. I nicknamed it "Dumb Yoga." After each class, we could help ourselves to the excellent hot herbal tea from the big urn in the foyer. The gals who worked there were sweet, though, and spoke reverently about a famous energy work healer who was coming. They were scheduling individual appointments with her. "She's amazing," they whispered. Well, I could sure use some amazing healing. I had some cash from the severance settlement, so when they said that the hour would be $300, I gulped but forked it over. It was a leap of faith, and I was desperate for relief from my hatred for Randall. It was eating me up. I did not want to rot from the inside out.

At the appointed hour, we met in a separate, individual room, more peacefully and tastefully appointed than the workout studio. I lay on my back on a comfortable mat on the floor, and the healer knelt beside me. She nodded her head, and I closed my eyes. She did a laying on of her hands, adjusting my posture, and spent a long time with her hands skimming just above my body, then landing on my solar plexus. There she rested for a long time, at my center, the center that I had learned years ago when I took a series of Esalen-style massage classes. I felt good when I left the dim room, and she encouraged me to come back, but I did not think I should spend that kind of money. But what I found after that session, and for about a year afterward, was that her work did have a profound and surprising impact on me. Each time my thoughts returned to Randall and that pain, I was interrupted by the sensation of a warm, glowing light in my belly, in my center, radiating out, obscuring the dark image of Randall. The light overpowered the negativity, and I felt that he could not get at me to hurt me. I did not consciously call up the light with each of my mind's unbidden, bitter thoughts of Randall; rather when my mind would go there, and it did quite often, what I would find instead was the light. I gave in to the light, and I was able to move forward. The healing, as strange as it was, as skeptical and desperate as I was, had helped, and the money was worth it.

So there I was back in Houston with Richard, taking on the big, creative, important project of reinventing high school and making it a reality at Rainard, bringing my dream that I had started twenty years earlier to its complete fruition, its final destination. And as I get when I am creating, all my senses are alive and stimulated. I wanted to jump in the sack, but Richard had retired from sex before we went to Michigan. I was not indiscriminate. I wanted somebody safe and discreet. I didn't want to start something new. So I called, once again, on Jack.

December 2005

For a month, Richard and I lived in a residential hotel near Rainard, cramped while we waited to get into the house we had chosen very close to the school. I would be able to take a five-minute bike ride to work, and we could look out our back porch to the flood-control dam instead of neighbors' windows. The house had terrazzo floors, giant oak and mulberry trees, and plenty of room. But the move from Michigan back to Houston had left us frugal, so we could not visit relatives for Christmas. I had brought a tiny fake tree with me and lit it up on our room's kitchen counter, but it was still a lonely holiday. That holiday week we visited our friend Patrick Green at his home tucked deep into the hills outside of Austin, Texas. It was outside on his deck where I finally got a signal on my cell phone and learned that my father, at age 89, had died the night before. He had called each of his children that night, as if with prescient foreboding, to say one more time that he loved us. Everyone—except me; because of the move, he did not know how to reach me. I had changed cell phone numbers in the move, and he could not find it. Not being able to say that final goodbye to my father was one more painful blow from my exodus from Randall and Michigan. My bile for Randall rose (this was before the healer's touch), but not as fast as my tears there in Austin. There was no need to come right then, as family members were scheduling two memorial services, one in Winona, Minnesota, where he had lived for the past 20 years, and the other in our hometown, Kenosha, Wisconsin. He was being cremated, so there was no rush.

My siblings agreed that I should write the obituary. "Why *me?*" I whined. "*You* know more of his past than I do! *You* have lived with him longer. I don't know much of anything about his life before me."

"But you're the writer," they explained.

So I did my best, sending it back and forth between my brothers, fact-checking, asking for information. I got some of the facts from the short biography that my oldest brother, Tom Jr., had printed out for a big party to honor Dad and the 50th anniversary of FPS, the electroplating shop that he had founded and that was now owned by Tom Jr., run by my youngest brother, Bruce, and also employed Tom III, who was Tom Jr.'s son. Nepotism had served my brothers very well.

The two memorials could not have been more different. First was the service in Winona, arranged by brother Keith and his wife Virginia. They are Baha'is and know how to keep things simple. Keith and Virginia had persuaded Father to move to Winona a couple years after my mother passed. In Kenosha, without Mother, Father had found that everything around him was about death—both Mother's death, and, increasingly, those of his lifelong friends. He wanted to embrace life, and Keith and Virginia would look after him and feed him home-cooked meals in the evenings. In Winona, Father had regular buddies with whom he shot pool at the senior center, and who bounced around in the swimming pool with him at his water exercise classes, ogling the young coeds who jumped through all the moves from the pool deck. So Virginia arranged for the memorial to be in a small chapel. As I did when my mother died, I put words to paper to reflect on Father's life, and I wept and halted trying to read them. Virginia and her daughter, Beth, came to my side and supported me until I could finish. The service was about heart and tears. Here is what I wrote:

Heaven

for Tom Laken, Sr.--Dad June 2, 1916-December 23, 2005

Dad didn't believe in heaven. When you're gone, you're gone and that's the end of the story--to quote Paul Harvey, to whom he used to listen religiously. No, Dad wasn't religious. At all. He'd drop us off at church and pick us up. He insisted that we go until we were confirmed, and then we could make up our own minds. He believed in good values and treating people right, but church-going had nothing that he wanted.

Dad didn't believe in heaven--but I do. So I am taking the time to talk about the heaven that I can see for him.

I believe in two kinds of heaven. First, there's the heaven on earth, the heaven that we can feel in the here and now when we realize that we are blessed, and we are grateful. I'm talking about the kind of grateful we feel when the cancer test comes back "clear" or when our grandchild gives us a smile that we know was meant just for us.

When did Dad have heaven on earth? Dad loved attention, and he had some favorite ways to get it. He was happy to host a big party for a family reunion, Mom's "Stitch 'n Bitchers" or a birthday, and he enjoyed seeing people milling all around the yard, eating baked beans with bacon, taking turns on the tennis court, and later he loved pulling the little kids around in the cart behind his tractor. And he loved the attention that he got when he got a rise out of you, when he could get you take the bait in an argument. He was masterful at that! Archie Bunker was a flyweight next to Dad. He proudly sported his NRA sticker on his Toronado during the Vietnam years, and he wore his bigotry and racist ideas with the conviction of a man whose personal experiences supported negative stereotypes. He was clearly disappointed if you turned a deaf ear. I thank him for those early years of arguing at the dinner table, because I learned early the fruitlessness of arguing with somebody whose intention is to get you worked up. Dad had to be in heaven when he talked with his buddy, Bob Kueny. I would wait for Dad's twinkle-eyed reports about their latest arguments, because Mr. Kueny would take the bait, and Dad enjoyed the back-and-forth and relished Bob's comebacks. I would cheer for Bob, because he had the patience that I lacked.

Right up there with the attention that Dad had when he was in his heaven-on-earth, Dad had a love of food, and plenty of it. He would try anything and delighted in the exotic as much as the everyday. No gathering or conversation was complete without a drink and a snack. Nuts, chocolate, fruit, sausages, cheese--there was always food to be snacked on. There was no such thing as junk food. He loved to try his hand at things, like when he set up his own smokehouse in the garage, or drove to Illinois to buy eels for pickling. His pickled fish was the BEST, and I know we will miss the moose sausage he had custom made. No holiday has been the same without his "cannibal." When he found a restaurant that he liked, he would visit it several times a week until he was bored with it. An all-you-could-eat buffet line was that Viking's Valhalla.

Dad was in high heaven when he got a bargain. He loved to negotiate, and we all remember his Flea Market years. Even my first marriage was a negotiation for him--I was allotted $1000 for a wedding, or he would double that if I would take the money and run. Ever his father's daughter, I ran.

With the money that he saved, he enjoyed his toys. Heaven for Dad was being able to pursue his passion to play. He messed around with hunting and guns, and traveled all over to bag the big ones. But he loved the hunting most for the time to spend out in nature. He found homes to live in that brought the beauty of nature to his doorstep, whether in Beverly Woods or on the Mississippi River. He was the one who most enjoyed the flowers in the garden, and in summer, he always cut a rose for the windowsill. But back to playing: he took up scuba diving and model boat building. I remember the very noisy summer when Dad and the boys took up gasoline-powered model airplanes, making endless circles above the tennis court, barely missing the oaks, but occasionally punctuating the buzzing with thrilling crashes. His antique car restoration hobby was much quieter--but that, too, fed his love of attention. There wasn't a pretty gal in town or an excited kid who wouldn't wave to him. Half the town must have gotten a ride, and Beth & Carew sure looked charming in their wedding gear riding behind Dad.

But in Dad's heaven on earth, the pleasures were not all his alone. He really liked giving to charity and to seeing good things happen because of his contribution. He gave to more than we'll ever know.

But I said that I believe in two heavens, and besides the heaven on earth, the heaven as a state of grace, there's the heaven that's waiting for us after we die, the one that Dad could not fathom. I get the biggest kick out of thinking what Mom has to say to him when their souls are reunited. Imagine Dad and Mom, and Roger and Kueny, and Truls and Astrid and all Dad's brothers and sisters. Now there's a reunion.

12-25-2005

The next day, we headed from central Minnesota to our hometown in southeastern Wisconsin, swerving from one memorial service for our father to another, from the home of his senior years to the home where we had spent most of our growing up. There would be a service the next day that was arranged by Tom and Nancy. The two memorials were scheduled closely so that those of us from out of town could attend both. His heavy urn was swaddled in a blanket behind the back seat.

Tom, Janet, Janet's son Ronnie, and I were passengers as Bruce wove his giant SUV along the interstate, between dawdling tourists and looming 18-wheelers, as the five us leaned and swayed with the lane changes. The speed limit was at least 15 mph behind us. Our little brother was Master of the Interstate.

Tom, the eldest of us six kids, tried to reason with Bruce. "Could you slow down? That's our poor father back there and I hate to see him killed twice."

That would likely be our last get-together until a niece or nephew should marry, or until another of us bite the dust. One of our six had been tragically killed almost twenty years earlier, and cancer took Mother a few years later. With both parents gone, what else was to rouse us from our scattered corners of the country to get together again? We were enjoying that rare time together, between the tears and reception lines: when we siblings gathered, we knew how to party. If Janet and I were lucky enough to get back north once a year, then the family would gather for a picnic and stay up late into the nights catching up with gossip and shared memories.

Bruce and Tom had stayed up most of the night before, finishing a bottle of their favorite bonding agent, Jack Daniels. It was a catharsis that completed the one begun that afternoon at the memorial service, when we relished the old photos sliding by on the screen at the front of the chapel, a beautiful slide show assembled by Janet and set to music that Dad loved. I had wept through my own tribute, and Big Brother Tom said that he had been able to keep it together up until then, but my words had released the dam in him. And when the sweet a cappella "Amazing Grace" was sung in clear, lush tones, it had wrung us all dry, and not a twitch of mascara remained.

The funeral that next afternoon was an entirely different affair. Hundreds of my brothers' friends and business associates filed through the reception line to extend their sympathies, a parade that took hours. Folks liked the giant poster photos of Dad posed with the grizzly that he had shot, or smiling with his arm around our mother. Big Brother had hired a guy to sing "My Way" as our father's theme song. It felt surreal that the singer was the cousin of the guy who had tried to punch out Dad's lights at my sister's wedding. Later in the service, he sang "Danny Boy," a song I had suggested because I alone knew that it could always bring a tear to my stalwart's father's eyes, as he would remember his own father and the loss he felt at his passing.

Years before, there had been a full-page advertisement in the *Houston Chronicle* that had a list of hundreds of songs. For a small fee, you could record a sentiment, choose one of the songs, and the company would phone that person at the designated date and time to play the song. Back then, I had chosen "Danny Boy" and arranged for it on Father's Day. Father phoned me after he listened, and he was choked up. "How did you know?" he asked, and I said that he had told me years before. "You know," he said, "when you were growing up, you were the only one of the kids that would greet me and ask how *my* day had gone. And you listened."

After the funerals, I settled back into Houston and put together Rainard High School. I had returned with that sole task but was quickly drawn into the politics of the school. The director we had hired prior to my Michigan move did not last through the first semester, so David Steakley had taken over, and then the board had placed Margaret, one of the teachers whom I had hired years before, in the position. The board was unhappy with her, and I tried to stay out of it. Margaret asked me how I had managed to deal with the Steakleys, who she said were constantly interfering and crossing boundaries of good practice for how a board and the school executive should share the responsibilities for the school. They were not interfering with me at that time, had saved the school, and then had saved me from unemployment. They had gotten me back to my beloved Houston. And I recalled that in the past, I had joked that I would give myself to the first person who would donate $10,000 to the school. Steakleys had given much more than that, but there was nothing remotely sexual in the relationship. However, I was indebted to them. They had kept my dream alive, giving it a new campus so that its mission could continue. Margaret was not as grateful as I was.

Eventually it became clear that the Primary teacher was not doing her job at all well, and Margaret had to be chided to observe the teacher before she, too, came to that conclusion. The board then told Margaret that she needed to take over the class, but Margaret refused. Paula Steakley begged me to assume the post, telling me that they needed somebody strong in there to restore parents' confidence. So I taught the PreK-K-1 Primary class each morning, and I worked on the high school in the afternoon. There was a small building that had once been a house and then a therapist's office at the far end of the campus. I worked with a contractor to remodel it to house the high school, and I hired a reliable man to expedite the plans through Houston's Byzantine City Planning Department. I put a lot of thought into creating the branding image of the high school. The image had to match the spirit of what the program would be like as well as what type of student we wanted. I carefully designed the marketing materials, and even bought a special typeface. I wrote the press releases and gave presentations.

And we all know what that creative process does to me....

Back to Jack

Now I must jump back in time a bit, to my separation from Jack. Our divorce hearing was on September 19, 1976. The judge went through the usual questions and formalities. It was a no-fault divorce, so there were no arguments to be had. I paid all the lawyer's fees, using half the money I inherited from my grandfather's bequest. But when the judge asked if the marriage was irretrievably broken, I said yes, and Jack said no. The judge looked up, surprised: that was not the right answer for him to grant a divorce.

"But you are here for a divorce, sir. *Do* you feel that the marriage is irretrievably broken?"

Jack looked flustered, ready to bust out of his skin, like his joints were going to fall apart. "No, but she does," Jack said.

"Jack," I whispered, "he won't do this unless you say it is."

"Yes," Jack croaked in a voice filled with torture. The decree was granted, and I watched Jack hurry past me down the hall of the courthouse, and my heart ached with the pain I saw.

I spent another four years in St. Louis but never ran into him once. He recovered and married an Asian woman from work, a widow with a daughter. When he had found his happiness again, he brought her and her daughter to visit my mother. Mother took photos and showed them to me. I was glad he was all right. Through the grapevine, I heard that they had a daughter together, too, and that he finally finished college—at Webster.

Years passed, and one day in Houston I got a phone call from Jack. His voice was slurred, and we talked a long, long time about his life. He just wanted to see how I was doing. He was living in his brother's basement, as his marriage was breaking up. He was between jobs and depressed, and he just wanted to see how I was doing. I tried to cheer him up and said that maybe the next time I came to St. Louis to visit Richard's family, we could grab a cup of coffee. So a few years later, we did. We met at the St. Louis Bread Company and sat there and drank gallons of coffee. All that caffeine did nothing for our nerves, and we jittered and twitched there for hours.

"I never stopped loving you, Jack. Never. I only stopped being your wife." I spoke earnestly.

"It felt the same, though. I was angry and confused for a long time."

"I'm sorry." The tears trickled down my face.

"You have nothing to be sorry about. I forgave you. You know I always wanted the best for you. You found somebody who you loved more."

"Not more, no! But it was different. It was bigger than all of us. It had to be."

We sat there for hours until there was nothing more to say. We were like detectives of our own lives, dusting for fingerprints as evidence of the love we had. That long talk made it clear that love was there, despite the crimes of the heart.

Months or years went by. I would try to call him, track him down by calling his brother's house, and a couple times we connected and talked. So we had maybe three or four conversations over the course of nearly twenty years. But it was comforting to always know that he was there if I needed him, as he had said in his farewell letter.

When I moved to Michigan, he came to the area to attend his niece's wedding, and we made arrangements to see each other there. I met him at his hotel and had the heart-pounding, awkward experience of meeting his whole family in the lobby. God, they must have hated me. But they were pleasant, and Jack's brothers kept sending him sly glances, but Jack kept grinning and being a gentleman. We left in my car and found a Taco Bell for lunch. Once again, we talked and talked, but I had an ulterior motive: I wanted to seduce him.

I flirted shamelessly, smiling coyly, making suggestive remembrances of our good times in the past. "We were *wild*," he agreed. I had set my libido radar on him because he was a known entity. I'd not had sex in several years, as Richard could no longer perform, and when he could not get *his* satisfaction through penetration, he just stopped all activity—no touching, no helping me, no letting me satisfy him. I was frustrated and so ready, but I was in a delicate position because of my work. Educators, after all, are expected to be sexless, moral exemplars. I could not be seen with other men in compromising situations. I had to be discreet. I had no desire to become wanton, to risk my job, my marriage, and my health by being indiscriminate. I was not a whore if I was monogamous, and after all, Jack had been my husband whom I never stopped loving. And he had been damn good in bed. His way of pleasing me was the benchmark against whom all other men were judged.

I won. Besides, I was driving, and he was my captive. I got us a motel room while he waited outside. I stepped out the front door and saw him peek around the corner, standing shyly, nervously, waiting. In the room, he was clearly anxious, and sat in the chair opposite the bed while I undressed for him. He stopped and dropped his pants and his excitement was visible, his length hard and ready. He looked like he was planning what to do. "Don't be nervous," I said. "Come here."

"I haven't done this in a long, long time," he said hoarsely. "I may not be any good."

"Me neither. Let's try."

He crossed the room and I knelt up on the bed, and he bent down and kissed me. He laid me down and took my foot, kissing it, working his way up my body, brushing over the hips, taking my nipples one by one in his mouth. I reached down and stroked him, then kissed it, taking it deep into my mouth. I'd forgotten just how long and narrow he was, and I remembered how deeply he would penetrate. He pushed me down onto my back, then grabbed both my feet and held them up in the air, opening me for his entry. He was being thorough, touching me everywhere, trying to hold back, but I knew he wanted to burst, so I met his hips, matching his thrusts, and sent him into that wonderful, warm release. He caught his breath, and we both giggled. "Ah, I remember you," I smiled. In our youth, I could count on a 20-minute recovery period for him. *What would the years have done to that interval?* I wondered. *How long would we lie here limp before I could climb aboard and have my way with him again?* We did enjoy an encore, and then he insisted that there would be scandal back at the hotel where all the guests were waiting for Uncle Jack to rejoin the prenuptial festivities. He'd already missed the golf outing while he was with me. He checked his phone, which he'd thoughtfully turned off during our time together, and laughed. "Thirteen messages! Oh, I'm going to hear from them!" I thought it best that I drop him off at his hotel without once again greeting his family, as I was now in a rather disheveled and flushed state.

I wanted more, wanted to get together again. We began to speak weekly, on Saturday mornings after my yoga class, as I sat in my car. And it was that October that I lost my job in Michigan. I turned to him for comfort. "Could I visit?" I asked. "Sure," he said, and I found that there were cheap round-trip flights between Detroit and St. Louis. I made several trips. He comforted me when my dad died. Jack had had a few accidents with the truck at work and was in danger of losing his license, but he had no health insurance to get his eyes checked. I insisted, and we stopped and got him tested and ordered glasses. I paid and told him it was from the Tom Laken Fund, part of the money I had inherited from him. His daughter Amy and son-in-law Jeb lived with him, and once I made them all a big batch of my famous lasagna. It weighs a ton, takes three jars of sauce, a pound of sweet Italian sausage, fresh spinach, fresh basil, and five cheeses: mozzarella, ricotta, parmesan, provolone, and romano. They ate it ravenously. We drank a lot of excellent Chianti. His daughter had gone up to bed, and Jack and I sat and listened to Jeb talk about how in love he was, how overpowering love is, how it just keeps going. My eyes teared up as I looked at Jack. His look softened into mine. Jeb saw this, got up abruptly, if a bit wobbly, and said, "Well, that's my cue. I'm heading up."

And one of my visits was during my creation of my high school. I brought my writing materials with me and worked hard while he was at work during the day, then ravished him at night. We spent a lot of time in bed, but we also frequented his regular Starbucks, where he knew every barista and they all knew his regular order, a *venti* caramel macchiato, upside down. When we went out to eat, he always charmed the waitresses and insisted on telling them that I was his first wife, and that we were divorced, but can't they see how well we get along? He thought our story was a surprising one, and with the help of a glass of wine, he shared our date with anybody who would listen.

"Where do you see this going?" he asked me one afternoon as I lay in his arms and Sarah McLachlan sang "In the Arms of an Angel" on his sound system.

I grew very still. Richard still needed me, and I did not suspect that he would live much longer. I would like Jack in my life again, would like to take care of him, as he had that air of a guy who had taken care of himself for too long. "What I would *really* like is if you would move to Houston. You could live at our house, have your own room. You could get a job in Houston, or work at the school. You'd be great. I'd love for the kids to experience The Jack."

He laughed in disbelief, held me at arm's length, and studied my face. "You want *what?* For me to move in with you? With Richard there?"

"Yes."

"My home is here. I have friends and a job and my daughters are here. That's crazy. All of us *together?*"

"Think about it."

Our visits grew longer apart. He was notorious for not answering his phone or leaving it in the car, but I figured that he was screening my calls. I sent him a few sexy, funny, romantic cards. In one, I let him know that I would be flying in for the weekend. The card would arrive in time to give him several days' notice to prepare—or to tell me not to come. He did not meet me at the airport, and I called him, but got no answer. I rented a car and drove to his house. His daughter, who shared the house, answered the door. Jack came to the door, looking very, very surprised. He invited me in. It was all very awkward. The house was a mess. The big puppy was careening around, jumping up on me, barking. Jack sat down.

"You didn't know I was coming?" I asked.

"No!" he exclaimed.

"You didn't get my card?"

"No. You sent a card?"

I looked up at the overflowing mash of letters, bills, and circulars in the basket by the door. I saw my handwriting on the pink envelope in the collection of unopened pieces. "There it is," I said.

Jack laughed. "I don't look at the mail. It's usually bills." Jack was in the midst of a protracted argument with the IRS, who wanted a lot of money from him that he did not have. The mail was usually not good news.

The next year, I made arrangements to spend a few days with Jack for my birthday over the Fourth of July. I wanted—needed—to feel special for that day, as I've always been neurotic about my birthdays, anxious with anticipated disappointment that I knew was certain to come. Everybody was always celebrating the holiday, and recognizing me was secondary, an afterthought. People would tell me that I was lucky because I always got fireworks on my birthday, but as selfish as it is, I wanted something that was mine, just mine. Maybe it's part of being the fifth of six children, and an introvert at that, the oddball of the gregarious family. Whatever it is, I recognize my anxiety as pure selfishness and feel guilty about it, which makes me more anxious. Yes, I'm a bit psycho about my birthday, but not the getting older part: that's out of my control.

It was my Worst. Birthday. Ever.

No cake, no present, no surprises. We spent the day—a very, very long day, from noon until about 10 at night—at his boss's house. Sitting around. Jack talking and cutting up with them, socializing. Now, I can socialize with the best of them, but after three hours or so, I am used up. There just wasn't anything to do. They all knew each other and had plenty to talk about. He abandoned me to talk with them. The conversations were not stimulating. He did not seek me out to see if I was OK. They did not sing to me. It rained that afternoon, and he evening was too foggy to see fireworks, so that was out of the question. By the time we left the party, I was pissed. When he finally asked what was wrong, I told him. He was quiet. That night in bed, we clung to each other, lying face to face. I remember that it was eerie, like talking to Cyclops, because at that closeness, I could only see one eye, right in the middle. It felt like that scene in the movie *Jurassic Park*, when the tyrannosaur's giant eye shows in the window behind the terrified children. Jack said that he did not want a relationship with me. It was one thing to get together, but he did not want a relationship, and he feared that is what I wanted and expected, and he didn't have it to give. He was rejecting me. And yet we lay there, clinging without anything between us. Just words, words, and more confusing words. None of it made sense.

It felt like a very long time before my flight would take me back to Houston. I'm sure that I made several pathetic tries to understand why he cooled toward me. I called him and wrote to him. But it was over. We kept in touch with a couple of phone calls per year after that, and I would find myself calling him, usually after an emotionally unsatisfactory rendezvous with the opposite sex and when my contract in Virginia was not renewed. We went out for dinner in St. Louis, stayed late talking and closed the restaurant, then got into my car to make out. I wanted to find a more secluded place than the parking lot of Macaroni Grill, so we took off on a hunt, fueled by way too much wine, but my route was circuitous, and a squad car made me nervous, considering how erratically I was driving in search of a dark spot. Then Jack was gone, no longer following my car. Gone. I called his cell phone. No answer. I headed back to where I was staying and reached him half an hour later.

"Where did you go?" I asked. "Did the police officer get you?" I was worried.

"No, I went to the Side Tap." He had gone to his local bar, his hangout. Left me high and definitely not dry. He had run away from me.

I struggled to accept his rejection gracefully. "Thank you for a great dinner."

"You are most welcome. I enjoyed it. Now be safe."

Ha, I thought. At least *you're safe*.

Rainard Redux

Upon my return to Rainard, I was very careful not to step on Margaret's toes. She was the Principal, and she did not need my shadow hanging over her, threatening her authority or her own vision. I wanted to stay out of the politics and the maneuvering with the board. I just wanted to launch the high school. But Paula and David Steakley saw that with me there, he did not need to run the school and could turn it over to me. They made me the director and her the principal. I reassured Margaret that I did not want her job. I didn't! I'd been there, done that. I just wanted to run the high school. That lasted just a few months, until Paula decided that Margaret was not doing a good job. So Paula would call me often, fretting about Margaret. And Paula liked her wine, which made her fretting go on and on, and she would call me on the weekends when I was trying to get chores and errands done at home. Margaret could sense all this, and she had that desperate look we get when we know we are on *terra infirma*. That summer, they fired Margaret and put me in as head of school, doing both jobs. Margaret was sure I had lied to her and betrayed her. While I did not think that she should ever have been principal, I don't think that they should have set her up like that, then behead her. But the Steakleys were accustomed to getting their way, and they would manipulate and use people to get it. They could afford to get what they wanted, and they held absolute power, which they wielded freely and without input, and certainly without collaboration from affected parties.

The board was not interested in a partnership with me as the head. They saw themselves as running the school. I was not invited to board meetings but finally convinced them that it would be in their best interest to get a report from me each month about what was happening in the school. While I no longer had to create the budget or financial statements, I felt the need to work with them and make recommendations. So they let me come to the meeting to give my report, and then they conducted business after I was dismissed. I had not only founded the school, but I had been the president of the board for 18 years! It was insulting, and they made decisions that I was not party to. The worst of it was when they decided that my position as head of school job would take my focus off the high school, so they hired another woman to run the high school. They did not talk to me about it in advance, and they certainly did not include me in their interview process. Thereafter the high school—the reason that I returned, the vision from which I started the school—slipped back into a more traditional model.

Paula, it was rumored, had driven off my first replacement with constant interference, and Margaret, too, complained of Paula overstepping. When David Steakley was president of the board, Paula interfered and criticized her husband's work so much that he threw up his hands and turned the presidency over to her. Paula, as board president, believed in an open-door policy for the parents. She encouraged them to bring their every complaint to her—about teachers, about the principal, about the other children. Parents in private schools complain a lot, and our parents were particularly high maintenance. Their children were exceptional, and most of them had endured bad experiences elsewhere in schools where they'd had to fight to get their child's needs met; that was not how they had to operate at Rainard. I understand that a parent feels empowered to be able to go to the highest level in an organization and get results; they feel like this access is getting them their money's worth for their tuition dollars. But what that does is cut the knees off the manager on the ground—the school principal. The board should be telling the complaining parents to work it out with the teacher or the director, and if the parents don't get satisfaction there, to bring it to the board at that point. The board is supposed to be about policy, funding, and big picture, and the executive—in this case, the school director/principal—is charged with carrying out the vision and making it happen within the budget and according to policy. If needed, the board can mediate a joint meeting of the parent with the teacher or principal. Instead, the parents loved to go to Paula, who welcomed the conversations and wine. But by not going to the source of the conflict, the complainers send the message that the teacher and the principal are unapproachable, despite not having been approached.

I tried to help the board to understand that there are best practices for board-management relations. I forwarded articles from nonprofit management and professional organizations to them, which they would not discuss with me, stating that their way was how businesses run. They had all worked in business, never for a nonprofit, and they saw no difference between them. They saw themselves as the managers of the school and me as the lead staff person. They had power, and they held it tightly.

At one point, Paula had been avoiding my calls to work out an issue. When I approached her, she dashed into her car and drove off, although she denied it later. She spoke ill of me to the board. One board member, Jodi, was the mother of one of the school's former students. I had dinner with her, and she let me know that Paula had been spreading poison and untruths about me to the board. When Jodi learned the truth, she was very upset. But rather than convincing the board of their error, she was so upset that she resigned from the board. And the board continued to run the school without involving me, all the while cultivating the complainers.

I got the school stabilized. Straightening out the office that had been David's took several days, as his filing system was to put everything—bills, advertisements, bank statements, licenses, correspondence, and so on—in big cardboard boxes, unfiled, with no system resembling anything other than a landfill. When one box filled, another was started. There were five such boxes under the desk. Margaret's office was better organized. My binders of board minutes were in the closet, but nothing had been added in two years. They had kept no minutes of their board meetings, although they are required to do so by law.

I stayed there until the spring of 2008, got the school accredited, and watched their appointed high school director turn my vision into a school like any other, except smaller. I kept my eyes open for a better opportunity and found a position to help open a high school that would at last let me try to put my beliefs into action. I accepted the assistant principal position for the debut Ideal Schools High School in northern Virginia, just 30 miles outside Washington, DC. I put my house on the market and waited to give my two weeks' notice. But a neighbor saw my "for sale" sign and brought it to the attention of the Steakleys, who confronted me. They knew I was unhappy with them, but this infuriated them. I finished the year, despite their refusal to pay me the vacation pay that we had agreed to prior to my return. They would not allow me to send out any emails or newsletters without their prior censorship. It did not end well. From the time the Steakleys took over the school's board in 2004 until they left in 2013, they churned through seven heads of school.

A Do-Over

I wasn't able to put my ideas for a high school into place in Houston, so it was a gift to be able to try again in Virginia. It was a miracle to find another person who felt as passionately about what high school could be, and who also had the wherewithal to put his ideas into action. Deep Sran was a 30-something, tall, dark, hip former corporate lawyer who decided to follow his dream and start a school. He flew me to town for a weekend for us to talk and talk and talk about our ideas. He listened with his laptop in front of him, typing as I spoke. I slept in the basement guest room of his large, suburban McMansion. The basement was filled with every kind of toy, especially electronic toys, that his two young daughters enjoyed with abandon. His wife, a corporate lawyer for a large IT company, was supportive. They were a handsome couple, both high-achieving first-generation Indian Americans. He offered help with the move but would not cover it completely; however, he had a friend who had a place where I could stay rent-free for up to a year. We drove out to the country to meet her. Juanita Koilpillai had an enormous estate in the foothills of the Blue Ridge Mountains about 30 minutes away. On her estate, she had a carriage house that she had remodeled in antiques and "shabby chic." It was adorable, surrounded by English gardens, grazing cattle, and beautiful vistas. She and her husband had made their fortune in IT, having sold their company to Symantec. She was from Sri Lanka, and she and Deep teased each other about their heritage and Americanization. Juanita desperately wanted education reform and offered to help Deep in any way that she could. Housing me was one of those ways. She also taught computer literacy classes for free at the high school.

It was thrilling to move to the DC area! I fell in love with the city when I took my Rainard students there as one of our regular Middle School road trips. The city captivated me, with its beautiful architecture, its rich history, and the fact that *this was where important things were happening.* Its citizens made America happen. Every kind of arts event of the highest caliber came through there. *The Washington Post* was dense with interesting things to read. Each time I crossed the bridge and the Washington Monument came into view, I gasped at the beauty. The traffic was murder, but not that much worse than Houston's. It had been a dream of mine to live there. And Loudoun County, where the high school was located, had the highest per capita income and fastest-growing young demographic in the country—the perfect place to start a forward-thinking private school. The cost of opening it had been multiple times higher than planned, thanks to the bizarre county requirements that would only allow a school to open in a business park, and that space could not be leased; it had to be bought. If Deep had declared that the school was a religious school, it could go anywhere in Loudoun, in leased space or not. So Deep had had to buy the spot in the business park. It was just ten minutes north of Dulles Airport. When the wind was coming from the right direction, you could look out the floor-to-ceiling windows and see the enormous jets heading directly at you as they prepared to land a mile away.

And then the stock market crashed in September 2008, the month that the school opened. Portfolios lost their value. People hung on to their money because of the insecurity. And the folks who would have been interested in the school were mortgaged to their last dime, in homes for which they had paid too much. I was told that just a few years before I arrived, people had waited in line to buy townhomes that were not even built yet. People offered more money for homes than what the homes were listed for. Now the economy was not great for people to take a risk on an unknown—unless they were desperate to leave their current schools.

Who are the folks who will enroll their children in a brand-new, untested private school? The first and most eager families are those whose children were not successful elsewhere. These were usually students with behavior and motivational issues. As the school founders, it was hubris to persuade ourselves optimistically that those issues would go away once the students were in our school—in a better, smaller, more responsive environment. Sometimes they did. That was true for about 30% of those students who had been unhappy and unsuccessful elsewhere, but the remaining 70% would last for maybe a year of stumbling about or distracting the others with terrible behavior. And those miscreants would scare away some of the serious prospects who believed in the school's mission. This was true at both Rainard and at Ideal. One had to be careful not to fill up the school with students who, although they would pay the tuition, would cost the school dearly. Sometimes those to try the new school would be the progeny of parents with perpetual dissatisfaction: no school had the magic bullet that would turn their underachieving student into the reflection of the parents' own success, and to them, it was always the fault of the school. Those parents were always shopping around, and the students moved many times.

But it was glorious when the right match came along: the student who needed what we had to offer to be free to bloom into their potential. Those were the students whom you held up as models for all others. There were the girls who found the standard school fare to be too boring or unchallenging for their hungry minds—and yes, they were nearly always girls. There were the boys who wanted more hands-on projects and fewer papers. There were those students who thrived in Socratic seminars, from having a voice and hearing their strong, adolescent opinions challenged and honed. There were those who could breathe more deeply in the relaxed, flexible, playful atmosphere without the crowds and regimentation.

Deep had advertised for my position on a website for the gifted, but his school was not just for gifted learners. He himself was gifted, and he knew that the gifted would thrive in his design, but he also believed that the average student would benefit from provocative round-table seminars, projects, and a convivial atmosphere. His belief opened the school to more students, which was good for the budget. But his decision not to advertise the school as being for gifted students was not a financial one. It was an open-hearted, philosophical one: that all students deserve a great education. There are those who see specialized education for the gifted as elitist; they rail against the identification of gifted students because they believe that all children are gifted. These critics hate the idea of treating gifted students as special, as more deserving than other students of a better education. They want those same resources available to the nonidentified students, and they speak up for it with the same fervor that they defend American democracy and equal opportunity. Juanita and I would go around and around about the gifted label: she hated it. She found it polarizing. Her own children had not been identified, and she saw that teachers could not see her children's gifts. Our biggest rows revolved around the gifted label.

Back in high school, I used to argue, like Deep, that the type of dynamic education that I envisioned was good for all students. All students need challenge and the opportunity to develop their gifts. All students need to learn to debate complex issues. All can benefit from meaningful projects, from a school that cares as much about heart and art as it does for math and science. I believed that the schools I envisioned were good for everybody. I still believe that, but I believe even more strongly in specialized programs for gifted learners. And trying to provide for the gifted learners in the same classes as average students is not optimal. I have found that maybe only 1 in 50 teachers can provide both the pace and challenge for the strongest learners while also providing the slower pace, support, motivation, simplification, and repetition required by the average learners. To do so takes rare depth of understanding of the subject matter to pull off, and even more rare organizational and planning skills. Such work is not easy with more than 20 students in the room, and it is even more difficult with a student load exceeding 100 students as is found in secondary schools.

The tagline of the charter school at which I worked in Florida was "for gifted learning." In Florida, charter schools could not discriminate in their admission, even for suitability to the school's mission. The other public schools did not want their top students cherry picked away, leaving the lower-achieving students behind to lower the school's test averages and reputation. In Ohio, the gifted charter school that I led for a year was able to test for qualifying students because Ohio recognized the value of charter schools designed for students with special needs. While most places think of special needs as those differences like autism, developmental and behavioral challenges, Ohio recognized gifted learners as having special needs.

Deep found out what I knew: that despite the program that we believed was democratically best for all students, it was the gifted population that took the ball and ran with it. Several years after I left his school, he renamed it Loudoun School for the Gifted, and expanded into a gifted program for middle school students to grow into his high school program. Schools grow students with bad habits that prevent them, once they are of high school age, from being able to rise to the type of challenge that requires motivation from within rather than from externally motivating factors like grades. Regular school is a place where students jump through others' hoops, where they have very little choice in projects and even fewer choices now that the current drive seems to be to prepare every student to take all the advanced math and science necessary to create future engineers. What Deep was doing at Ideal, and what I was doing at Rainard, still provided advanced coursework, but it also included a great deal more choice, more meaningful projects, and more current and topical resources. It made tremendous use of the rich resources of DC and in Houston. Both schools incorporated frequent educational travel with students.

Our schools strove to help students to thrive in a more relaxed atmosphere with couches, access to snacks, and open study spaces. The commons area at Ideal had a ping-pong table, beanbag chairs, and gamer chairs. But that first wave of new students came from traditional, restrictive environments, so when exposed to the freedoms, some went a little crazy at first and abused the freedom with wildness, carelessness, messiness, and irresponsibility. They had to be reined in and taught that the environment was there for them to enjoy, but the priority was their learning. For example, students whose schools may have taken only one field trip a year, as was often the case, would see those first field trips as opportunities to bust out and go crazy, yelling out the bus windows, playing chase in the museums. Students who get out and are given more freedoms from an early age make more responsible choices. Students who grow up in Montessori schools, for example, handle freedom and choices very well when they move on from those early days, and they chafe when others make seemingly arbitrary choices for them that traditionally schooled students take for granted.

The reason I designed Rainard from the high school backward, but opened with the youngest students, was because I knew that I would have to grow the types of students who could do what I wanted them to be able to do in high school. When I accepted transfer students from traditional schools, I observed that it usually took six months or more to "unschool" them. In time, those students began to enjoy learning and to see their teachers not as prison guards, punishers, or dolts. Once a student experienced being known as an individual and having the teacher take them from where they were academically and challenge them appropriately, they began behaving like a reasonable person. They were no longer just one of many, a person who is constantly being evaluated against a narrow, rigid set of expectations. When they stopped being herded like cattle, they stopped behaving like beasts.

Progressive education is fairly well accepted by parents when the students are in elementary and middle school, but that appreciation for project-based, interdisciplinary learning and social-emotional learning seems to evaporate when the student reaches high school. High school becomes a serious business: the child's entire future seems to be riding on the best possible high school experience to lead to the best possible college to lead to the best possible career. While parents are expressly caring about their child's happiness in the younger years, when high school looms, the benchmark is no longer the student's happiness but rather the student's success as measured in grades and the school's success in college placement. Rigor is measured by Advanced Placement (AP) courses and college credits earned while still in high school. Why is AP the gold standard? The cost of college credits earned while in high school is usually less than their cost at college, so the push is on to save money by knocking out college credits in high school. AP classes cover a ton of content, and the work is geared to earning a high score on the challenging AP exams. Parents demanded the opportunity for their students to take AP classes to prepare for those exams. That was their benchmark for rigor, and that was how they thought that colleges would know that their child was capable of the challenges of college coursework. But the push to offer AP classes and exams in high school has resulted in many students passing the exams. There is an economic force at play here on the college's side as well: colleges are not all happy about this and do not guarantee that they will award college credit for passed exams. The colleges want students to benefit from the richer experiences that they feel come from tackling the advanced subject matter delivered by professors with a deeper knowledge of the subject matter and mulled over as more mature college students. In addition, the college benefits from having a student attend for all four years of matriculation.

Our approach was to offer rigor and depth of thinking in our high school classes without making those classes official AP classes. Rather than "pile higher and deeper," we chose fewer books but took care to milk them for great thinking.

One thing we could do that traditional programs did not do was to offer cross-disciplinary, multi-disciplinary, or interdisciplinary classes—I use the terms interchangeably. And what I came up with, for which I remain very proud, was a way to award credit for more than one subject. While the rest of the world is stuck with an English class being an English class, and a history class being a history class, we could offer a class for which the student could earn partial credit in multiple subjects. For example, I designed a class around Trevor Corson's excellent non-fiction book *The Secret Life of Lobsters*. The book teaches extensively about the biology of the crustaceans, but it also leads the reader along to learn about the clash between the politics of fisheries regulation and the science that only recently uncovered what the regulators needed to know about the mysterious life cycles and population rhythms of lobsters. The book is also an excellent sociological case study of the population in a particular fishing community. The school was on a quarter system, so a student who took my *Lobsters* class would earn one-quarter credit in English. In addition, depending on where the student chose to focus further study, the student could also earn one-quarter credit in sociology or biology. We offered the same split-credit for a number of classes that combined reading and writing instruction with geography and history. I designed a transcript that would communicate our nonstandard classes in the language of Carnegie units that the colleges could understand. Part of my job duties was to serve as the college admission counselor, and I participated in national college admission counselors' conventions to meet with college representatives to make certain that our unique approach would not confuse the colleges or disadvantage our students in any way.

What should high school graduation *mean?* What should be required of a high school graduate? Traditional programs require that a certain number of classes be taken in order to earn credits, and those classes are designed to give the student the knowledge and skills needed to survive as an adult and to handle college courses. Graduation requirements in public schools generally consist of earning a set number of Carnegie unit credits in subjects, such as four credits of English, three credits of math, and so on. Private schools have the freedom to tack on other graduation requirements, too, and they will often require a certain number of hours of community service. Some schools, such as those that offer the International Baccalaureate, require an extended essay. Schools that are part of the Essential Schools network will require a senior exhibition, and that is what we required at Ideal Schools; Rainard did not pursue it to the same extent. But starting a high school gave me the opportunity to think about what we should and could make of these formative years for a teenager. Surely it should be about more than courses. What should be required, and where was the flexibility for individual interests and abilities? The Roeper School took an interesting approach: high school students were expected to carry a full load each year, but the class choices were at the student's discretion. The students were well informed about what colleges expected of their applicants, but if students chose to take a different path or to find a college with different flexibility, those students were supported.

What if high school graduation could signify something less nebulous than course completion, but rather the acquisition of a set of competencies? Those could be proved competencies in reading, writing, and working with numbers. It could include demonstrating knowledge of civics, science, and geography. Some students could knock them out more quickly than others, and graduation would not be just a factor of spending a set number of years in school. Competencies could be earned in any number of classes. I imagined students working with advisors to set goals for competencies to be achieved each quarter; the teachers would attest to those competencies demonstrated in their classes. You could look at a student's record and see that she had demonstrated a particular competency, for example, in evaluating conflicting perspectives of a historical event while taking a class on the Civil War. You might see that the student had demonstrated the skill of organizing data into a clear and meaningful graph while in a class on the science behind nutrition. Not all the competencies would have to be attained and demonstrated through coursework: maybe the student had proven competency by taking a standardized test. And you might see that the student had not yet demonstrated the required competency of planning a realistic budget for an event, so you would encourage that student to be the treasurer for an upcoming overnight class trip. At

Rainard, I was able to require the competency of first aid and of being able to save one's own life by being able to swim. At Ideal, we had begun work on a competency-based graduation requirement, but we did not finish the work. To debate and discern just which competencies within the various disciplines should be mandatory, and how to keep records without being overwhelmed by an enormous document, were not tasks that we were able to finish in my two short years in Virginia.

But we were able to think outside the box when it came to requirements. For example, I designed a course called Fine Arts Survey. Its goal was to expose students to performances in a number of the arts. For each one-quarter credit hour, the student needed to be an audience member for 28 hours from at least seven different types of performances, ranging from theatrical, dance, and musical performance, to art galleries and studios, and even comedy shows. They had to accumulate a total of four hours of response, reflection, or research related to those performances.

Another unusual requirement that we had at Rainard was to require each student to enter competitions. Each student had to enter what we referred to as a "personal best," in which that student entered as an individual. It could be a tennis tournament, a writing contest, an art show—the suggestions were wide open, but the intent was to have to rise to a level of competency and quality that made the student reach for their highest level of accomplishment and be judged by somebody from outside the school. In addition, the student had to participate as a team member in a competition, whether that be in something like Model UN, Destination Imagination, or the trebuchet competition at the Renaissance Festival. Once again, the suggestions were wide open, but the intent was to learn to be accountable to others, to learn to work cooperatively, and to divide and conquer to reach for a goal. It didn't hurt the school's public relations, either, to be able to publicize our students' successes.

The ethos of both schools was for students and staff to support one another as individuals and as members of the community. Another way this was done was for each member of the high school community to commit to tackling a personal challenge and to ask for the encouragement and help of the high school team. For one girl, it was to conquer the fear of speaking before a group. For another, it was to get to school on time and awake. We celebrated successes together.

Foreign language was a true challenge. Learning a foreign language is important for us because we need to be prepared to be world citizens. It is arrogant of Americans to presume that learning a second language is unimportant because the rest of the world is all learning English. It is a pompous attitude because it implies that if others want to play with us, they will play by our rules, for which we are at a very distinct advantage. The stupidest among these folks are those who justify the claim that learning English is easy because, after all, they can speak it! They do not put much stock in their advantage at having been hearing English since they were *in utero*, nor do they recall how many years of baby talk they babbled before becoming a fluent speaker.

But which language to learn? In the early twentieth century, French was called the international language of diplomacy, so choosing French made sense. Some of our nation's neighbors to the north spoke it. But our neighbors to the south spoke Spanish, so that was also popular. During the Cold War at midcentury, schools scrambled to find Russian teachers. When the Japanese and Chinese economies took off, the push was on to learn those languages. As our connections to the Middle East grew, so did the need to be able to speak with them—but in which language? The United States is connected to the world, and we want to be able to speak with all of it. To limit ourselves to one or two languages does not make political or economic sense.

I would strive to provide exposure to many languages for our elementary students. We would sing songs in verses of French, Spanish, and German. The language we offered was at times dependent upon the availability of a teacher. But then grouping the students was a challenge. Once again, it takes a rare teacher to be able to challenge the fast learners without losing them while the strugglers catch up. There would be such a range of skill in one class, to say nothing of the range of attitudes. One of the challenges of teaching gifted students is that they are morbidly allergic to repetition: they simply will not sit still for it. And repetition is a necessary evil when trying to learn a new language. If they are not stimulated by the class, then elementary students, especially little boys, make their own stimulation and can be very disruptive. During foreign language classes, that is when I would be very busy as a principal dealing with rowdy and disrespectful boys.

I am a practical idealist. When there is a solution that makes perfect sense to me, I seize it and am very upset when others do not see the sense of it. Mother once pointed out that I do not suffer fools gladly. A prime example of this for me as a teacher was when, in the 1970s, our nation debated switching to the metric system. I found wonderful activities and games that got all my students competent in the system. But our country dismissed the change as too expensive. Although our economy depended on working with the nations of the world, most of whom used the metric system, we once again chose the low road of arrogance and kept on with our confusing, outmoded, "good old American way."

My same practical idealism kicked in when I learned about Esperanto, which is like the metric system of languages. Here is a proven language that is simple, politically neutral, and spoken all around the world, albeit in small pockets. There are free curricular materials available and eager teachers. The language was invented by L. L. Zamenhof, a doctor who grew up in a part of Poland where five different languages were spoken in his neighborhood, and where he saw how misunderstanding, suspicion, and fighting happened when people could not communicate. He studied the major languages of Europe, especially those with Latin and Germanic roots, and created a language that distilled those, simplifying them for ease of speaking and use. The language is phonetically regular, so that there is only one way to pronounce each letter and each word; there are no silent letters, and the accent is always on the second-to-last syllable. Words are grammar coded; for example, nouns all end in -*o*, adjectives in -*a*, plurals with -*j*. Words themselves do not have confusing genders as they do in French, German, and many other languages. There are none of the irregular verbs and nouns that turn English into confusion. There is a handy set of affixes and suffixes that can be added to root words, and sometimes more than one can be added, making it "agglutinative." If you cannot remember a specific word for something, in Esperanto you can usually piece together a combination that another Esperantist will understand. A person can get to survival fluency in Esperanto in a matter of months, compared to the years necessary in one of the traditional languages. Learning Esperanto has also proven to be extremely helpful to understanding English and its nuances; learning Esperanto also has proven to make learning modern languages easier.

I once stopped by a poster session at a national gifted conference, where I learned more about the language from one of the Esperanto Association's top education ambassadors. An article he wrote about the language was published in one of the gifted education journals, where I had read it. He persuaded me to take the free correspondence course lessons in the language and to accept free phone practice. That led to my receivng a scholarship to participate in a three-week language immersion program to learn Esperanto with students from all over the world. I did that immersion program twice when it was held at San Francisco State University. I taught Esperanto to students at Rainard and at Ideal. However, I was sensitive to the fact that Americans are very skeptical of the language for the political reasons that I described earlier. The language is better accepted elsewhere in the world. I would find myself sheepishly defending the language, aware that to most Americans, my embrace of the language branded me as a ridiculous, idealistic, and impractical hippie.

It is worth noting that the language has its greatest promoters in the gifted community. That is ironic because it is simpler than the traditional languages, so one might expect it to be more heavily promoted to students who have trouble learning a foreign language. But because Esperanto is regular and sensible and can facilitate international and scientific communication, it holds great appeal to hungry minds that want to learn from the rest of the world. It was striking how many mathematicians found its regularity appealing, and how many poets and creative artists chose the language for its expressive potential. There were four PhDs in my class of ten in San Francisco. What does that say?

Although I would have liked all my students to study Esperanto, I only planted the seeds with them and instead found Spanish teachers in Houston. But when I got to Virginia and the high school there, we invested in the Rosetta Stone foreign language program for the school. Students were able to choose from eleven different languages and could proceed at their own pace. I was responsible for supervising their progress and setting goals with each student. The choice and individualization made great sense.

At Rainard, one of the graduation competencies that I required was for the student to reach at least a practical, survival, conversational tourist level of fluency. As an incentive, the school would take an international trip each year, and we would depend upon the students of that language to be our guides and translators. Unfortunately, that never happened.

Between the high schools in Houston and Virginia, I was able to try out many of my ideas. If part of my reason for being on the planet was to put my ideals into practice by providing alternative education, especially for gifted students, then my mission was successful.

But my contract was not renewed in Virginia for financial reasons, and I was out of work. Again. First from my friend's private school in Missouri, then in Houston, after the personnel agency. Next was in Michigan, after the Roeper School debacle, and now in Virginia. And once again, my release came in June, a very bad time to find a senior administrative position in a school. For the first time, I applied for and received unemployment compensation. I tried very hard to find a position that would allow me to stay in the DC area. I was keen to work at one of the

Smithsonians, or at a national organization's headquarters. I was a finalist to help open a charter school in DC, but the "winner" had a better sense of the local politics.

At Thanksgiving, I took a job taking over a sixth-grade advanced academics language arts class in Reston. Actually, I was taking over five classes and had a case load of 137 students, which is more than high school teachers have! It was a ridiculous number of students to teach. I was out in one of the trailers, without restrooms or running water. To get to the main building we crossed a wooden boardwalk and the staff parking lot, then climbed a set of stairs, then ascended another set of stairs to get to the office, and climbed yet another set of stairs to get to the library and arts classes. It was a very snowy winter, and the walkways could get dangerously icy. My classroom floor was always filthy as the janitors would not mop it because they could not get water buckets out to the buildings. I cut way back on my coffee drinking that year because it was such an ordeal and distance to get to the restrooms. It was hard work to teach that many students, and even harder to edit and grade all those papers. I kept track, and one writing assignment took me a total of 37 hours to grade.

It helped that I was working with a wonderful team of seasoned professionals. The students were great and the parents very supportive. I had a few interviews for administrative positions around the country, but nothing came of them, so I was looking forward to returning to Reston in the fall. The money was great—fifty percent more than I was paid at the high school. But in May, the charter school for the gifted in Cleveland brought me in to interview for their head of school position. I was very, very cautious and shared with them my concern about the relation between the board and the head, as I did not want to get burned again as I had at Rainard. Individual board members said that they were learning how to do that better, and they desired to improve, so with my help, they knew that they could get there. And it was a chance to bring gifted education for free to students. I accepted. School got out the end of June in Reston, and the next week I reported to Cleveland.

I did not want to return to the Midwest: I had grown up there. Cleveland and its rust belt, recovering economy felt a lot like my childhood home in Kenosha, Wisconsin. Cleveland did not have the energy of Houston and certainly not of DC. It did not have the ocean, which I craved. Perhaps I could see Lake Erie as a suitable substitute. After all, growing up along Lake Michigan had whetted my appetite for the big, ocean-like bodies of water. Maybe it could work. I felt that I had one last, big project in me. Teaching was satisfying, but I knew that I could run a school for gifted again. They needed me. My confidence, my ego responded.

I hated to leave DC. Beyond the fun that I had in the schools, my personal life had blossomed. I was free to have a life outside of school. And what a place to have a life! Our home was in Leisure World, a gated community of high-rises overlooking the Potomac. It was a senior community for active adults, and our 7th-floor rental had a wonderful view of woods, the golf course, and the river that was visible in the winter when the trees lost their leaves. I could take long hikes through the hilly woods, observe deer, watch the wildflowers through the seasons, and collect errant golf balls for fun. But the most fun of all was the water volleyball team. Three days a week, folks met in the pool for three hours to bonk the big beach ball around. I thought it would be lame, playing with the oldies with a big, soft ball, but I was wrong. There were some very competitive players, but they were considerate, too, careful of those who'd had heart surgery or knee problems or did not want to get their careful perms or makeup wet. One white-haired gal always played with dangling, fancy earrings. But it was vigorous exercise, and I slept soundly on those days when I could join them. It was a gorgeous pool, a very long one in a room with three-story windows through which we could watch the planes on their landing path to Dulles; even better was watching the snow fall so beautifully that winter. It was nice not to have to drive to the community's clubhouse, so the walk uphill after swimming was easy exercise. The community was good for Richard, too; it was safe for him to ride his scooter all around, and he was a regular at the bar in the clubhouse. A hospital and our doctor and dental offices were all just across the street from the community, and it was an easy 15 minute drive to the high school, or 25 minutes to Dulles. The best grocery store on the east coast, Wegman's, was in that same zone. It didn't take me long to understand why that store has an almost cultish following.

Living in Virginia, I was able to get back into theater. I ushered regularly in downtown DC at the Studio Theater, which I loved. Once I even got to serve Pierce Brosnan and his wife! I got back on stage in Gaithersburg, Maryland, in a period production of *An Ideal Husband*. It was a fun stretch to use a British aristocratic accent as an over-the-top society woman. A perk of that show was getting a custom-made corset! The lead actress had taken costume design and construction classes in college, so she sewed one for each of us. At first, getting laced into the beast made me feel elegant with my smaller waist and straighter posture, but wearing it for five hours every night took a toll on my back that only a month of serious massages could unkink. It was a harrowing 60-90 minute drive to the theater through DC rush-hour traffic, in the winter—the winter of Snowmageddon, as the locals called it. That was the year that the federal government had to close down because of the massive snowstorm that buried the city. We had ten snow days out of school that winter, and many more delayed-start days. We never made up those days. I also did two summer productions in Charles Town, West Virginia, which was an hour's drive over the Blue Ridge along winding roads, past wineries and over rivers. Those long drives to rehearsals gave me time to listen to my lines over and over through the car's sound system. For one show I had to learn a Baltimore accent, and for the other I used the Maine accent I had learned from my husband, a native of Maine.

Moving from Virginia to Ohio was quite an adjustment. Besides the culture, energy, and convenient lifestyle of the DC area, there was another thing I was going to miss in Ohio: my sex life.

Swinging 2009

Abstinence does *not* make the heart grow fonder. The heart gets damn resentful, in fact. Because Richard had retired from sex back around 2004, I was forced to take matters into my own hands. But that wasn't enough. By then, my San Antonio lover had been long out of the picture, and Jack did not want a relationship. I did not want to replace my husband, but I did desire to be a whole person, a person who was as sexual as I wanted to be. I did not want to retire from enjoying life, and sex is a way that I really enjoy life! I need to touch as much as I need to be touched. As an introvert, I prefer to get to know people one-on-one, and sex is one route to an intimate connection. So there I was, settled in northern Virginia, but without sex. It was time to open my mind.

How *does* a person get into "the lifestyle," as it is called? My introduction was gradual. Perhaps you recall Bob, the boy I was dating in high school. His nickname, given to him by one of my gal pals who had dated him before I did, was "old hands and mouth," a tribute to his aggressive sexuality. He was the one who taught me to give head. Well, he kept his energy into his midlife, which is when we reconnected. Shortly after my father died in 2005, I got an email from Bob asking if I was the same person that he knew in Wisconsin. His mother read my father's obituary in the

Kenosha News, and the obituary gave the whereabouts of Father's children, including me in Houston. She remembered me and told Bob. It turns out he had been living in Houston for several years, so we were in the same town again—a remarkable coincidence. We got together and had many a long conversation about our mutual dissatisfactions with work and the state of our lives. I told him that I wanted sex, and we played a bit, but it did not work out. Bob, however, was no longer able to stay hard, but that did not stop him from playing. And he told me about swinging.

It seemed so tawdry, meeting strangers online. What kind of scum were these people? Weren't they all afraid of catching a disease or getting caught and shamed as sluts? Weren't they all just using one another?

Bob responded, "Am I scum? Sure, there are some losers, but word gets around about them. There is a code of behavior in the lifestyle world. It's all about the woman. She calls the shots. No means no, at any time. She sets the boundaries, and the man is expected to help her to feel comfortable. Everybody is expected to be honest about what is OK and what is not. It's fun, and I think it might be your solution."

"Eww, it just seems so wrong. I'm not a slut. It's supposed to be about love, and about the relationship. There has to be trust."

"Most people like to meet in public and see if there is chemistry," Bob explained. "People understand that everybody has preferences, and no offense is taken if there is not a follow-up to get together."

"God, I want to get laid."

"Another way to get your feet wet is to go to a house party. People socialize, bring food and drinks, and sometimes they go off and play, then rejoin the party. I can invite you the next time we go to this one guy's house. He likes to have us over, and he really likes my wife," Bob explained. His wife was an equally eager lifestyle woman.

"So it's an orgy. You go to orgies."

Bob giggled. "Well, I guess you could say so. But it's not out of control. Nobody is doing anything without their consent."

"What if somebody finds out? I have a very public position, and it could hurt my reputation."

Bob was reasoning very calmly. "So do a lot of these people. It's about respect and trust."

I would need to be very careful. "OK, let me know when there's a get-together. Maybe I will come and see."

I thought about it for months, and about a week before I moved to Virginia, Bob invited me to a house party. It was at the home of a low-key couple in their 60s with whom Bob and his wife had played before, and another couple or two would be there besides Bob and his wife. I figured, what the heck, I was leaving town that week anyway, so if it were embarrassing, I would be gone. The house was nondescript, and the pool was inviting. I absolutely love to skinny dip, and they invited me to enjoy the pool. I luxuriated in the sunny blue waters and watched the men playing with Bob's wife's breasts while she moaned with pleasure. Bob swam over to me, kissed me and played with me under the water. Another man swam over and played with my breasts. I was an underwater sex sandwich. The man entered me, large and enthusiastic. The water carried our motions along, but he stopped before he climaxed, saying that he wanted to save himself to be able to enjoy more activity that afternoon. It was all relaxed, fun, and no pressure.

And then I was off to Virginia. I behaved myself that first school year, but my desperation and desire grew too much. It was time to look into this lifestyle thing that Bob was talking about. I went to SwingLifestyle.com and read all about it. I looked at people's profiles and pictures. There were a lot of skanky-looking people and lot of them without pictures. Icons in the profile told which members were OK with alcohol, and which were OK with smokers. Some were paid members, and some were lifetime members. Free members like me were limited to five messages per day and could not have access to nude pictures. I created a profile and screen name but posted no pictures. In my profile, I was honest about my large size—a BBW (big, beautiful woman). After all, I did not want to endure the rejection of somebody who was unpleasantly surprised.

I was barraged with responses! That was shocking. I don't get second glances in bars. There sure are a lot of horny guys out there on the Internet. The program has a canned rejection response with which you can reply "Thank you, but I am not interested at this time." I sent that to the smokers and to those who were bi-curious; I was open-minded, but the idea of getting together with a guy who has been with another guy just got me too afraid of AIDS. Yes, that is a silly and ignorant prejudice, I know. I rejected those who were horrible spellers or who wrote in text-speak, e.g., "Ur profile got me xcited." If they could not spell, I decided that they were not of a mental caliber that would give us anything to talk about between rounds. When I was feeling particularly particular, I would rule out those who said that they were "discrete" rather than discreet; I wanted to sarcastically commend them on their independence, but I refrained. Aside from my quirks about bisexuality and literacy, I was open-minded: black, brown, or white, young or old, I would give them a look-over.

There were a surprising number of men who want the thrill of the hunt, the naughty talk, and the planning, but then who never want to get together. They say they want to, but something always interferes. Those are the married guys who just want to know there is something else out there, and they want to stay safe. Good for them, but they waste my time. There are those who won't continue a conversation without photos. Some of them just want fresh images to whack off to, while others have preferences that they will not voice. Occasionally I would send a face picture if we had exchanged some emails and things were going well. Some fellows wanted to get together but had done no planning beyond that: they did not have a place to play (married) and did not want to spend the money on a hotel. More time wasters.

And so I was able to have adventures in Virginia. There was the guy who rode his bicycle to the motel and told his wife that he was out for a ride. His pubic hair was so thick that it was like riding a trampoline. Another guy whom I met at a Panera read that I liked doing it outdoors, so I followed him to a nearby park, where we walked into the woods and he spread a blanket just off the trail. There was the sleazy roadside motel outside of town, where I found a pair of dirty men's underwear under the bed when I went to retrieve my shoe. Yuck. That fellow helped me to overlook my prejudice against tattoos, as he had three constellations on his arms, one for each of his three children. At our second visit, we were interrupted no fewer than five times by calls from his three children, whom he had left at home alone. That was our final visit. There was the young man who left his mop and vacuum in the middle of the living room to show me that he had cleaned for my visit. There was the fresh college graduate who was so overweight that his dick wouldn't extend past his belly, ruling out most positions. This was the case with the nice lobbyist, too. He got us a fancy suite at a nice hotel and insisted that we shower with Cetaphil soap before playing. He fed me well, served nice wine, and brought me a fancy silk scarf from his Chinese trip, but there was no satisfaction for me. Another was a colonel who would look me up when he came to town for Pentagon work. There was the NASA contractor who explained the new radar system to me. One fun fellow looked just like Santa Claus, with a round belly and full white beard. There was the black man who took me back to his office and pounded me on his desk, making me fear that we would collapse in a pile of lumber. Later, he was my first MFM— male-female-male encounter. But most of the guys were not all that memorable. I enjoyed the variety. If I had my druthers, I would try somebody new every week as well as see a "regular" each week, giving me a few days between engagements to recover.

It was cool how so many of these DC-area guys were doing interesting things. Many worked for one of the many "three-letter agencies," like the CIA, NSA, DOD, or they did contract work for them. They had some very interesting stories to tell. There was also a professor, a psychologist, a judge, and an insurance executive. The caliber of men was higher than I would expect in other parts of the country.

How did I decide to see someone more than once? If I could get off easily with the guy, I would see him again. If he made a valiant effort to please me, I would give him another chance. If he made little or poor effort, I wouldn't see him again and would often find myself seeking succor on my way home by calling Jack or another regular, or downing a bowl of Ben & Jerry's Coffee Heath Bar Crunch. But if he got me off without my lending a hand, then I would tell him my real name. Until then, I was just Ella Bush. That was the name I invented when I was in college, writing about my illicit relationship with Richard. It was a play on my first initials (Lorraine Ann was my birth name) and the first syllable of Richard's name (Bouch > Bush.)

John was a regular. He wrote the most wonderful, over-the-top note to me on Swing Lifestyle. After reading my profile, he would die if he could not meet me, he said, he was in love, my profile sent him into spasms of lust. He had to meet me. Despite the appeal of his writing skill, I replied skeptically because I could see that he and his wife shared a profile, and I did not want to play with her, too. Then *she* wrote back to me to say that I seemed like a great match for her husband, that they both played with permission, and that she thought I would really like him. I let it go for months until I had to be in his neighborhood anyway to usher at the theater in downtown DC, so I agreed to meet him for coffee at his neighborhood coffee shop. He spoke often of our first meeting, of seeing that "wonderful mane of white hair" and my beautiful, friendly smile. He was retired, so he could meet anytime. His wife still worked, and they had an arrangement to give each other the apartment when one had a tryst planned, but the host had to clean the whole apartment. That was motivation to clean house! While one of them played, the other would run errands or go to a movie or dinner with friends. John told great stories and gave me excellent advice about business. He was a world traveler and collected beautiful Haitian art. He treated me to meals, and we saw a couple shows together.

He gifted me with music that I had enjoyed during our play sessions. And he always complimented me with superlatives and hyperbole, which I ate up with a spoon.

John prodded me to share my fantasies. And before one visit, he asked me if I liked surprises. Sure, I said, and when I got to his place, there was another man there, too, and they offered me a glass of wine from the bottle that they had begun to share. Chris was a large, handsome black man. John said, " I thought you two might like to meet." So Chris and I played, John watched, and then John and I played. "Did you like my surprise?" John chuckled. "Oh, yes," I admitted sheepishly. Chris was great. I later invited him up to my place, and he played like he was an insurance man coming to sell me a policy. On another visit, John arranged another surprise. We were playing in his bedroom when I felt a cool hand on my rump that could not, for reason of distance, have been John's hand. I turned my head and saw a strange, naked man stroking my backside. John had contacted him, told him what time to get there and how to get into the building without buzzing, had left the door unlocked, and told him to just come on in. And come in he did! He left, and John and I resumed, only to be interrupted by a different fellow! That one was kind of nervous, and I picked a big piece of toilet paper off his rump, but he was fun and enthusiastic. That was a busy afternoon! John had tried to arrange a third guy, but he couldn't make it. Whew!

But it was Marty who was my most regular lover. Charles Martin's profile was unassuming and understated. It was all about respect and mutual fun. He was 63 and he invited me to meet sometime. I was noncommittal and said that we could get together for coffee. But one Sunday morning, I was quite horny and wrote to him. I said that I would come over if he made me breakfast. He agreed. And he dropped his drawers right there in the kitchen, with the spatula in his hand, and we began to play. Over breakfast, he told me that he was divorced but was in a long-term, loving relationship with a woman who had moved to South Carolina to be with her grandchildren. This did not concern me but let me know that I had nothing to fear about him getting overly attached. They agreed that each was free to play while apart, and they enjoyed hearing about each other's lusty adventures. It threw me for a loop the first time he dialed her while we were in the middle of noisy playing. She chattered encouraging words, then he listened to her get off. I was not accustomed to another woman joining us, even if it was on the phone. I felt my privacy was invaded. If I asked him not to call her, he wouldn't, but eventually I found it to be a frequent addition to our play. They each enjoyed knowing that the other was not suffering while absent from one another, and keeping things above board and open prevented the suspicion that comes from not knowing.

Marty welcomed me over anytime, and sometimes we got together on an evening, but usually we connected on Sundays. He liked me to call him after I met another man, as my details would appeal to his prurient interests. It was also a good safety practice that women in SLS (swing lifestyle) observe: always let somebody know where you are going and that you are safe. If I had a very unsatisfactory encounter, he invited me over for a better finish to my evening. He was pleased that he was the one that I turned to and chose over some of the younger guys. His town home was large and tastefully decorated, and clean for a bachelor. It smelled good. Too many single men are absolute slobs, and I find their lack of cleanliness to be a red flag: if they take such poor care of their home, they will take poor care of me and our connected health. Marty indulged me by keeping a bottle of sodium-free sparkling water, my favorite drink, in the fridge. So for the couple of years that I was in Virginia, we had time to get to know one another. It was an easy intimacy, and we shared our traumas and insecurities, steadying one another during transitions, he from working for the government to retirement, me from working in the high school, to unemployment, to public school.

It was an odd balance between playfulness in our open relationship and intimacy that was ours alone. How did our feelings for one another as just one of multiple lovers evolve to something more? He shared that he had feelings for me. He wouldn't usually say it so much as express it, and one of those ways that he expressed it was choosing a music playlist of songs that were about love. I knew all along that Cathie was the queen of his heart, and told him so, but he squirmed at the suggestion. He was clearly connected to her, but he wanted to think of himself as unattached. He chafed at the idea of his being part of a couple. He'd been married twice before and wanted none of it. His ex, the mother of his two boys, was not a kind woman and had been insulting and insensitive to his feelings, according to him and confirmed by his grown sons' observations. Cathie had been with him through that traumatic divorce, and she was patient with his withholding, noncommittal ways, knowing they were a result both of his dysfunctional former marriage and the traumas he had experienced serving in Vietnam.

Cathie called him multiple times a day without necessarily having anything to say, which drove him nuts. But in her defense, when she left Virginia to move to South Carolina, Marty had committed to Cathie that once he retired, he would move down to South Carolina to be near her. Yet as his retirement neared, he made no move to find a place there. She was frustrated that he was not living up to that part of their agreement. They argued and made up. He hated that she would cry when he would leave to return home. She suspected that he had feelings for me, and she felt threatened. He would visit her for a week or ten days at a time, then get anxious to get back to his own home, his own space. He would stay as long as he had projects to do there, such as painting her garage or laying tile for the kitchen floor, but then he would retreat and return to Virginia, where he and I resumed.

He could not or would not commit to her. He wondered aloud about whether his quest to keep trying new pussy was just to build his self-esteem, which had been battered by his ex-wife and his mother. He wanted to have many new experiences, but he was frustrated that he did not get the kind of responses to his Swing Lifestyle profile that younger, more studly guys enjoyed. He wondered why more women didn't give him a chance. His lack of satisfaction with what he already had—Cathie, me, and another regular local woman—got on my nerves. Why couldn't he see what he had? One afternoon, immediately after a particularly satisfying and intimate round in bed, as I lay in his arms, he began, once again, to gnaw that bone of frustration about why he couldn't get more women. I scoffed at him in disbelief: how could he not acknowledge that what he had was good? And how could he disregard what we had just had as not enough? We had just had a lovely, playful, generous romp, but he wanted more? What was I, chopped liver? I was hurt and slid off his tall bed to dress without a word, crying. I trotted downstairs, gathered up my things, and he followed me down. "You're leaving?" he asked weakly.

"Goodbye," I said hoarsely, and walked out the door without turning back. He did not pursue me.

And he did not call or write to me. I was hurt and angry, and his silence and lack of pursuit or understanding just made me more upset. How could he be so intimate and so obtuse and insensitive at the same time? But as the weeks passed, I felt compelled to explain to him, to try to help him to see that he had hurt me, and that was why I left. I tried to contact him but learned that he had gone to sea, volunteering with Operation Smile, a charity he'd worked with before, which sailed to Third World countries to give free cleft palate repairs to children. Marty would do their paperwork and help out however he could. He had accompanied a trip once to Vietnam and found that being able to help the Vietnamese children, after having been a soldier there, gave him a profound healing that abated his deep anger and fear over his war experience. So going to sea on the hospital ship was a healing retreat for him.

When we finally exchanged emails, he admitted that he had been terribly hurt by my leaving him that day. He saw that women left him, as Cathie had left him to choose her grandchildren over him, and didn't want the pain of being rejected. We made plans to get together to talk it over when he returned. We sat down at his square teak kitchen table, and we held hands across the table. He had no idea that he had hurt me; he could only express that I had hurt him by leaving him.

"I want you in my life. I missed you. It hurts me when you talk about wanting other women while you are with me," I admitted. "I know you want to pursue them, and I don't need to be exclusive, but I don't want to hear about them in a way that makes me feel like what we have is not good. I feel rejected and dismissed when you do." And with that, our regular relationship picked up again, and he was more careful not to bemoan his dismissal by other women while we lay in each others' arms.

I did try to help him to enjoy new playmates. I wrote him a very positive certification on SLS. When we went to house parties, I spoke to the other women about how satisfied they would be if they gave him a whirl. I went to a group party and was pleased to see him getting attention from other women, while I enjoyed attention from the other men. But he still never had enough. Some people just don't know what they have. And if you are fearful of commitment, what you have is too scary.

He was looking for meaningful ways to spend his retirement. He was a pilot and owned his own little Cessna. He loved planes, and his house had multiple large prints of paintings featuring aircraft flying over beautiful countryside. He volunteered often at the Smithsonian's Udvar-Hazy Air and Space Museum close to his home. Early in our relationship, I told him how much I missed the beach and was dismayed at the horrible traffic to reach it from Virginia. So one day he flew me in his little plane down to Virginia Beach. We walked along the cold and breezy deserted beach, then stopped for delicious boiled crabs. He hates all seafood, so he was very tolerant and patient while I tore the crustaceans apart with gusto. He promised to take me back again but never did. He sold his airplane a couple years later, torn between its constant expense, what with parking, fuel, insurance, and inspections, and the freedom it offered him.

He found another volunteer opportunity at the Badlands of South Dakota and spent a summer there. I connected him to my daughter, as she just lived up the road, and he stayed overnight at her house to have a shorter drive to the famous Sturgis Bike Rally. He also visited her a couple times to get massages, and he wanted to help her out by paying in cash. In this way, he got to meet my family. Later, when Emily figured out that he and I were more than platonic friends, she had a face to go with his name. She said that he was definitely not the kind of guy she imagined me choosing.

Marty was restless in northern Virginia. He liked his home but did not like how built up the area had gotten, and how there were always sirens sounding from the fire station down the street. He wanted to be near his two sons in town, but he wanted to go someplace quiet. He feared that if he moved away to a nice, quiet small town, then his sons would finally get married and give him the grandchildren he was eager to enjoy. Should he go to South Carolina to be near Cathie? He enjoyed their times together but wanted his own space. Should he spend a year in Europe? Do a house exchange? He was in as much flux about his life as I was, changing jobs, searching for something better.

When I was offered the position as the charter school director in Ohio, I decided to take it. It had looked like I had made up my mind to stay in northern Virginia and enjoy continuing to work in the public district there, but I felt compelled to lead again in gifted education, so I changed my mind. When I told him, I was taken aback by his reaction. He was upset that I was leaving and wished I would not go. We held each other, and I cried into his shoulder, stunned that he was expressing his feelings for me. He asked if I was sure this was what I wanted to do and could not understand why. And yet he offered me no compelling reason to stay. I knew that he would always put Cathie higher than me. What did I see our relationship being when I moved? He asked me. I said that I wanted him in my life for always, and that I hoped we could visit back and forth, hopefully monthly. He would be my beach, my retreat and restoration. And there was always the phone.

When I was in Ohio, he did visit. He drove up a few times and even flew in once, which felt very romantic and Casablanca, meeting him at the little municipal airport in Ohio and seeing him fly off, tilting his wings in farewell as my skirts swirled around my knees in the breeze. And I drove to visit him, too, enjoying the spectacular Pennsylvania scenery for the six-hour trip. A couple times I found bargain airfares and flew in, and he would pick me up in his sexy, bright-yellow convertible Ford Mustang. It was fun. I would be fine with monthly visits, but true to his form, he did not want to commit. He said that he would come to ride the famous Cedar Point roller coasters with me, as they were just a 40-minute drive away. He was not willing to book in advance or save any dates. He was always open to something better coming along.

I eventually told Richard about Marty, that we were close friends and that we liked to get together. Richard was happy for me and liked Marty. Richard knew that he could no longer make love to me or make me happy, and above all else, Richard wanted me to be happy; he never pried about details or even mentioned sex. He met Marty when we lived in Virginia, and I told Richard when I visited him. When we moved to Ohio, Richard insisted on welcoming Marty to visit, and he would move into the front bedroom to let Marty and me have the master bedroom. It was unconventional, but it worked. One helpful element that made it work was that Richard took long naps, and his hearing was terrible. In our wedding vows, Richard presaged the challenges our age difference would present in his later years, and he wrote into his vows to me, *I promise to hold you close, but with open hands.* And so he had. Marty was never completely comfortable sharing the house with Richard on his visits. The three of us would usually sit down to dinner together, and Richard would get very garrulous, telling how he could see that Marty loved me, and he should take good care of me, and he loved me and wanted me to be happy, and how glad he was that Marty was there, and what a good guy he was. Richard would say that he knew that he would die soon, maybe that very day. That was a lot of drama for poor Marty to go through to be able to come and bed another guy's wife.

When I quit my job in Ohio, it took me a year to find another job. I had a lot of time on my hands, but Marty and I did not see each other any more frequently than when I had been working, despite my availability. We talked about Europe and began to make plans for that summer: he would spend half his time with Cathie and the other half with me. When he asked me what I wanted to see, my preferences included the islands off the Italian coast, where I researched for the best snorkeling spots. But Marty did not like the ocean—too salty, stinky, and sandy. But then something came up in Cathie's family life, and Marty decided not to go to Europe. He said that his decision was based upon wanting to stay there longer and not wanting to be there alone for such a long time after I left. I would not be able to stay for the month that he wanted to be there. His decision made me angry, realizing that he would not go for the time with me and that I had to miss out because of Cathie. Again, he would not admit that she outranked me in his priorities.

Yet he was hanging on to me, and in such subconscious ways. Twice when I was traveling around the country for final interviews with schools, he would call me late at night and engage in serious, long conversations, pitched way more intensely than when I was parked at home. It was almost as though he were realizing that I was spinning away from him again, and he was hanging on, or testing me, or trying to sabotage my visit by disturbing my rest. It was mystifying.

I tried very hard to find a job in the DC area again so I could be near both him and that exciting city. It was during that year that he finally decided to make the leap to leave the DC area, if only experimentally for a year. His friends offered to have him stay in their lake house for a year while they continued to work another year before they retired. He offered to let Richard and me stay in his house rent-free until I got my financial footing again, but I declined because Richard would not do well with all the steps to get into the house and even more to go up to the bedrooms. But I did take Marty up on his offer to stay with him when my house in Ohio sold before I was offered a position somewhere. I visited him and arranged for a number of interviews in the DC area.

It was a ten-day visit, the longest we had been together. I was very anxious about overstaying my welcome and of giving him his space and not expecting him to entertain me. I told him so, and he reassured me that he wanted me there and that I was very welcome. I knew that he had a lot to do because he would be leaving at the end of the ten days to move to North Carolina. He had been packing for a month; he had packed up all his cooking supplies and had no food in the house. It upset me that he had no pots and pans, so I searched online and learned how to microwave an egg. It worked, but he refused to try it. There was a lot of tension between us, but when we parted, he did say he loved me. He seldom said it.

When I moved to Florida and he moved to the lake house in North Carolina, something changed in him. We still talked almost daily, but nothing was coming of my desire for us to make plans to get together. There were issues with his move-in there, and with closing out his house and making repairs. He would not commit. But he did see Cathie about every other weekend, or for a week at a time. They were seeing a lot more of each other, and she was happy, no longer getting upset when he would leave. They were now only a couple hours apart, an easy drive. So he had his space and his woman, too. She followed my postings on Facebook and kept him informed, as he did not want to use Facebook. She told him of my postings of loving the beach at sunrise. And then he called me one Sunday and asked about the beach: did I love it more than I loved Galveston? He had often heard me rhapsodize about my love of that island, of how I made monthly pilgrimages there when I lived in Houston, about how I needed my beach fix to make everything better. I thought hard about my answer and said that I like this beach even more. And then somehow he switched the conversation completely over to something about freeloaders and welfare abuse, and how they were taking his hard-earned money, feeling entitled. Where the heck did that come from? We'd had that discussion before, but it was annoying and strangely timed for him to start ranting about it. I groaned and said, "All right, Archie," which turned him to ice. I could hear the anger in his voice, and he ended the call.

Then I didn't hear from him. He didn't answer my calls. I finally emailed him a short message: *What the hell happened?* to which he responded:

I think I finally realized that as much as I care for you and love you and as interesting as our talks are sometimes, at basic core I am an old, racist, right-wing conservative who is angry at the problems our country has, the direction it's going, and I want change. On the other hand you're just happy with the way things are because you don't want to hear about BAD stuff. After we last talked I had an image of you as the kid who when he/she hears something they don't like sticks fingers in ears and yells "Lalalalala."

The old right-wing racist may be Archie Bunker. But Archie worked a job, raised his family, and paid his taxes. He didn't live off welfare, abandon his family, or not pay taxes. I'm sure in that statement could be a hidden racist agenda so let me say I have that same feelings about a white, yellow, or green person who lives off welfare, abandons his family, or doesn't pay taxes.

I am what I am and you are what you are. We have some fun together. But we're just too different. That's what I finally realized.

Having a conversation will not change my being an old, right-wing racist. Do you really think there is anything more to discuss? There is no changing who either of us is. Is this breaking up? I'm not sure what that means when you're married and I'm non-committal. I will be a friend and help if you need anything. But I'm just through with being the old, right-wing racist. Maybe you think it's a joke. I don't and I'm finished.

I was reeling and sad that it was ending like that. I missed our daily chit chats. As much as they were often about the mundane, the calls were also a way of reaching out and touching, caring. I sent him this note:

A little boy came up to me with a sad, long face today. He pointed to a little girl sitting cross-legged on the floor with another little girl, reading. He looked up at me and said, "I want to be her friend, but she said she doesn't want to be my friend. She doesn't want to be mine." He wanted me to fix it. Instead, my heart just burst. "I know how you feel. Let her be. Try again tomorrow. Maybe she will feel different."

Should I keep trying? I sent him this note:

Who is worth keeping in our lives?

- *Those who bring out the best in us, who make us want to be a better person, live up to our potential, spread the love.*

- *Those who see the good in us.*

- *Those who help us to enjoy our lives, make us smile, experience the joys of pleasure, help us through the tough times, keep our perspective positive.*

- *Those who have something to teach us, whether it is enlightening or uncomfortable, growth is good. Confrontation and discomfort, when one pushes through it, brings clarity, drive, and purpose.*

Are you worth keeping in my life?

You bring out my patience, and your fucked-upness gives me an opportunity to develop empathy, so in those respects, you help me to be a better person. I enjoy our sex. You are entertaining and make me laugh. Our conversations teach me. You know a lot of stuff and I learn from you.

You're a keeper.

But you need to know that you have abandoned me in my time of need. Here I was in a new job, new home, without your comforting little calls, knowing that you cared.

And on Friday I lost my job. I was let go, no reason given.

It is humiliating, and I cannot imagine anyone, especially you, thinking that I am anything less than a failure. "Here she goes again, fucked up."

I just cannot work for other people, it has become clear. I'm tired of looking for a good match. I will not spend another year like last year!! It's time to do something completely different, or finally write that book I've been threatening to write.

So I've got some flexible time on my hands. I've got performances the weekends of the 25th and Nov. 1st. Thanksgiving I'll be in South Dakota.

If you should want to connect to me again, I would like it to be in person. I remember when you returned from the Comfort, and we sat across from one another, touching hands, discussing the pain we had caused one another. That is such a more comforting way to reconnect, to forgive, than words in cold, distant cyberspace.

I still love you.

But if your life is better without me in it, then do not respond. I wish you well.

Oct 23, to me

I'm sorry to hear about your job. I am at my sister's then going back to NC via the Blue Ridge. The owners of the house are there and I wanted to get gone. After rehearsal and a concert next Monday I'm headed to NoVA to do some repairs to my home. Perhaps you could come to the lake for a few days in early

November. If you'd like I can send a check to cover air fare or I'll pay you while you're here.

While it was not an affectionate letter, it was opening a door, so I made arrangements to visit him for a few days. I got Mike the security guy to look after Richard, and I flew up with hope and trepidation.

We talked, and we didn't talk, our conversation proceeding as if nothing had happened, and then one of us would mention something raw and startling; it was as if our connection were a wire, and the insulation had frayed off in parts and sent shocks of negative energy out, expressions of frustration and hopelessness; then we would go into a shop in town and admire the varieties of olive oil. I told him the tale of woe over my job situation, and he tried not to push or condemn me or offer too many suggestions. Sometimes we held hands, sometimes we played. The lake house was really lovely, with a spectacular vista over the cove of the sprawling lake. I had alone time down on the dock, and he took down a kayak for me to paddle around by myself. The sunsets were breathtaking, and I took photos. We cooked, and cuddled, and made small talk.

I used to believe in signs, search for signs, thank heaven for signs. Signs are poetry that jump up in our face and tell us to *pay attention: the answers are here! This feeling is true!* Maybe I still do believe in them, but all the negative shit in my life has left me feeling skeptical. So when Marty and I were sitting on the porch, bluebirds kept flitting up to the window and clinging to the screen in front of us. Bluebirds! These are not common birds. "My grandmother wished all her life to see a bluebird," Marty said in wonder. I looked again, trying to see if perhaps they were actually nuthatches, little gray birds that cling easily to screens. Bluebirds like boxes and meadows: this was a heavily wooded property along a lake. Were they purple martins, small birds that like to be near the water, where they fly out for the insects? No, the wings of these birds were not so pointy, their bellies clearly rust-colored. Bluebirds, the symbol of happiness, were right there in our faces. A sign, or irony?

My departure felt tender, our hold still there but fragile. "I hope I see you again," he said.

"So do I," I replied.

A few weeks later, I asked Emily if she believed in signs. "Signs are from God," she said. "Have you seen a sign?" So I described the bluebirds, clinging to the porch screen, showing up in a place where they don't usually frequent.

"So they were clinging, in a place where they don't usually go."

Her alternate interpretation thunked me in the heart. "How did you get so wise?" I asked her.

But it was over with Marty. Although we connected a couple times after that, it was like trying to scrape that sticky residue off your window left by an expired decal. I don't handle being dumped very well. It's almost as if the guy has to run over my dog on purpose (if I had a dog) for me to decide that I should stop thinking about being with him. I thought about Jack for way too long after he didn't want a relationship. I thought about Art for way too long after he didn't want to continue. I took a long time to heal. I prayed a silent wish to be able to end the relationship gracefully. I don't believe in wishes any more, and my praying lacks impact. I need a new mantra. How about *Adios, muchacho.* That's much more empowering than just telling myself *Take the hint, idiot.*

2011, Ohio

I left Virginia in 2011 to take over Ohio's only charter school for gifted children. I had run a private school for gifted children, so the idea of finally not having to turn away gifted students who could not pay private school tuition really appealed to me.

"You're *not* going to buy a house again, are you?" my friend Jodi asked with a cautionary tone. She was aware of my previous home-selling debacles: the tens of thousands I lost selling in Michigan, and the money I lost selling in Houston, and how each home had been on the market for over a year.

"It turns out that you can use the VA home-buying credit more than once, and we can get in with zero money down, so what's to lose?" I responded. We bought half a duplex in a senior community in Avon, west of Cleveland and an easy 20-minute drive to school. It had its own nature trails through a private, protected wetland, plus a clubhouse and social center with pool tables and a swimming pool, and it was an easy, safe scooter or bike ride to a large shopping center. I had my own office just off the kitchen, and the home came complete with an herb garden and volunteer plot of rainbow chard. I seldom saw the home in daylight except on the weekends, when it would surprise me how different it looked than in the dark evenings.

I was devoted to giving the new job at the gifted public charter school my all, with long hours to get adjusted. Some infrastructure remained to be put into place since the charter was only in its fourth year and had experienced exhausting growth. What worked for the school when it was half its size had to be adjusted as the school's enrollment grew each year. There were connections to forge and tons of reporting to do for the board and the school's sponsor. It was a challenge to figure out just how much information the board needed and how much leeway I had in my decision making without requiring the board's blessing. It was frustrating to me to have my hands tied in so many ways; the board only met monthly, so weeks could go by before I could make a purchase, hire staff, or institute procedures until they would vote on a matter. And the board wanted a great deal of information before making a decision. There were no committee meetings before the board meetings that could be used to inform them of all the factors that went into my recommendations, so there would be extensive discussions and debates at the board meetings, the result of which would often be that no decision would be made until they could continue the discussion the next month. I tried to prevent that stalemate by sending out extensive reports prior to the meetings in the hopes that the members would read them in advance. They were asked to institute an email thread in which discussions could carry on and information be acquired before the monthly meetings in the hopes that decisions could be made and the meetings could end before ten at night. But all the board members were volunteers who had busy jobs in addition to their board obligations, and all but one had children at the school, so their time for attention to lengthy reading and discussion was limited. They complained about how difficult it was to keep up with all the reading, and I complained that I needed to be able to run the school without these frustrating delays. I begged them to follow Robert's Rules of Order, which they agreed would be a good idea, but they did not follow the procedures, and debates continued. I reminded them that I had run a school for over twenty years and had been board president for many of the years, so I had a proven sense of what was board business and what should be at the discretion of the person whom they hired to run the school. They demurred that it was a matter of helping them out by building trust, that they would let go of the reins as they got to know me and my decision-making process.

I could understand their hesitation to let go: the school was their collective baby. The school had started under another name, owned by a charter school chain and in a different location. The previous charter school chain decided in the spring to close the school when they saw how little money serving gifted children could get them: there was much more money to be made in serving children with learning disabilities. These parents rallied, as parents of gifted children are forced to do all over the country when the programs for their children are cut. They persuaded the charter chain to turn the charter over to the parents, and they miraculously got the school open again in just six months. I was their third director in four years. It was clear that they really didn't know what to do with a director. In fact, they had kept the original director on from his time with the original charter. He was a leader beloved by the parents and children, but the teachers found him lacking. The board kept him on to take charge of strategic initiatives. He made no money for the charter and kept a very messy office. When I came aboard, they wanted me to deal with him. I had no projects to entrust to him because I knew that if he could do what needed to be done, he would have gotten something done in the last couple years. I asked the Board to organize some kind of formal farewell for him to show appreciation for his years of service, but they never did. It was all very awkward. Eventually, we let him know that we needed his office, and he cleared out. There was no formal parting, public communication, or goodbye. He asked me in confidence not to make it known that he had been released. It turns out that his wife was best friends with the folks who lived behind me, and he was worried that word would get out: his wife still believed that he worked for the school. He was getting unemployment benefits, so he was getting by.

The biggest mess of all that brought out everybody's true colors was centered on services for exceptional students. Yes, gifted students can have issues that warrant counseling and accommodations; believe it or not, there are those who think that you cannot have a brilliant mind and also have troubles with reading, or they believe that having a quick and logical mind means that a person is exempt from anxiety or problems with focus and organization. The common question is, "If they're so smart, then why don't they..." But rather than lead to an answer, what the question does is highlight the questioner's ignorance and insensitivity. It's akin to asking a tall person, "If you're so tall, why aren't you playing basketball?"

At Rainard and at Roeper, both private schools, we did not have anybody on staff designated as a special services provider. We had quite a few students with behavior issues, dyslexia, ADHD, and sensory integration issues who would have qualified for services in a public system. What we did in the private schools was simple: we accommodated for them. Most of their problems became very manageable in our smaller classes. We worked as a team of teachers to keep an eye on each student and to plan together how to meet the student's needs. We involved the parents and, if necessary, would ask them to get professional outside assistance. Our academic and social goals for the students were geared to the individual. We could vary assignments and expectations to ensure a challenge without being overwhelming. Our mixed-age groupings of students set the expectation that not everybody would be in the same place. When one student would remark that "it's not fair" that his fellow was only expected to write one page while he had to write two, our responses could vary. "We want everybody to be challenged. One page is a challenge for him. Let me know if you think the challenge for you is too much." And we would build a community in the classrooms that celebrated each student's progress and successes. Even the youngest students caught on to this, and it would warm my heart to listen to a six-year-old praise a four-year-old, "Hey, that's the roundest *o* you've ever written!"

Another important factor that helped these students with issues to succeed in the private schools was our reporting system. While individual assignments might have rubrics and letter or number grades, the quarterly progress reports did not. Rather than report cards filled with letters or numbers, ours had scales and personalized comments. For the subjects and major assignments, students' progress was evaluated on two scales: "meets expectations for quantity and quality" and "meets expectations for effort." On those scales, a check would be placed somewhere between "exceeds expectations" and "needs improvement." Those qualities were far too subjective and loosey-goosey for the measurement-obsessed public system. But good private schools and their parents have a contract, made clear through the tuitions paid, to communicate and work things out for the benefit of the student. It is a relationship built on reputation, communication, and trust.

Public schools are institutions with bureaucracies and are forced to deal with things like special education in ways that will stand up in a court of law. The public schools mandate that the students be serviced in some way. The public schools have specific rules about who is qualified to identify what needs the student has, who will meet them, how the progress will be measured, who must be notified of the evaluation, and how often the plan for services will be reviewed. The system makes this compliance mandatory by means of layers of bureaucracy for oversight. A public school can get poor marks for noncompliance, but a charter school can be shut down and go out of business. The slim budgets of public schools mean that class sizes are too large to easily accommodate for the differences in the way that the smaller private school classes can accomplish. Even though the charter school had smaller class sizes than the public schools, there were still 50% more students in the classes than we had at Roeper or Rainard. Despite the earnest intentions of the public school teachers, the assignments they give to students tend to be one for all, all for one, and too bad for the students for whom the writing takes three times as long as it does for the other students. To help the struggling students, the public schools are mandated to provide assistance to the student and teacher via a prescribed number of hours of homework help, classroom assistance, or counseling services. Communication with parents gets mandated. Behavior gets charted and recorded. The records are permanent and follow the students everywhere.

Parents who came to the private school from public school were taken aback when we told them that we did not have a resource room or special education teacher. "Don't you *have to* provide for them?" they asked. "We *do* provide for them and accommodate them, but not in such a formal way," I stated. I explained that we work together; that I am successful at counseling the students. We've been at this a long time and know when something is going on for which we would ask you to get outside help. We can't cure dyslexia, but we can adjust assignments and be sensitive to their needs. We aren't physicians, but we know when behavior is too far outside the norm and is deleterious to the student's learning and ability to make friends. We can adjust our class schedules; if we see that the kids need a break or a different type of experience because they are getting rowdy or exhausted, then we can change things up or step outside. That was why we had such large playgrounds and intentional natural spaces. Gifted kids tend to be intense, and they need breaks, especially breaks that either release a lot of energy or provide a respite. Even the middle school students got recess.

The special education challenge in Ohio was due, in part, to the school being small and new, with few students in need of services. They had nobody assigned primarily to serve those students, and parents were complaining. One of my first priorities was getting the special education services in place. We had an exceptional counseling program, provided by Dr. Sylvia Rimm and her associates on a part-time basis. She was an internationally renowned psychologist who specialized in gifted students. Upon the renewal of her contract for the year that I was there, she agreed that her team would be responsible for the special education program. However, neither she nor I were well-informed of the requisite bureaucratic details.

The charter school's sponsor is responsible for seeing that the charter school abides by the state's regulations and reporting. The sponsor collects the reports and passes them on to the state or receives copies of what is submitted to the state. The charter pays the sponsor for these services. The sponsor assigns one person to the school to see that things get done. Our sponsor representative was a tall, elegant, gorgeous, and smart woman. She was patient and savvy but overworked. She had several schools under her domain, and most of them were on the other side of the state. They had bigger problems than ours, according to her, so they got most of her attention. We were going to be audited by the state in special education services, but she did not make clear to us just what we had to provide for that area. And we were backlogged in referrals from parents and teachers about students for whom they wanted evaluations for special services. There were deadlines to meet and paperwork and a great deal of paperwork to do. I needed to hire somebody who knew these regulations and was qualified to provide the services, and Dr. Rimm's team could not do that.

As I mentioned, I did not have the authority to hire an employee without the board vetting the candidate and voting. In an emergency, we could call a special meeting. But being a public institution, those emergency meetings, like all meetings of the board, had to be made public, so phone meetings via a conference call were out of the question. And getting the board together as a quorum proved challenging. I found a woman to hire who was experienced in providing special education, but by the time the board got around to approving her, she had moved on. I found another candidate, and he was hired, but he was an incompetent liar who made no progress in organizing the files. He and Dr. Rimm's team pointed fingers at one another and did not get along. He was with us during the preliminary audit, at which he was able to pull a few sample student files that were in fair condition, and the auditor was gentle and gave us very workable suggestions for improvement. Still, our new hire was not working out, and he required extensive counseling from me to try to get him to rise to the position. He did not show up for work several days before admitting that he could not do the job. And so the search for help began again, and we contracted with a company that provided us a wonderful candidate, Lila, who put all the files in order, assessed the situation, and gave a presentation to the board about what exactly was needed in terms of manpower and resources to get us in compliance by the deadlines pertinent to each case. She put together an exceptional presentation, replete with graphs, numbers, and cited regulations.

Dr. Rimm's team came to that meeting, a response clearly in defense of the fact that they had said that they could meet our special education services, and here was Lila pointing out that things were not right. Now, a well-organized board meeting is one in which a given number of minutes is prescribed for presentations and for discussions. The 20 minutes allotted for Lila went by, but the 20 minutes allotted for Dr. Rimm's team stretched on to a volatile 80 minutes. They argued that what the school was supposed to do was to provide homework services, and that we were not doing that. I argued that, in fact, we had a supervised homework program each afternoon that was voluntary but that we strongly urged parents to partake of if the student had issues with completing work during class time or at home. A member of Dr. Rimm's team argued that to be effective, it should include only those students with the special needs, and we should hire people just for those students. Nothing was accomplished. Teri, the board president, let the argument go on long after all the facts were revealed. I was exhausted, having already put in a twelve-hour day there that was not ending well. I rolled my eyes and needed a break from the long meeting, so I got up to use the ladies' room and get a drink of cold water. It would do no good to get angry, so I needed to step away for a few minutes. I knew that we needed to hire Lila's firm to launch our services at least into the coming year, until we could manage the program on our own. I was pleased at last to have somebody competent and knowledgeable who could help us to get it right.

I was surprised that the board could not see what I saw. Why had Teri, the board president, let things go on for so long? Why didn't they see that Dr. Rimm's team was being self-protective? Didn't they have the facts and history needed to do the right thing? Why didn't they fall to their knees and kiss Lila's hand for saving us? Instead, what I got the next day was an angry verbal reprimand from Teri for my unprofessional behavior of rolling my eyes during the meeting and for walking out of the meeting. Worst of all, according to Teri, was that I thought it was appropriate for Lila to "school them" about the special education staffing needs because Teri said that they already knew all that. If that were so, I asked, why hadn't we provided it? How could she say that she knew it and had never shared that information with me? Teri was clearly trying to protect the school by trying to make it look like the board knew what it was doing. And once again, I needed to hire somebody to be our special education resource teacher, because Lila and her company were approved by the board for just long enough to transition to a new employee. And the board decided that it was better for the new employee to report to one of the board members rather than to me, as retribution for how upset I was. Insulting. This was stepping over the boundary of appropriate board-management roles.

Then again, I did have enough on my plate. There was one other administrator in the school of nearly 300 students. Connie Lindemann was a classy, experienced woman who juggled a buffet of plates and kept them all spinning for the school. She was the operations manager, which meant that she oversaw everything related to facilities, including the janitorial staff. She was responsible for payroll and for managing all things in the personnel files, including insurance. In addition, she supervised the employee who handled all the attendance and scheduling reporting to the state, a position that required communication with the 42 school districts from which our students were drawn. Connie was responsible for the accounting and financial statements. She was also responsible for all the volunteers needed at the school, including accounting for their hours. Considering that every family in the school was required to serve 20 hours *monthly,* she was, in effect, responsible for about 200 families at twenty hours each, meaning 4,000 work hours. The volunteers were crucial to keeping our payroll and other budgets workable within the paltry sum provided in funding by the state and local districts. She organized the daily lunchroom supervisors, playground supervisors, fundraisers, and work crews. She was charged with organizing a committee of volunteers, including an architect, to evaluate options for providing more classroom space to accommodate the planned growth of the student body. She was stretched thin, but she gave it her all. She was one of the first employees there each morning, and she worked from home nights and weekends. And she did it all in high heels, with a big smile and a professional persona.

But the board rode roughshod over her. They invariably criticized her reports, her interactions with parents, and her interactions with them. They always wanted more than she gave. She was even criticized for freak weather: in August, boxes and boxes of the new, school-wide math curriculum were stacked in the hallway when a freak thunderstorm sent two inches of rain through the back door and down the steps, flooding into the hallway where the books were. She called a neighbor for help, and the three of us and her husband sloshed through the flood and moved carton after carton into the cafeteria, set up all the tables, opened every carton, and laid out all the hundreds of books to dry. Rather than commending her for her quick action, they criticized her for stacking the boxes on the floor in the first place! They pooh-poohed the work of her committee for refurbishing the school's facilities to accommodate the growing student body. They did not appreciate her, so she resigned in January for a better job with better pay. They did not replace her. They did authorize the temporary hire of a part-time accountant. The rest fell back to me. The board offered to take something off my plate, so I asked for help with the facilities planning, and a board volunteer took responsibility. However, that person did not have time to follow up and get the answers needed to accomplish anything. Each time she came up with a plan and recommendations, including the addition of two portable classrooms to the playground, the board would come up with questions, and decisions would be delayed until the next meeting. Because I had been responsible for the acquisition and setup of four new portable buildings in Houston, I knew this would take six months. We were already beyond that. The school had committed to increasing the school population with no place to put the new students. My secretary and I got involved in pricing a better security system and procedure for enabling access in and out of the building for access to the portable structures, but the board would not approve it.

There was a pattern: because key founding board members did not trust anybody but themselves to do the research, whether it was about a security system, additional space, special education services, or a modification of the daily schedule, they discouraged the employees as well as the new board members from pursuing plans. No matter how comprehensive the material provided to them ahead of the meeting or during the meetings, they would not act on it unless it was their own idea. And because the board was divided, if the facts were presented by one faction of the board, the others would raise questions and delay action. It was dysfunctional, to put it mildly.

They hired a consultant, Ed Bernetich, to survey the faculty and parents about their satisfaction with the school that spring. He met with me off campus, and I let him know how frustrated I was with the board. He was taken aback by their negativity and interference. I had met with Ed prior to starting the position and asked if he felt that the board was ready to step back and let a strong, experienced leader take the helm. He said that they were, for the most part. The fact that things had not gotten better, despite his advice to them, seemed to dismay him.

He met with each teacher individually, then met with me to summarize their feelings. I was feeling good about the progress that I was making with the staff. His report was positive, but he said that a few teachers were discouraged by how negative and griping their colleagues were in the staff lunchroom, to the point where they did not want to go in there. It is normal for teachers to need to vent and to share their frustration, to let off steam so that they can go back to class feeling supported and less stressed. But I hoped that they could take it down a notch so that they could take a more positive and proactive stance toward their daily problems. I wanted all teachers to be able to spend positive time in the lunchroom so that the faculty did not break into cliques or isolate any member of the team.

After school that day, I had a regularly scheduled meeting with a team of teachers. I wanted to use them as a sounding board for what Ed had told me, to get their ideas about how to make the lunchroom a place that restored them and did not drag them down with negativity. I raised the following question: At what point does healthy venting turn into griping? How does our expressed frustration impact others? I asked them to think about it for a couple minutes and make a few notes for a discussion. The teachers looked at each other uncomfortably. Shannon, the reading teacher, was most upset, began to cry, and stormed out of the meeting. This made the remaining teachers even more uncomfortable. We got through the discussion, but the tension remained high. I asked each of them to post a positive note in the staff lunchroom, a word of inspiration, or something that made them feel good. A couple of them did. The next day, a teacher who had not been at the meeting asked to speak to me. She had heard about the heated meeting and said that I needed to do something about Shannon. So the incident was blowing around, stirring up people. As it happened, Shannon approached me first and she said that she had overreacted, and we made peace. I told her that I understood that everybody was strung tight: it was April, and they had not had any days off in some time; spring break was very late that year, and there had been no snow days. Snow days are a great relief valve for teachers, and they had not had any.

Two weeks later I was meeting with Teri, the board chair. We'd had several talks before that day, and we met for over an hour, convivially discussing the next board agenda and various issues around the school. At the end of the meeting, she handed me a piece of paper for me to sign. It was a formal, written reprimand:

Specifically on Tuesday, April 3, 2012, you had a meeting with Mr. Ed Bernetich where he provided some feedback from the interviews he held with staff members. After that meeting, you led a Language Arts team meeting with several faculty members. You chose to use this time to reprimand the faculty members for comments that were made to Ed "behind your back" and followed with an "assignment" where you proceeded to mock those comments.

This vindictive behavior is directly opposed to the professional and positive atmosphere that is core to MPA. As we discussed during your mid-year review, positive communications and "rallying the troops" behind you will be key to your future success. This negative, retaliatory act has further alienated the staff members and compromised the work of a paid consultant.

I was incensed. "This is not accurate," I told her. "You never even asked me what happened that day. You took two weeks to write up this reprimand without once mentioning the incident." I refused to sign it because it was grossly wrong and an insult.

"Well, think about it," she said.

"I don't need to. It is wrong. How were my questions insulting? I did not mock them. If the teachers feel that they can't talk to the consultant because I might get some general feedback from his meetings with them—which I should, as that is the point of hiring him—then why even hire a consultant? I did not insult them. Yes, Shannon was upset, but her crying and overreaction were not caused by me."

Two weeks later, Teri waited until the end of a meeting and brought out the paper once again. Because I had not heard about it from her in the interim, I figured that she had come to her senses. "No, I will not sign it," I told her, "because your insistence on it is the last straw. I will sign a resignation later instead. I won't be back next year."

"Don't tell the staff," she said. "The board will want to be there when you do."

It was just a couple days later that we held our Final Friday staff meeting. This was a morale-booster that I had started at the beginning of the year to bring the staff together. A different pair of teachers each month took responsibility for planning a brief, fun or funny game or activity that would take no more than ten minutes. It closed out the month with a smile. The teachers were nervous because that afternoon, they saw a critical mass of board members in the hallway; that always meant some terrible announcement, one of the original teachers to the school said. I asked the board to wait outside during the fun part of the meeting. After we had all enjoyed a great activity, with lots of laughs, the board entered and lined up, and I told the staff that I would not be returning, and that if any of my actions had caused them distress, I apologized, and I wished them well. There was stunned silence. A couple teachers cried, and one came up and hugged me. My dear office manager was very upset—we really liked working with one another and were a great team. She completely understood my frustration.

The board insisted on an exit interview, so I met with two of the board members who seemed cognizant of the issues. It should be mentioned that those two members later resigned in dismay from the board, while Teri and her compadres continued their reign.

In Ohio, a person may qualify for unemployment compensation, despite having resigned, if they can prove that the atmosphere was hostile, inappropriate, and prevented them from doing their job. I did not think I had a chance, but as the development director whom I had hired and who left won her appeal, I gave it my best shot. What follows is my appeal.

Appeal for Unemployment Compensation

Reason for denial: "Claimant did not inform the employer of his/her concerns, or allow the employer reasonable time to correct the situation."

1. When the written reprimand dated April 16, 2012 was presented to me by the board chair, I let her know at the meeting that it was inaccurate and insulting, and that her writing it up without checking with me first about the situation described therein was inappropriate and disrespectful. She made no move to correct the misrepresentation therein but presented it to me again for my signature about 10 days later. This indicates that I let her know of my concern, and she had time to correct the situation, but did not.

I was given responsibility of hiring and evaluating the workers at all levels within the school, and the board would approve hires. I was to supervise the workers and recommend rehires. This is standard practice. However, the board members did not adhere to this, which made it difficult to achieve my goals. I made the board aware of this problem on multiple occasions: I did, in fact, inform the employer of my concerns, yet I observed a pattern in their behavior that saw no improvement or in their willingness to correct the situation. Among the **multiple occasions in which I made the board aware of my concerns,** are the following:

2. The operations manager formed a team to evaluate the options for creating the classroom space needed to meet the growing enrollment. The plans were presented at a board meeting (in January?), but the board put off deciding and instead started researching the options themselves

from scratch, thereby causing the school to open in August without sufficient classroom space. They did not follow the well-researched options, causing great waste of time, discouragement of volunteers, disregard for the operations manager, and most importantly, unsafe and inadequate accommodations of classes throughout the fall semester. I made my concerns known to the board at the meetings by letting them know that their timeline was not going to allow the classes to be operational in the fall.

3. The operations manager left February 17, and the board brought somebody on part-time at the end of February to cover only a portion of her duties. The replacement was hired through a temporary placement firm. The board did not want to pay retirement taxes so the board would hire him for 30 days at a time, release him, then rehire him in order to avoid paying the retirement. This was disruptive to getting the job done. I asked that the person be hired permanently and full time because he worked out well. They did not acknowledge or follow my preference or the needs of the school. This undermined my staffing authority and left the operations in disarray. I made my concerns known to the board chair in our individual meetings, and at the Board meeting of April 5, 2012.

4. When the board refused to pay the operations manager her earned vacation pay, I objected at the board meeting, but they did not correct the situation.

5. When the board refused to change the administrative assistant position from an hourly position to a salaried office manager position, I objected, but they did not agree.

6. When the fund development subcommittee of the board held fundraising planning meetings without coordinating with the director of development staff member, I objected that the meetings should be planned in tandem with her, and in consideration of the limited hours for which she was hired. They did not agree and continued to meet at their convenience without coordinating with her, and they chose to supervise her work directly without going through me. I objected to this, but they persisted to overstep.

These examples illustrate a slice of the pervasive history of the employer's unresponsiveness to my concerns that they correct the situations. The persistent disregard for adhering to best practices may be interpreted as a constructive discharge, in which the employer's behavior became so intolerable that the employee had no choice but to resign.

My appeal was denied. And Menlo Park Academy went on to hire its fourth Director for the school's fifth year. They opened that fall holding classes in stairwells and cramped rooms.

Crybabies

The world can be divided into two kinds of people. The first kind sees crying as a call to action, a signal to soothe and save the crying person. No matter what preceded the waterworks, the cryer is the aggrieved party, and whatever or whoever set the tears flowing is an insensitive brute who should take it back, whatever it was. The second kind see crying as a distracting character flaw—a bit of theatrics or a sign of unprofessionalism. An example of this second kind is Tom Hanks's character, the coach of the women's baseball team in the movie *A League of Their Own.* As he is loudly reprimanding the team for their mistakes, one of the players sobs, and he gets exasperated and shouts, "There's no crying in baseball!"

This dichotomy has caused me as much grief as anything in my life. If only I could always work with people who are on the same side of the dividing line as I am, because no matter on which I side I fall at any given time, my superiors or my employees are on the other side. It's the partisan politics of weeping.

The divide became clear in college when I had written an opinion paper without any outside support for my opinions. In my other class, my writing was a reflective journal, so I had taken the same approach for the sociology paper and received a D. I met with the teacher to try to understand why. When he explained that my opinions were fine, but that I should know better to include evidence from research to support them,

I broke into tears. The heartless man just went on and didn't soften a bit with any sympathy, just kept his jaw as square as Dudley Do-Right's. I felt like he didn't care about me as a person.

Now I know better: my tears were my own, not his. His job was not to take care of my feelings but to craft me into a better scholar. While I wished he had done both, the dichotomy, for the most part, puts people on one side of the line or the other, with little dancing between the territory. My tears did not make the sociology teacher wrong, and he did not deserve to be chastised by anybody. I was feeling ashamed of my ignorance and grieving for the fact that my arguments were not to be accepted as the gold standard, no matter how smart or right I was, if I could not support them with the wisdom of others before me.

But I have worked with people who have seen my tears as the professor's problem, and who see a colleague's or student's tears as my problem. Shannon's teary exodus from the staff meeting in Ohio was a result of her own stress and shame. When I chastise a student for playing with the materials and distracting the class rather than listening to the instructions, and that student breaks into tears, those tears are a good sign that the student may be feeling remorse enough to correct her error. The student who cries when the teacher makes red marks on his paper shows that he cares and may be motivated to do better. If a team loses a game and a player cries, does the coach get fired?

For many folks, crying when they are in trouble or have done wrong brings in sympathy and soothing, and it may even deflect from the fact that they screwed up. The aftertaste from the warm and fuzzy remedy of comfort may be pleasant, but does it take away some of the energy that will motivate the person to avoid getting in trouble again or making the same mistake? I think back to the wild child at Roeper who had punched his teacher with a right to the jaw. Staff members were aghast that I spoke with him sternly. They were worried about his feelings. If he had any empathy or feelings of remorse, they did not bubble to the surface until he looked uneasy under my gaze. I learned later that when I left the room, the staff rushed to rescue him from his discomfort. They were giving him positive reinforcement for his bad behavior.

It is OK to feel lousy when we screw up. It is OK to feel lousy when we grieve. Feeling lousy proves that we care. Sociopaths and egocentrics do not care. Is feeling bad a necessary prerequisite to reform and improvement? No, but it is quite the impetus!

And here is where attribution theory comes into play. Once again, there is a dichotomy that places us into either the camp who attribute their success or failure to their own doings or the camp who attribute their problems to the machinations of others. Those who mess up and see themselves as the reason for it will realize that working harder or making amends are things within their own power to change. Those who mess up and attribute the fault to their poor genes, lousy teacher, or unsympathetic spouse have a "get out of guilt free" card, and they are less likely to change because they view the problems as out of their control. This idea of where the control lies, whether in ourselves or in others, determines who works hard and succeeds and who gives up and wallows.

But if our locus of control is internal, if we take the blame, then we feel the shame, the guilt and the grief. If our locus of control is external, then we place the blame and feel the anger and resentment. Am I attributing my failures and job losses to my bosses, or am I taking responsibility?

I let my students feel lousy and my teachers feel guilty—up to a point. Once I know that they feel the pain of the error—or the guilt, the remorse, or the shame—then it is time to switch gears to go into proactive mode. How can you fix the problem? How can you write a good, meaningful apology? How can you make amends? Because, I tell them, you are a good person, you want to be a successful student, you want what is best for the students. We focus on the person's wonderful core and great intentions, and I work with them to do better. I am on their side. I believe in them and that they can and will do better. And I see to it. The praise and reward come from doing good. But others do not want people to feel bad at all, especially children. Their little psyches will be damaged and they will be discouraged, they say, and they will hate school or live in fear or be oppressed or tyrannized. But they won't. Not if they get to the next step after the uncomfortable feelings, the step in which growth and productivity and connection happen.

This is related to the "everybody gets a trophy, everybody gets a participant ribbon" philosophy. They don't want kids to feel left out, and they don't want kids to feel less than wonderful and perfect.

Have I grown from the frustrations and disappointments in my past jobs?

Again

I next took a job in Florida, and it turned out to be absolutely fatal to my career. I had been heading steadily downward, but this disaster nailed my career coffin shut. How did I get here?

I had quit my job in Ohio after one year, fed up with the board that ran the charter school I had been hired to direct. I was their third direc- tor in four years, which should have tipped me to the fact that they were poor at either managing or hiring. I resigned in May, which was the wrong time to find employment as a school administrator. Searches for heads of schools begin in the fall, one year prior to their start date. Schools try to make their decisions by December, or February at the latest. Starting a search in May put me way behind, and I knew it would be a year before I found a placement, or January if a school was desperate.

I put our Ohio house on the market and, despite five open houses, got no offers, except from a dozen different companies explaining that we qualified for a lower interest rate if we refinanced our VA loan. It would be processed in 30 days, and we would have a lower payment to help us through the lean times. I did not qualify for unemployment because I had quit, so we cut corners wherever we could. We were required to take the house off the market while the paperwork processed; but instead of the promised 30 days to process the refinance, it took four months. When the paperwork finally went through, we put the house back on the market on a Thursday and accepted an offer that Tuesday. We paid several thousand out of pocket to sell the house and then had to clear out. The last couple of moves we had hired a moving company and packers, but I could not afford them this time. My daughter and her husband flew in, and I rented a couple of PODS, which are portable storage units that could be moved anywhere—once I knew where that would be. I left my home with no destination. We hit the road to visit relatives while I kept applying and interviewing for positions. In July, I had Skype interviews with two schools. The Florida school made me an offer, and I asked for time to finish speaking with another school in North Carolina. Either way, it looked like I was heading east. I started driving in that direction as their deadline for making me an offer loomed. North Carolina shied away, so I turned right and showed up at the Florida job in two days.

That was mid-July. They were so happy to see me! They knew that I was interviewing elsewhere, and the principal said that she was on pins and needles all weekend, waiting for me to call back to accept. She said that the teachers in the interview were excited to see me, and that they kept writing each other notes during the interview, *How do we get her here? We want her!* I was hired to be their gifted instructional coach, making considerably less money than I had in my previous positions. When they let me encamp temporarily in the counselor's office that summer until I got my own office, those teachers perched on the desks and chatted and chatted away, dangling their feet, happy to fill me in and cozy up. I was introduced to everybody with great fanfare and excitement, so happy that they snagged me with all my administrative experience and expertise in gifted education, to help them to do great things with their gifted students, because they sold themselves as a school for gifted learning. They wanted more help to walk the talk, to differentiate for their brightest, because it was tough to do right by them when the school accepted everybody who applied, space willing. It was an odd feeling, to be so revered and respected. It reminded me of the movie *Jewel of the Nile.* Michael Douglas and Kathleen Turner thought that they were after an enormous emerald or something, but it turned out that the Jewel was actually a beloved spiritual leader of the people whose presence was desired for the good that it brought them. I felt that they saw me that way. It was a daunting expectation. But I was determined to do whatever it would take to make this the last big job that I would ever take on.

Be careful what you wish for.

Ninety days later, on a Friday afternoon, the principal, with her long bleached-blond hair pulled up into a tousled bun, asked to see me before I left. When the office manager slid behind the office table, too, I knew it was bad. You bring in witnesses when you let somebody go so that the victim does not kill the one doing the firing. The principal minced in on her high-heeled sandals, the paperwork all ready, that bitch, after I had asked her earlier in the week what was going on. I suspected something, but she kept reassuring me and asking how she could help, saying that she wanted me to succeed and that she knew it would take time. That bitch had lied to me, knowing that she wanted to get all my information and organization before she let me go. I had spent a lot of time in those first three months setting up the individualized, computer-based instruction for the entire student body, with several different software programs. She had said that she needed it all documented so that when I got called away to district meetings, they would have what they needed to keep things running. And not 30 minutes before, when I asked her how her day was, she had the nerve to smile and whine that it had been so hard because she had a workmen's comp case now from a teacher who had to deal with a disruptive student, and a lawsuit from a parent who felt that the school was not meeting her son's needs. She smiled her squeaky little whine and wanted sympathy from *me?!* I was seething. So you did know, I confirmed to her. You lied. She ignored me and showed me the settlement agreement. I had nine months left in our agreement, and she offered me two weeks.

But Florida is an at-will employment state, and agreements mean even less than the paper that they are written on.

I was out about $8,000 in moving and relocation expenses that the school had not covered. And I knew that I would never be offered a job in education again. Any potential employer would deduce that my job hopping could only be a factor of my own poor judgment. This principal had not terminated me from her school; she had effectively terminated me from education. My life's work. It would be the last big job that I could ever take on. My desire to make this the last big job that I would take on? Wish granted.

December 2013, Florida

There is nothing like the burning humiliation of leaving a job against your will. And this Florida debacle was my third time. The first was the headhunter. That gave me the opportunity to start a school, to exorcise my old school demons and set the universe right, to live out the child life that I wished that I could have had. The second time was in Michigan. Nothing great came from that. In fact, I still live with the reverberation of it. And now this third time was far, far from charming. What seemed like it would be a classy, idyllic final chapter of my professional career turned out to be the beginning of the end—a very tawdry, expensive, downward spiral.

So how did it feel to be unemployed again? Well, as I write this, it is one of those days when it is 1:32 in the afternoon and I am wearing only a dirty nightgown and flip flops. I had started to get dressed but got distracted with making lunch. I'll have to get dressed to take Richard in for a checkup, but I'm fighting inertia. Failure to launch. Feeling like nobody will ever hire me, nobody will ever love me again, no jobs look interesting, or they look like too much work, or I'm not qualified. Why didn't I learn to fall in love with online teaching? If I want to teach at a university, I'll have to do it online—that's what they all want. Why didn't I keep publishing? Why didn't I learn to play the game? Why didn't I learn to keep my mouth shut? Why do I have such strong opinions that have to get me in trouble all the time? Must Richard keep belching and hocking up loogies?

So I finally write a few thank you notes for Christmas gifts, load a stack of dishes into the dishwasher, eat one too many slices of pizza, chat with my daughter on the phone, try to open files for the songs for rehearsal and fail, read too many Facebook posts, try too many times to beat my old score at Speed Tiles on my phone—my phone that is forever with me, waiting for somebody to offer me a job, or to want to get together, or to make me laugh. I check a few of the career websites, check Florida, check the gifted posts for jobs, check LinkedIn for jobs, send off an inquiry to a connection there. I watch the osprey soaring outside the window, water the beautiful blooming Christmas cactus, pick out clothes, wish I didn't feel so upset with Marty, the asshole. It's probably my anger to him that's got me so mucked up today. They say that depression is anger turned inward. Yeah, I'm pissed at him. I deserve better. But where is Mr. Better?

Blast from the Past. Bewitched. Shall We Dance? I watch three movies in a row, on my ass, noshing on the gift of chocolate-covered pecans from Richard's son and the summer sausage from his other son. I do not recommend the combination, but to be fair, they were hours apart. Let the good times roll. Lovely carols are now playing from the TV. I am struggling to keep down tears or panic.

Skim the email advertisements again. Airlines announce great deals to places I shouldn't go: I need to hold on to those dollars to get me through the winter. I scroll past recipes and lots and lots of shopping sales. Groupons. Living Social. Upworthy. Blech. And then a brief email from an old friend, wishing me well. There *is* life out there.

I click through to one of the educational placement firms to update my profile per their request, sweetened with the opportunity to win an iPad mini. It says that I must resubmit my application, cover letter, and resume, but when I click those links, I just get errors. I skim the list of administrative positions at schools, but they are a lot of schools with *Saint* in their titles—that won't work. There's a school that rejected me this year. All the others just look so normal, so traditional. I would curdle their blood.

I don't like them, and none of them have liked me. Why torture myself by looking at them again? Blech.

Richard stops to ask me if I know where his money is. He has asked me that dozens of times in the last couple months. "Yes," I tell him.

"Where is it?" he asks.

"In the bank," I reply.

"Which one?" he asks.

"PNC," I tell him.

He explains, "I need to get it out to give to you for Christmas." (This is a new twist: usually he just wants to make sure that I have it.)

"I already have it," I tell him.

"Oh, good!" he answers.

That is the extent of our conversation for the evening, except when I try to offer him something to eat. He gets most excited when I offer him a glass of wine. "Oh yes! I always like wine!" he says. Today he slept until 11 this morning. He took a two-hour nap this afternoon. It's life in the fast lane around here, I tell ya.

I have nothing to look forward to in the coming year except the expense of moving when I run out of funds to stay here. Nobody will buy this book. If they do, I'll probably get sued. Those who don't sue me won't speak to me. How is that any different from now? Nothing to lose. Nothing likely to gain.

I have one present to open tomorrow on Christmas, from my buddy Joni. I opened my present from Emily over FaceTime the other day, so she could see my reaction when I opened her painting of a barn in the snow. We opened our food gifts from his sons as soon as they arrived so they would not spoil.

I heard Richard open the refrigerator door and pause a good while. It was 2:30 in the afternoon, time for him to eat something. I shuffled down the hall to the kitchen.

"I noticed that you did not eat your dinner last night, or the night before. You should eat something. Would you like the boiled dinner or the spaghetti? Peanut butter and jelly? Crackers and cheese?"

He swayed around, off-balance. "Yes, cheese and crackers." He headed toward his well-worn spot on the sofa where he spent 90% of his waking hours. "But we don't have any wine, do we?"

"No, you drank the whole bottle in one sitting last night. One bottle is to last two days—"

He cut me off and raised his angry voice. "Fine! Then I don't want anything! Nothing! I don't deserve anything! I'll just sit here and shit!"

"OK. Fine, that's good," I said and put the box of generic crackers back on the pantry shelf. "You do that!" I would not bring another wine bottle out from hiding, and besides, there were no more: tomorrow I would shop for groceries and his favorite sustenance.

Friends would point out to me that he's 87—what the heck, what's it going to hurt him? Let the guy enjoy his final days! But I was the one who had to clean up his messes when he'd had too much. I had to listen to his lugubrious, alcohol-fueled words of love, love that was evidenced by no deeds or other communication. I was the one who took the worried phone calls from the building security man, Mike, who reported that Richard was, once again, lost, and he had helped him back home. But Richard never remembered Mike, which hurt Mike's feelings. Richard had dementia and remembered very little about anything. Last month, he had forgotten to call our daughter to wish her happy 34th birthday, despite the fact that he had it written down on the little pocket calendar he carried with him, its entries densely packed, filling the pages with jittery notes. He never took his medicines without prompting, and he never once asked why I was no longer going to work. When I did work, he was baffled and never understood what my job was here in Florida, so he stopped asking. Every other day he would say that we needed to go to the bank to take out his money so that I would have it if anything happened to him. "I have $900," he would insist. "I want you to have it."

"Why do you need to take it out? I already have access to it. You signed over the power of attorney to me. My name is on the accounts."

"Well, which of these cards can I use to get my money?" He pulled an array of cards from his well-worn wallet: a senior pass to the national parks, his Social Security card, his AARP membership card, and his Virginia ID card. I had taken his credit card and bank card away in the spring, as he was withdrawing $60 a week to spend on drinks and on bottles of cheap vodka that he would hide in the garage. It was an unspoken game of hide and seek, and when I won, I poured the vodka down the drain, wishing I could mix myself a small drink but knowing that if I kept any alcohol in the house, he would find it and down it, then he would stumble, perhaps fall, and need an expensive emergency room trip. We'd already been through that.

"None of them, honey. You don't need money. What do you need money for?" And he would get agitated and angry.

Word from Mike was that Richard was a well-known regular at a neighborhood bar, the Wet Spot. Richard was running a tab or drinking for free, having hinted that he had a lot of money. I did not want to pay his tab, and Richard never admitted to visiting any local bars, although he would disappear on his mobility scooter for large chunks of time. Why were they giving him drinks? Should I just pay the bar a visit, give them ten dollars a week and tell them to stretch it as best they could? I chose to just let things be.

"Aren't you afraid for him drinking and driving his scooter around, Mom?" asked Emily, concerned.

"Well, it could be a fast and painless way for him to go."

Appalled at my callousness, she pointed out, "But what about the poor family that hits him, and how they would be injured, and how bad they would feel?" She had me there. I decided that I would hide his scooter key after dark in a concession to save the rest of the innocent world.

I was out for dinner with a friend and shared my woes dealing with Richard.

"He's quite a bit older than you, isn't he? How much older?"

"Twenty-nine years."

Her eyebrows raised. "And you were how old when you got married?"

"Twenty-one."

"So that means he was...fifty?"

"Yes, but the age difference wasn't a big deal then."

"Didn't anybody tell you that he was too old?"

"Yes, everybody. He wasn't too old then. He was just right. He was very lively. It's really just the last...fifteen years or so that he's gotten too old. I really didn't think that he would live this long. He just keeps living! His parents died before we got married, his baby sister is dead, his baby brother is dead, his ex-wife is dead. When we got married, he had high blood pressure and was wild. I really didn't think he would live this long! He's been telling me for the last four years that he thinks he will die today, but he just keeps on going."

In Florida, we could pay the rent and groceries with Richard's Social Security and his annuity. We could pay the minimum on credit cards and live very frugally. When I flew out for interviews, Mike could look in on him, or Richard's sons came to town to keep an eye on him. I could not afford health insurance, but his Medicare and supplement took care of him.

Head for the Hills

I was glad that we had moved to Sanford, Florida, despite the job fiasco. Richard could scoot around town and all along the lakefront. If he got lost, all he needed was to be redirected toward the lake, then find the tallest building. I loved the flat, old city where I could bike everywhere. I got involved with two community theaters. I even crossed off one of my bucket list items: to earn acclaim for singing solo in a show.

So how did we end up in South Dakota?

Sometimes it is as if a right decision just forms itself, without deliberation, without a clear event to which one can point and say *this is when we made that choice*. So it was with South Dakota. There was Emily, getting to the hospital at six in the morning each day for her work as an anesthesia technician. And there was her husband Joe Bob, working on his research at all hours at the School of Mines. Between their schedules, it was not easy getting the kids off to school on time. Emily was trying to have a child with Joe but enduring miscarriages, and I shared her grieving from afar as she struggled. She could use my support, and they could use a hand with the kids. We both wanted to reduce our living expenses. I had no job prospects in Florida. I wanted Emily and the grandkids to have time with Richard before all his brain cells were mush. All these factors told us: live together in South Dakota. Emily found a house large enough for all of us to live together, and that summer we moved in together. Richard and I paid the lion's share of the rent, but it was still less than we had paid elsewhere on our own.

Richard and I took the downstairs, which had a walk-out private entrance. A man from Emily and Joe Bob's church built a ramp over the step in the sidewalk so Richard could get out and go for a ride on his scooter. The kids used our living area to watch movies, practice cello, and play video games, while Richard and I shared the upstairs kitchen and living room. We had a roomy deck for grilling and picnics, a big yard for Sage to kick the soccer ball around, and a fruitful apple tree that gave us pies and applesauce. Our basement bedroom stayed cool year-round and cold in the winter, but it was cozy to snuggle under the down comforter. Richard learned his way across the house to find the bathroom and managed the stairs fine.

The scooter, however, became a problem: he went riding and could not find his way home. Twice, people drove to the house and asked if we had lost an old man. They would find him a mile away, he would give them our address, which he kept in a little black notebook in his pocket, and they would lead him back. On another of his forays, it began to rain, so he hustled back into the front door—but it wasn't our door. Luckily, the strangers did not shoot him. It wasn't as easy as it was in Florida, where folks could point him to the big building along the lake. Even if we went out with him, watched him, and told him not to cross the street, he would cross it anyway. We had to stay right with him. On one of his expeditions, the scooter's battery died, and the kids had to push it uphill to get it back to the house. I replaced the big, heavy, expensive battery, but we had to accept that it was more trouble than we could handle in that setting.

The idyllic bonding that I imagined for our extended family unit did not happen. Richard's hygiene was poor, and nobody wanted to sit by him between his weekly showers because he smelled bad. He hocked up loogies all day, spit on the floor, and spit into the food on his plate. On the other hand, he was kind to the kids and said sweet, appreciative things. He loved to listen to Chloe practice her cello and Sage practice his drums. Emily took him to church parties, and her friends liked him. We could take him to the grocery store, where he could ride on one of their scooters that served as our grocery cart. He loved to go for a ride and enjoyed a dish of ice cream. Every morning, he microwaved his Jimmy Dean sausage, egg, and cheese croissant. Throughout the day, he would make toast when he was hungry. He napped a couple times a day, either sitting at his spot at the end of the sofa or stretched out shoeless on our bed, covered with his favorite navy blue fleece blanket. He could not work his phone, and the TV remote confounded him. We would turn the TV on to the westerns channel before we left the house. He worked sudoku puzzles by flipping back and forth between the answers at the back, then filling them in on the puzzle page. I bought the books by the dozen through the mail, as well as refills for his favorite Uniball medium point black gel pens. He asked for nothing except our company. We saw that he took his pills, and his doctor maintained his heart. Even with hearing aids, he could not understand what we said because he could no longer hear most consonant sounds.

So he was not really connecting to people. We could not induce him to trip down memory lane and regale us with stories of his youth. He was not a wise old listening ear. He often asked if we lived there, why were we there, and whose house was it. He wanted to know when we were going home. He was confused, withdrawn, and worn out. Even his beloved Barefoot Pinot Grigio tasted disgusting to him, and he no longer asked for, nor accepted, a drink of alcohol. I could not make him happy except by being near.

I showered him once a week, the limit he could tolerate and I could bear. I had to hide his clothes so that he wouldn't put them on and avoid the shower. He yelped and whined and moaned. He felt so very insecure in the shower. My soapy hands or sponge felt like sandpaper to him. He begged to be released, he promised to be good. He pleaded to know why I had to torture him so. I gently helped him from the shower, dried him, and trimmed his hair. Shaving hurt him too much, so I trimmed his beard. I cut the hair from his ears and cleaned out the wax. I lotioned his dry, tissue-thin skin. As he redressed, he thanked me profusely, every time, for taking such good care of him.

Merciless

I have never made a more difficult decision than the one to put Richard in a nursing home. It isn't as if he were combative. I could handle his medications. But I felt that he needed more care than Emily and I could give. He was alone for stretches of time, and I feared that he would fall or wander out. Richard's sons knew his condition, and Peter, the youngest, did some research about VA nursing homes. Because Richard had been a veteran and had lived in Missouri for at least eight years, he qualified for acceptance in the VA home in St. Louis. I did not know where I would end up after that spring in South Dakota, after Joe graduated. Joe would accept a job somewhere else in the country, and I did not plan to follow them because I was looking for a job somewhere around the edges of the country, to be near the ocean. I could not afford any nursing home, so the VA was the most affordable. If Richard were accepted into the St. Louis home, the cost would be reasonable, and he would have two of his three sons nearby. They were both retired and had the capability of looking in on him on a regular basis. I began the lengthy and cumbersome application process and spent six months on their waiting list. When a spot came open that May, I had to accept it right away or lose it. I talked them into giving me two weeks to make arrangements so I could drive him there.

Oh, that was a grim, two-day drive. I told him that we were going to St. Louis. I packed his scooter, his clothes, and photo albums.

"Where are we going?" he asked.

"St. Louis."

"Oh, I like driving with you."

We stopped for the night in Oklahoma. The phone in the motel room rang about 1:00 am. "Your father is out here, and he is lost and confused," said the annoyed desk clerk.

"Could you please bring him back to the room?" A few minutes later they appeared at the door, and I thanked the clerk. "Where were you going, Richard?"

"I don't know. I got up to find the bathroom and I got lost," he whimpered.

"Go back to sleep."

The next day we rolled into Phil's, his eldest son's home in Brentwood, Missouri. That is when I lost it, when the years of grief overwhelmed me, when the realization of the finality of our long life and love together was over, really over. The man I had loved was gone. Only a tiny kernel of him remained: the tiny hot spark of love. Not the man "with his hair on fire" and ready to go, not the righteous fighter for children, not the passionate lover—all of them were gone. This husk, this wispy-haired, grizzled-faced, rheumy-eyed shell was all that was left. All he wanted, all he asked for, was to be with me, just me, just to be near me, and I was dumping him, leaving him, abandoning him. I wasn't moving nearby, visiting him at a regular time each day, spooning pudding into him and decorating his room with afghans that I hand-stitched. I wasn't one of those devoted spouses who adoringly wiped his chin and tidied his bed. I was selfish and self-loathing. He wanted just one thing, and I wasn't giving it to him.

I sat on Phil's shady front porch with his wife, Sandra. I sat weeping and sobbing and grieving. I was a bad person. I was losing him forever. I betrayed him and left him behind. His sons were there, his sweet, devoted sons, but it was me he wanted, and I was going away. Sandra comforted me, told me that it was the best for him, that he would be fine, that I had work to do, that one more move for Richard would be so hard on him, that having him in a safe place was best for him. She said that I was welcome to their home any time.

When I had tried to break up with Richard at the end of my undergraduate days, my whole soul and body flung itself into paroxysms of grief, despite the sensibility of the break. Now here I was, trying to make another sensible break, and I was wracked, wrecked, and inconsolable.

The next day, we all traveled to the VA home, where they were expecting us. I settled with the finance office, with the social worker, and with the VA officer. The home was up on a hill, away from traffic and dangerous places, should the residents wander off. The complex was one story but sprawled out via ridiculously long hallways—hallways with enough square footage to ben thirty more rooms had the space been used better. Only the most mobile vets could get from one section to another alone. I had brought Richard's scooter and was glad he would be able to get around the huge place.

But there were glitches. As the workers did his intake assessment, they determined that he was a 'flight risk" due to his dementia and he would need to be in the memory care unit, not the regular unit they had reserved for him. Fortunately, a semi-private room was available. Unfortunately, they could not allow him his scooter. He could not leave the locked unit without an authorized attendee. His meals and all activities would be in the dim "Liberty Lane" wing, not the big, sunny, airy cafeteria. The irony of the wing's name was nauseating.

Before we left, I had refilled all his prescriptions, a 90-day supply, about $400 worth out of pocket. The home could not accept them but had to get them prescribed by their own doctors, although there would be no cost to me for them as his VA benefits would cover them while he was there. I tried to find a way to donate the medicines—anywhere— but nobody could take them for safety reasons. It was painful to toss out hundreds of dollars' worth of perfectly good medicines that could have helped somebody, or that he could have used up. Couldn't their pharmacist have determined that they were good? Somewhere in the admissions papers it should have told me that they could not accept his medicines. What a waste.

We settled him into his room, set up his hearing aid dryer, stacked his sudoku books, hung up pictures on the bulletin board. The clerks at the desk took all the clothes that were not on his back and sent them to have his name tag put in them. The twin hospital bed had a hard vinyl mattress and a thin cover. Would he be warm enough? Would he get comfortable, even if he did not get cozy? The floor was hard tile. His room was at the end of the hall, farthest from the common sitting area. That is where residents slumped in a circle of mismatched lounge chairs, recliners, and wheelchairs. Disinterested attendees stared at soap operas. Even the fish in the tank looked bored. Across the hall from his room, a man repeatedly yelled out, no words, just an angry, frustrated and alarming cry that never ceased. The residents did not speak to one another. The attendees did not speak to them.

"What is this place? Why are we here?" Richard was baffled.

"This is where you live now, Honey. This is your home."

"What? No, no, I'm coming with you." He resisted; he was agitated.

"I'm sorry. No, this is where you'll sleep now. I'll visit you. I'll be back tomorrow. Peter and Phil will visit you, too."

"I don't want to stay here. I'm coming with you," he insisted, and grabbed his jacket and cane.

"No." My heart was breaking. I tried not to cry. I took his hand and sat him down on the bed. "They will take care of you here. I need to go back home. I'll sit with you a while."

We sat at the edge of the bed, at the edge of the abyss. Oh God, am I doing the right thing? Oh please, please take care of him. Oh please help him to make friends. Help him to find peace. Let these people love him.

He deflated, relented. "I'm tired. I need to lie down," he said. I helped him with his routine. He removed his hearing aids, sliding open the battery covers so that they would not squeal and drain the batteries. He ripped open the Velcro straps of his black tennis shoes and removed his belt. He placed his smudged glasses on the bedside table. He lay gingerly down on his back and arranged his blue velour Columbia jacket over himself. He clasped his hands on his chest and closed his eyes. I kissed his forehead and told him that I would see him in the morning before I left town.

I had to find an attendant to open the door so I could leave. I walked down the endless hallway, weeping along the way, avoiding the eyes of those I passed. I sobbed all the way to the car and sat in the parking lot, bawling my eyes out. *Please, please take care of him. Please don't let him feel abandoned. Please forgive me. Please please please.* Finally, my sobbing slowed, and I could clean the salt spots off my glasses.

It had been a very long grieving process, and it was not nearly over. Over the years, as each infirmity stole away a piece of my husband, I grieved for what he had been, for what we had. Now my grief was palpable, and my guilt infected my soul like a damned flu. I felt guilty for not being there for him, for not always being patient, for not being able to bring him happiness. I felt envy for those whose partners had their wits about them even as their bodies failed. I was envious of those whose partners' deaths came suddenly and without suffering. I wished that somebody could understand my grief and reach out to me. Emily understood, all three of his sons understood, and everybody supported the decision to put him in the home. Yet I grieved, and I missed the Richard who slipped away so long ago. I could not tell people that my husband died, and work through the grief. Instead, my husband was alive, and I had abandoned him, and so I grieved alone.

Beautiful Black Hills

Life in Rapid City, South Dakota, was unlike any other living I'd done. Emily had moved to the Black Hills years before when her first husband was stationed in the Air Force in Rapid City, South Dakota, so I visited every year. It was small-town to a Houston gal like myself, but I embraced its charms. What had once appeared to me as a depressed, dried-up place turned out to be a lovely place to spend a year in transition. The sky was the most vivid electric blue you can imagine, owing to the 5,000 foot altitude and the winds that blew away any pollution along the front of the hills. There was more sunshine there than in California, I was told. Clear, rushing and bubbling creeks wound through town and out into the canyons just outside the city. While temperatures could drop below zero in the winter, two days later it could be in the 40s. Cloud formations stunned us with their ever-changing, colorful sculpture show.

I applied to teach in the school district's gifted program and was offered an interview. The money was about half what I could make elsewhere in the country. They say the cost of living is less in a town like that, but don't believe it. Rent was still high, groceries were not cheap, and other necessities like insurance, gasoline, and restaurants were just as pricey as in Houston. But the day before the interview, I choked. I just could not go back into the public system. What if my supervisor was as awful as the

Florida bitch? The pain of that experience grabbed me by the throat, so I cancelled the interview. I could not do it.

Instead, I recalled a stop on one of my earlier visits to a beautiful winery up in the Hills. I'd had lunch there and fell in love with the rustic yet elegant ambiance. It seemed like it would be a nice place to work, so I applied and began my year at Prairie Berry Winery in Hill City, South Dakota. I'd gone from being a school principal to a tasting room associate. Why not?

The down-to-earth staff trained us well in the history of the winery, the variety of wines, and how to sell the guests on becoming wine club members. It was high tourist season when I started, and we were busy serving the hundreds that walked through the door, drawn by the enormous billboards that advertised Red Ass Rhubarb wine. Each guest could choose five of the wines to sample for free, and I would determine the best order to serve each of the half-ounce pours. I watched the more experienced associates pour, then swirl the wine to aerate and enhance its flavor, all the while talking about the wine's ingredients, flavors, and food pairings. "Do you like barbecue? The fruity blackberry notes in this wine are a perfect complement to a spicy, tangy barbecue sauce." Or we would bring around little cups of samples of frozen wine slushies, and sell the guests the $9.00 mixes to make them at home. We offered oyster crackers for between samples, and as snacks for the kids. We'd befriend each guest, get to know where they were from. Because I had lived so many places, it was easy to chat them up—"Oh yes, I used to live there, what have they done with the Fox Theatre?"—or we'd talk about the traffic. During the annual summer Sturgis bike rally, the drone of motorcycles was constant and the guests more colorful.

We did not work for tips, and were not allowed to put out a tip jar like they could in the same owner's brewery next door. When I would get the rare buck or two tip, it felt like a crisp $20 bill. Between guests we would clean, fill the racks of wine glasses beneath the counters, or roll the trays of dirty glasses back to the kitchen. We'd keep the floor displays of cases of wine full. At closing, every open wine bottle had to have the air pumped out of it to preserve its quality. All the pouring spouts were hand washed, the supplies refilled, the floors swept and mopped, and the bathrooms cleaned. It was very physical work. The cases of wine that we would stack and arrange weighed 35 lbs. We wore blue jeans and a black shirt of our choice, covered up with a denim apron with the winery's logo. I bought a funky pair of sparkly blue comfy shoes and some compression socks, but even those did not keep my hip from screaming or my legs from cramping up at night with spasms. Advil was my friend.

As the season wound down, I had hoped to be converted to a full-time, year-round employee with benefits, but that did not happen. I got hours through the winter and helped with shipping and retail, sometimes stirring big tubs of powders to make up packages of wine slush mix. No job was too menial, and the fellow workers were great. I got a discount on wine and food, so those lunches of homemade, gourmet soups, delicious cheeses, and crusty breads, eaten on the lovely patio looking out into the Black Hills, were a sensory delight.

That first summer, I took my daughter to the play *Motherhood Out Loud* at the Firehouse Brewery Theater in downtown Rapid City. I laughed and cried, and the familiar itch got me. When auditions rolled around, I showed up and got cast in not one, but two shows. They were juicy parts: Gertrude in Steve Martin's *The Underpants* and Sonia in *Vanya and Sonia and Masha and Spike*. I was recognized quite a few times around town and at the winery, which surprised the heck out of me, because that never happened in a big city like Houston or around Orlando. We were actually paid $40 per performance, which definitely helped and felt good. We got a discount at the brewery and restaurant downstairs, and I got out of the house nights.

Speaking of getting out of the house nights.... While Richard was declining, I was not going to just roll over. I met a local guy online, a very tall, well-educated but underemployed man just eight years my junior. We clicked, and I visited him twice a week in his apartment just five minutes away. He lit his bedroom with strings of Christmas lights that the city had discarded and he had retrieved in his job working for the city maintenance crew. We listened to music, talked a lot, and had a great time in bed. He wanted to be exclusive, and given the slim pickings in the area, the ease of access, and his long, fit ...body, it was worth it.

So my year in South Dakota was fun. I enjoyed making good breakfasts for the kids and sharing in the cooking of dinners. I'd like to think my presence took pressure off Emily and Joe, not just financially, but in knowing that they could rely on my help. They'd had several problem, incomplete pregnancies, and I wanted to mother Emily. It worked: they got pregnant toward the end of my year with them.

But while I was in South Dakota, I knew those days would end, and I did not want to stay there: I wanted to get closer to the ocean. I applied for jobs all over the edges of the country, but nothing panned out. Where was I going to go when our lease was up in June? My siblings invited me to stay with them, and Marty offered to rent me his townhouse. I chose to join my big sister in Phoenix, Arizona, while I kept applying and looking for a soft place to land. I loaded my things into a storage unit in South Dakota, packed my car with my houseplants and outfits for every conceivable adventure one could have in a few months, including job interviews, and headed down to Phoenix.

All this moving around was getting easier. With each move, I sold and gave away more stuff. Some things were tough to let go: my giant, beautiful oak French armoire, even though it did try to kill me by crashing apart on top of me after it had been incorrectly assembled by an antique "expert." The scooter, for which I got less than the cost of the new battery. The patio table and its matching chairs that rocked so soothingly as I watched sunsets from porches in Texas, Virginia, Florida, and South Dakota—and that even served as my kitchen table in Ohio. The bedroom suite Richard and I had used for dozens of years. The dresser had the burn marks from the candle that caught fire one Christmas, and I can still picture the armoire doors and drawers thrown open after one of our home burglaries in Houston. The sofa bed that welcomed many a guest. The super-heavy, long, blond Formica bookshelf that had been in Richard's office when he was a public school principal. So much stuff. You never get for it what you paid, but you do travel lighter.

But it was the emotional side of moving that got easier. With each place I lived, I embraced that place and found things to love. I welcomed new adventures and maintained my flexibility. "Barn's burned down, now I can see the moon," wrote the Japanese poet Mizuta Masahide. When I moved from Houston to Michigan, I thought that it would be my last move before retirement. After Michigan, I moved seven more times. All this hopscotching pretty much rules me out for high positions of authority because they see me as flighty or wonder why I can't keep a job.

Phoenix

Jan lived alone in her four-bedroom house, with a game room and a very private pool in her fenced backyard. She welcomed me that June for as long as I wanted to stay. She worked downtown, so I had the place to myself during the days and could apply for jobs in peace. I cooked for her and told her that if she had any meal favors that she owed people, or folks that she wanted to entertain, to invite them over and I would do the cooking. It was great fun, especially since she liked to clean her own kitchen. She was good at it. In fact, Dad once watched me cleaning up my kitchen and said, "You know, your sister is quite the good housekeeper." Jan's pool vacuum was on the fritz, so I took it upon myself to clear out the bougainvillea petals that littered the pool each day. I'd flip-flop over the hot pool deck, drop my towel, step gingerly from the flip-flop into the water to avoid second-degree foot burns, then enjoy the sensual delight of skinny dipping. I'd pluck petals off the bottom with my toes, then do side stretches to gather them and toss them into the trash. I got a great tan and stayed flexible.

Being sisters in our sixties is so much better than being sisters in our teens. In our teens, we did not share the same interests or values. She is four years older than I, so she could certainly get jobs and boyfriends before I could. Lots of boyfriends. Jan was very popular in ways that I never was. She ran for student council in high school and almost beat a boy, which was rare. She always had dates to every dance, back in the '60s when dances were still popular. She went to Sub-Deb, Homecoming, Prom, and Winter Formal. There was always a big hullabaloo around getting the right dress, the right shoes, and a fancy hairdo. The hair usually resulted in her crying and re-doing the lacquered helmet to her particular druthers.

Two teenage girls tended to tie up the phone, so our parents gave us our own princess phone with our own phone number. This was in the days before cordless phones, so to answer the phone's ring when we were not in our bedroom, we would bound up 13 steps, turn right, take four big leaps, turn the corner, and grab the phone; I could make it before the third ring. It amazes me that I had memorized at least a dozen phone numbers, while today I still have to double-check my own daughter's, being accustomed to our cell phones' memories doing the work for us. Long-distance calls were closely monitored. Either we had to reimburse the parents for their expense, or I would take my bag of change to the phone booth at the discount store a mile away and place my long-distance calls there. Everybody knew back then that weekdays after 10 pm or weekends were the cheapest times to call. Even now I will, out of mental habit, think that it is after business hours and a thriftier time to phone somebody. Similarly, when I am visiting another city, I will make an effort to phone a person who lives there in order to avoid the long-distance charges, despite the fact that long-distance charges are no longer charged.

Jan as a teen was a live wire. She got into all kinds of mischief and was grounded very often. Our parents were strict, but even so, my older siblings found ways to get into trouble, from something as innocuous as getting her ears pierced ("only tramps get their ears pierced") to coming home past curfew or drunk. We shared a bedroom, so my sleep would be interrupted when she'd stumble home on late nights. The worst was the time she drunkenly barfed all over our bedroom floor. It was not too hard for her and her friends to get borrowed or fake IDs to go out drinking. I occasionally borrowed her ID, but only to be able to go see R-rated movies, like *Klute* with Jane Fonda. It's not that I never drank; at theater cast parties, somebody would have a bottle of vodka for spiking our sodas. It amped up our sing-along of show tunes around the pianos. But nobody ever got more than slightly loose, never drunk.

Jan knew how to get what she wanted from me. She could turn on the charm to persuade me to write her English papers for her, or crawl into her bed for a summer-night giggle. She had mood swings and a temper that taught me to stay clear. Once, she had locked me out of our bedroom, so I stood outside our door, pounding furiously on it. She swung that door open and smacked me upside the head so hard that I have had diminished hearing in that ear ever since. I was, and always have been, incompetent at hair styling, so she would charge me to set my hair. When I did it myself, it would have random creases and crinkles and frizzy spots, but her attention to detail made me look great.

She tried to teach me to dance but laughed so hard that I have been forever intimidated and shy about dancing, convinced that everybody is laughing at me as she did. She tried to help me learn to drive but gave up after I turned too wide on the corner and drove into the neighbor's yard. She didn't exactly take on the big-sister-as-mentor role, ushering me wisely into my teen years. Rather, I would bump against her—literally—to learn what I needed to know. For example, I had no idea what boobs were all about. She dressed secretly in our closet, but I managed to "accidentally" bump against her and learn that boobs were squishy. In earlier years, I was curious about those big, puffy pads hidden on our closet shelf, so rather than talk about it with her, I borrowed one for a Barbie doll bed. That made her livid. Another time, I was about nine years old and gave her the finger because I had no idea what it meant and wanted to know. She became unhinged and yelled that I was never to do that ever again, never to her, never to anybody.

"Why? What does it mean?" I asked.

She was incredulous. "Don't you know what fucking is?" she asked.

"No."

"Well, that's what it is and you don't say that to people."

This left me as confused as ever, but I didn't try it on anyone until I was years wiser. Well, maybe not *that* wise, because when I flipped the bird in Houston to the monster pickup truck that was honking impatiently behind me, the driver tried to run me off the road and up on the curb as we turned the corner. After my heartbeat slowed, I remembered Jan's advice and did not use the single-finger salute in public ever again.

Jan doesn't laugh at me anymore. She is a confidante who listens. She may make suggestions or show her concern, but she doesn't lord them over me. She asks questions and lavishes unconditional, nonjudgmental love to me, her children, her grandchildren, and her friends. I wish I had her talent for talking with children. Yes, I may be a teacher, but she can strike up a conversation with any toddler, any six-year-old, any fourteen-year-old—any child—and make them smile and open up. She "gets them" at their level. She knows what they like. And she is generous to a fault. She shops all year for others, and dozens of children know her as Jama. Like our mother, she was born to be a grandma. It's a gift—to the world. While I may have learned things the hard way from her in our youth, I am now content to admire how graciously she gives of herself.

So in Phoenix, I pursued a job in earnest. How should I spend what were likely to be my last good earning years? Who would find value in my salmagundi of past jobs? More importantly, who would not be scared away? How do I revise a resume and craft a cover letter so that I do not look too old, too flighty, too indiscriminate? How do I explain my gaps and short tenures without sounding like a prima donna or a whiner?

Amongst my job applications, I applied to the school district in Virginia where I had worked for a partial year, having filled in for a promoted teacher, before I moved to Cleveland. Their pay scale was far better than I could get in a private school, and it would be nice to get health benefits, as I had gone without for the prior two years. While I was not eager to work in public schools again, the prospect of getting back to the excitement of the DC region outweighed that objection. In June, a school offered me a job, contingent upon approval from human resources. But my Virginia teaching certification expired the following week, on June 30th, so before they could extend the offer, I needed to renew it. This did not appear to be a problem, as I was currently certified in Missouri and Florida. When I first taught for the district, they accepted my teaching license from Missouri. Surely Virginia would acknowledge reciprocal licenses again.

Wrong.

Because I had an expiring Virginia license, I was required to renew it rather than be issued a new license based on my other existing licenses. The fact that I had moved out of state for the past four years was irrelevant to them. To renew it, I had to document 180 points of training. So there I was, working out of a briefcase at my sister's kitchen table in Arizona, with most of my files in storage in a warehouse in South Dakota, trying to get documentation from schools that were closed for the summer in Ohio and Florida, and from which I did not leave on the happiest of terms. There was no way of getting supervisor signatures on a list of workshops that I had conducted or taken. The school in Ohio had gone through several different principals and office managers since I had left, and they had lost all the training files, so they could provide nothing. After a month, the school in Florida was able to send a partial list. To get the ball rolling, I submitted to Virginia and to the school district in Virginia a partial list totaling about 100 hours.

Bureaucracies and red tape make me boil. Each correspondence with the state and the district specified that I could get a reply from them in six weeks, and they stretched that six weeks to the maximum. They sent out their reply at exactly six weeks, but sent it to my old mailing address, so I had to wait for it to be forwarded. When pressed, they would send a duplicate of their correspondence via email at the end of the six weeks. They never phoned to say that I had to submit more hours before they could proceed. And when I did respond with additional documentation, they waited another full six weeks.

Something that I have never understood is how a business or agency can justify taking six weeks to respond, especially in a time-sensitive matter such as this. Do they intentionally keep a six-week backlog of correspondence? Does it arrive at their desk, and then they file it under a date six weeks in the future to deal with it? The matter would take 15 minutes to analyze and respond to if they dealt with it right away. And because school systems anticipate a rush of renewal applications in the summer, why don't they schedule their renewal officers to work longer at that time, and take comp time during the slow season? Why do they let them take vacations during that critical time? Why aren't they bringing in temporary help or interns in the summer to help with the processing? The ethos of customer service is lacking in government agencies. Do they understand that people's livelihoods are on the line? Can they see that the quality of education suffers when teaching staff is unstable due to bureaucratic laziness and mismanagement? In the end, children suffer. There is no justification for allowing a six-week turnaround.

It was August, and school was beginning. I had never attended the district's orientation, but they could not allow me there until I was officially hired. I wanted to peruse the curriculum, but the same restriction applied. The principal assured me that they could start me as a long-term substitute teacher until the paperwork for the certification was cleared. The pay was less, and there were no benefits, but I could start the year. On that recommendation, I moved to DC ten days before school started.

Another round of correspondence with the state and the district took place six weeks later. This time, they denied me credit for all the training I took in the district in 2010 after starting with them because they said that my official license did not get issued until January 2011, despite the license itself stating July 1, 2010. Well, if that were the case, then shouldn't I have had the full five years until January 2016 to submit and have my 180 training hours on the record? No, all the training in the fall of 2010 went into a black hole and would not count. They only accepted points from the date on the certification, not per the actual issue date.

In terms of the dating of the license and the time frame in which one is eligible to earn renewal points, licenses are issued effective July 1 of the school year in which application is made.

> Renewal activity may not be earned until such time as a renewable license is issued. While the effective date of your license is 7/1/10 (July 1 of the 2010-2011 school year), your five-year license was not issued until January 27. This is the reason for the advisement that renewal activity completed prior to January 2011 (prior to the issuance of your five-year license) would not be applicable for renewal.

> (email from Lori Mann 8/11/2015)

Miraculously—hah—my license was renewed by Virginia exactly 90 days after I returned to the district. Ninety days was the limit that a long-term substitute could teach before having to relinquish the position to another long-term substitute, otherwise the district would have to hire that substitute or put another sub in place. So for those 90 days, I was paid an hourly rate of about one-third of what my salary would have been, the salary for which I had determined the move would be worthwhile. I was paid to work seven hours a day, despite the fact that I was working ten-hour days and weekends. Because I had performed as a full-time, salaried teacher, I requested back pay to acknowledge that my renewed license stated that I was certified as of July 1, 2015. The state and district would not allow this. I had joined the union and appealed my case to them. They listened and spoke to the district's union ombudsman, but they had no luck. I spoke with the union's lawyer, but he said that he did not handle cases like that. I spoke with the head of human resources, who denied my request on the basis that I had accepted the long-term substitute position. I appealed online to lawyers to take my case. I calculated that I was denied $11,000 in back wages and benefits, but I could find nobody to take my case. I wrote to my congressional representative, Don Beyer, for help in contacting people in Virginia's Department of Education, but I never received a reply. The district saved a lot of money on me. I quit the useless teachers' union. That spring, I was the first to be "de-staffed" at the end of the school year because I had been one of the last teachers hired—last in, first out. And because I had not started the school year as a certified teacher, I did not have the benefit of first dibs to transfer to open positions in other schools in the district. I had to reapply in the district all over again.

So from March of 2016, I was once again job hunting. I had no income after June, yet I was still paying for the move from South Dakota. In the summer of 2016, I accepted an offer from another school in the same district, although to work with third-grade students. The school was even closer to my home. I am with that school to this day but working with the older sixth-grade students where I am a better fit. So this is how I got here, back in public school where I started.

Summer 2019

The summer of 2019 was the first in a long while that I did not spend moving or job hunting. This meant I had the luxury of hopping around the country, visiting family and updating this memoir. When I had Rainard, it used to drive me crazy when folks would assume that I was enjoying a relaxing summer. I had to explain that our enrollment jumped from several dozen students to a couple hundred students who were taking any combination of classes over six weeks. Those were exhausting, sweaty summers, but important for both cash flow and publicity. Now I am enjoying the sort of summer that people assume teachers have.

Still, I get my hackles up when I get the impression that people think I am "just a teacher." I want to interject that I once had my own school, that I have been a principal at several schools, that I have published and have given presentations around the world. But if I point out my past, it only makes me look like even less, like I have come down in the world. Instead of being a teacher, as common as a roadside pebble, I'm more like roadkill. When people meet me for the first time and hear that I am a teacher, I generally get one of three responses:

1. *Oh, you are so lucky, you get three months off!* (Grrr, it's only one and a half months, and it's comp time, and we're attending summer training, and we don't get a paycheck for two months.)

2. *Oh, teachers aren't given enough credit, they work so hard, they have to deal with* ..... (This is not as aggravating a response, but I somehow distrust this pat condescension, as if they are talking about a garbage collector for the city.)

3. *Gee, I've always thought that I would be a good teacher* [after I finish collecting my six-figure salary and am ready to relax and enjoy the ego high of watching all those eyes light up when I've lit the spark of learning.] (Oh barf, yeah, it's so easy teaching one person at a time in your puny imagination.)

Public School Redux

If the system makes me so furious, then why would I apply to teach in it again? Once I hit 60, I began to worry about my retirement years. The district and state had paid toward my retirement, and if I could hang in there a few more years, I would be vested and able to collect what they had contributed. Although I would be the beneficiary of Richard's lifetime annuity from his years in teaching and administration, I needed more. Had I stayed in Houston in the house we had lived in for 17 years, the house with the mortgage of $500 per month, I could manage. If I had stayed at Rainard until I no longer wanted to work, I could have managed it. All the while Emily was growing up, I told her that my expectation was that she would take me in when I retired, because we were spending our savings in her youth. I planned to turn over my Social Security checks to her, and she would put me in a tiny house in her back yard. If I could contribute to Social Security for a few more years at a good rate of pay, it would pay off with a better income once I turned 67.

What exactly am I having to tolerate? For one thing, ridiculous class sizes. I had 29 kids in my class this year and last, although the district boasts an average elementary class size of 22. There is no cap. They turn no student away. Both of those classes were at center schools that accepted students from more than twenty different neighborhood schools. They should have been turned away from the center and served in their neighborhood school once the class size limit was reached.

Twenty-nine sixth-graders is different from 29 third-graders, although each has its own challenges. Sixth graders have the school routine figured out. You can give an instruction to the class, and most of them will follow it. Third graders somehow seem to expect personalized invitations to pay attention, and they will follow directions once you get in their face and repeat it to them personally.

Space is obviously an issue as well. Sixth graders take up a lot of room, and with 29 of them it is impossible to move around to all of them. Classroom size may accommodate desks, but not desks AND tables for working on group projects. If you level all the desks to the same height to enable table work, such as working on a poster or a shared document, you will have a 5'11" student next to a 4'9" student; either the legs don't fit or the arms don't reach. Another space challenge comes when implementing the Responsive Classroom practice, which starts each day with a morning meeting in which the students face one another in a circle so they can greet each other and have discussions to build community. If you leave an open area for them to meet in a circle, such as on a rug, then the desks are crowded together. If instead you spread out the desks so that you can actually walk around the room, you might move the desks aside each morning for the meeting, then replace them afterward; however, the cacophony of dragging desks and chairs will be deafening. If students have anything in or on the moving desks, those will spill all over the floor.

Of course, more students mean more work for the teacher. To calculate the extra work created by those seven students above the "average class size," add up all the papers to be graded in a week. I would estimate that they required a total of 10 minutes per student to grade. Seven students x 10 minutes = 70 minutes x 36 weeks = 42 additional hours of grading. This is one reason why I am at school for several hours each day after the students leave, and why my Sundays are set aside for grading and lesson planning. Perhaps I could take a page from the Virginia Department of Education's playbook and file the students' papers for six weeks before returning their graded work.

All those grades get factored into what goes on the quarterly progress reports. These require hours upon hours of labor. It isn't as easy as assigning a grade for each subject area because in our district, each subject area is broken into subcategories. In addition to the subject areas, there are the behavioral and social skills to grade, which makes for a total of 41 separate grades for each student. How long do you think it took me to do that for 29 students? Now double that at the end of the year when we had to report not just the fourth quarter grades, but final grades as well. While the district does not give grades on these progress reports like A, B, C, D and F, nor number grades like 93, the district does give a number of 1, 2, 3, or 4, which requires as much documentation and thought from the teacher.

For example, my students worked in teams of two or three to prepare a presentation about traveling cross-country to experience the different geographical regions. They had to map out a trip that would also visit key features such as major rivers and mountains. They needed to research the cost to travel via their chosen mode, such as airlines or trains. These are just a few of the elements that were contained in the project. When it came to translating their project evaluation to the progress reports, we had to consider their accomplishments in public speaking, geographic under-standing, organizational skills, effort, and ability to work with others. Do we record marks for each of these areas in our grade books for a project like this? Imagine how long that takes.

I've sometimes wondered if there should be a screening before one enters a teacher training program in order to determine if the candidate has a suitable constitution for the profession. I would not have passed because I am very sensitive to sound and am stressed by noise. Classes get noisy, especially large classes; and because we are trying to help our students to learn to be collaborative, many of them must talk at once. To understand what this is like, imagine your dinner table conversation. Now imagine a Thanksgiving feast with all your family, relatives, and neighbors. Now add seven more people. Now expect them to be quiet while you talk to the whole group. Then ask them to discuss amongst themselves the pros and cons of hosting Thanksgiving at somebody else's home next year. Imagine the voices rising as they struggle to be heard, or as they struggle to focus on just the conversations of their own little group. Now take them for a walk down the block, like students walking to the specials classes or the cafeteria, but instruct them not to converse with on another. "SILENCE SHOWS RESPECT" signs are posted all along the route.

How's that working for you? A big percentage of each school day is spent controlling noise levels and attention. It's tough to have a comfortable, welcoming atmosphere that does not turn into a militarized zone.

In addition to the ramifications of overcrowded classes, there are the expectations for the teacher to cover the curriculum. The focus is not on mastery or depth but covering all the subjects a mile wide and an inch deep. A spiraling repetition can be effective, but it leaves some serious holes. In the scope and sequence, many subjects, like early American history, are covered repeatedly. Virginia students learn about Jamestown and the Revolutionary and the Civil Wars in fourth and sixth grades, as well as in high school. Meanwhile, they cannot identify the states on a map but can sing the "50 States Song." Students do not know the countries of the Middle East or Asia, but they can tell you about Greek gods and the architectural accomplishments of ancient China. To ensure that the students would not be ignorant of the world as it exists around us, I secured the funding to subscribe to the *NewsCurrents* current events program in sixth grade on the condition that I share it with my sixth-grade team. None of them would use it because they said that they had too many other things to cover. But one of the aspects of the program that truly engaged the students was that it inspired animated discussions. Students love to argue and share their opinions, and the program gave them unbiased facts and data to inform their passions. I used the inspired debates to motivate their speaking skills and their persuasive writing. Their Language Arts assignments and assessments included their debates and writing generated from *NewsCurrents*. While I still taught American history to the sixth graders, I also gave them current, real-world awareness.

The principals push team planning. They want all the classes in that grade to cover the same material, give the same tests, and grade the same, because principals do not want to answer to disgruntled parents who have decided that the grass looks greener in the classroom next door, where the teacher assigned a project while their own teacher assigned a test.

What the team planning looked like for self-contained classrooms, like the third grade I taught, was that of the four-person team, each instructor takes on a subject to plan for the whole team. We shared our plans online in Google Docs. We would be responsible for running off the copies for each class, so I would come away from every meeting with a six-inch stack of papers for math, another pile for language arts, and another stack for social studies. I would organize those papers into folders for days of the week when I was scheduled to use them. I no longer have any grip on my fingers from handling so many papers; it's a wonder I still have fingerprints.

Does it really save that much money to photocopy the bejeezus out of everything, rather than use consumable workbooks or copy problems into a notebook from a colorful, thoughtfully designed textbook? The district can't afford one-to-one computing; I get it. But photocopying papers at half-size to be glued into composition books does not feel like it inspires engaged learning. I had a closet shelf full of five different consumable workbooks that we could not consume. Why didn't we just have one copy of each consumable and photocopy that one?

I have had an interesting change of heart about textbooks. I have historically been resistant to them after witnessing a depressing lack of inspiration on the part of teachers who formed a rigid dependence on textbooks. When the textbooks become Holy Texts from which one dare not depart, then we are less inclined to pursue exciting projects or alternative presentations. Now I see a good textbook as an attractive jump-off point, a skeleton on which one can build—and save trees. And with a textbook, when you have all those topics in one place, students can work ahead at their own pace or review as needed, with more ease than flipping through a notebook that may or may not be well kept.

Teachers are expected to keep parents aware of what students are learning via the online resource Blackboard, or FCPS 24/7 learning. I find the medium clumsy and inelegant and prefer Google Classroom, which is more attractive and easily tied to the many Google applications. The district, however, would not pay for the feature that would allow parents their own passwords and relied on their children to share their school logins and passwords. To compensate, the grade-level team would send home a generic, monthly newsletter informing parents of what was happening beyond what they could read from the school-wide weekly newsletters. In addition to these communications, teachers are expected to respond to parent emails within 24 hours.

Are you as tired of reading my whining as I am of writing it? Yeah, I thought so. So what about the positive aspects of teaching, in contrast with being an administrator? And what are the upsides to working in a public school rather than a private school?

I love the camaraderie of teaching in a team. We are all in the same boat, and we get it that when another teacher talks about wanting to punch a student in the face, that it would never happen, and that the teacher is just venting from a difficult day; they do not need to be reported to the principal. We watch each other's back, we find ways to laugh and help each other. The team is our platoon, our war buddies. As a teacher, I get invited to lunch. As a principal, my teachers did not invite me to join them if they went out for lunch. Conversations stopped when I walked into the staff lounge. Teachers looked worried when I, as a principal, asked to speak with them. I had to build trust that I was there to support them as their principal. As a teacher, I trusted my fellow teachers and worried whether the principal would support me. So when the principal would ask to speak with me, I, like my teachers did when I was principal, went into anxious alert mode.

Another benefit of teaching in a public school is that I am not managing the school's finances. While the public school's budget certainly impacts my class size and my access to materials I would like to use or trips I would like to take with my students, I am not responsible for seeing those dollars come into the district. As the head of a private school, I was responsible for the dollars that came into the school through tuition and fundraising. In a public school, I am not always worried about parents leaving, or gossiping, or not paying their tuition. If a parent left the public school, it only made life easier for me. In a small private school, even one parent withdrawing could have a substantial negative impact on the budget. For that reason, it was a big decision to ask problem parents and children to leave, which could be both good and bad for the school. In public school, you do the best you can with the hand you are dealt.

Abandoned, but Not Forgotten

Richard adapted to the VA nursing home. On one hand, it was good that he was so unaware and uncommunicative because he had no complaints about where he was and got along with everybody. The staff liked him. He did not keep inquiring about where I was. He lived in the moment. His mind had simple needs; he responded little to what small stimulation was offered, and he napped a lot. He was not agitated. On the other hand, that meant that my efforts to make him happy were not really satisfying. I tried to help him communicate with others by giving him little erasable whiteboards so he could have people write notes for him to read, as he could not understand what people said. Those ended up piled under the cards and letters that I sent. Decorations that I sent were hung by the staff. He never responded to them. I phoned him once, but he had no idea what I was saying. When I visited, he did not act surprised or delighted, but rather matter of fact: it was as if I had been there only the day before. He wanted to go for a ride anywhere in the car, but he quickly tired and wanted to go back and lie down.

I visited him that year every few months and did what I could to make his living space better, with a new blanket or a fresh arrangement of pictures. The staff did not seem to make much effort. I found a lot of dried spit gobs on the floor next to his bed. There was no system for collecting dirty clothes, and Richard was not in the habit of taking out clean clothes.

If he found the staff collecting his clothes from his chair when he lay down at night, he would protest, so sometimes the staff would sneak in after he was asleep to replace his dirty clothes with clean ones. That's how they trashed his hearing aids, by sending them through the laundry when they were in his pockets. They took no responsibility for their carelessness and would not help with replacing them. They also "lost" his wedding band. When I visited, his pants and shirt were stained, and he had dirty underwear stuffed into his drawer.

Like the dirty clothes, less valuable items accumulated. For example, each of his meals came with a pink note with his name and indicating that he received "mechanical meals" that were easier for him to chew with his loose dentures, as he no longer would use denture adhesive. He kept every one of those notes and packed them by the dozens into his ditty bag and drawers. When I asked why, he said he thought he had to do this to pay for the meals. I threw all those out each time I visited. I tossed out the dried-up flower arrangements. I found every box of cookies and snacks that I had sent him in care packages. He did not eat them, even though I wrote him to share them and offer them to any visitors and staff to help him make friends. Still, the snacks were there. I brought his harmonica, hoping that his playing would give him pleasure. He ignored it.

What kind of a life was this? Why didn't he rise up and make trouble? How did the life of a party, the one who enjoyed being the center of attention, devolve into a walking ghost? I kissed him goodbye and left each visit heartbroken and weeping. Yet he kept on going. Philip pointed out that he could live another ten years unless one bad virus took him out.

It turns out, Phil was right.

My phone rang late on Saturday, December 10, 2016. I had spent the afternoon with my nephew, Steve, who had come to Washington to see me in a play. After the show, we went for drinks with the cast. It was late when we got back to my place and my cell phone rang.

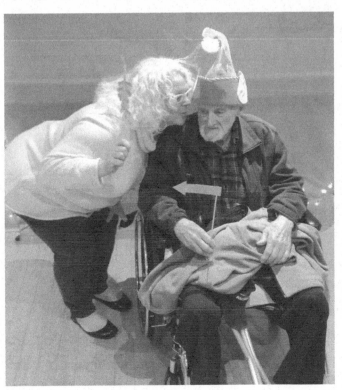

"Can I speak with Mrs. Bouchard?"

"This is she."

A man with a heavy accent continued: "This is Nurse Lungu. I am at the hospital here in St. Louis. I want to clarify your husband Richard's DNR."

"Why? What is happening?"

What happened, he explained, was that Richard was in physical distress, presumably from a bladder infection, so the home sent him to the hospital. The home had reached Phil, who gave them permission to administer antibiotics. The nurse on duty then called me for clarification: is that what I wanted?

"Doesn't the DNR explain that?" I had thought that by having a DNR, that I would not be forced at a time of stress to make tough decisions. There were to be no heroic life-saving measures. Were antibiotics in that category?

"The DNR does not talk specifically about antibiotics."

I asked for clarification: what was happening with Richard? Was he in pain? It was paramount to me that he not suffer. The nurse explained that his organs were starting to shut down as the infection continued. Without antibiotics, he would die.

"How long would that go on?" I asked.

"It could be hours; it could be days."

"Could his pain be managed if he were not in the hospital?"

"Yes, the doctor can release him back to the home with a prescription for morphine. It is late, but we would need to locate the doctor and then the ambulance."

"Please do that," I responded numbly. "Please keep me informed."

Why hadn't the home called me? Why was I just now hearing about this? I called the VA home and reached the desk attendant on Liberty Lane to ask why they had not phoned me. She said that she did not know who was on duty at that time, but that she was sure whoever it was called me.

"Do you all keep a record of when people are called, or when the hospital was called?" She explained that they do not keep records of calls. "What number do you have on file for me?" She looked up their number for me, and it was correct. "Then why don't I have any record on my phone that I missed a call from there?" She did not know. Their files indicated to call me, and if they could not reach me, they were to call Phil. It was he who gave permission to take him to the hospital and treat him. Phil did not go to the hospital, nor did Phil try to phone me. The shift working at the home at night was not helping me to understand why they did not reach me. I told them that he would be returning to the home, and that he would have a prescription for pain medication.

Nurse Lungu called back at 11:55 that night and told me that Richard was very agitated and in misery because he could not pee. The nurse was waiting for the doctor to return his call and authorize a catheter, as the nurse was not allowed to do this independently. I thanked him for keeping me informed.

At 12:45 am, the nurse called again to say that the catheterization was successful and that morphine had been prescribed, but it was not yet delivered. Once it was, they would forward the prescription to the VA home, and Richard would be returned to the home.

On Sunday morning, I spoke with the home again. The pharmacy at the home was not open at that time, so Richard was not receiving pain medicine. I took Steve to the airport, then drove to the matinee performance of my play. I told the director that I might be distracted or need to take a call because my husband was dying. He and the cast were phenomenally supportive and understanding, and the show went on.

On Monday morning, I went to school and told my team what was going on. During my lunch break, I got a call from the home and left the staff lounge to take the call in the restroom. The nurse said that Richard had passed, and the funeral home had been called. I returned to the staff lunchroom, crying, and my team whisked me away to my classroom to get my things. They insisted that I not try to finish the day and not try to make plans for my replacement, just go. And so I did.

I spoke with Peter. He said that he had gone to the home in the morning and found Richard at his breakfast table, eyes closed. Richard was dead, and he had clearly died just moments before, because the staff had gotten him up and taken him to breakfast. It was Peter who discovered his death. Bless his heart.

I made arrangements to fly to St. Louis, and for Emily and Bluebelle, her toddler, to fly in, too. Emily arrived Monday night, and I on Tuesday morning. Richard's son Steve flew in from Florida, and we all met at the funeral home late on Tuesday. We sat in a conference room with the funeral director, who went over what my prepaid plan covered. I had bought the plan years ago in Houston from a funeral chain that assured me that it could be used at any member of the mortuary chain around the country, if that was needed. We paid for it over time. It covered cremation, no embalming, a visitation event, and the simplest of caskets. We had no need for the viewing or for other items on the list, so it turned out that I would get a refund. The refund helped toward the airfares and the ridiculously priced obituaries in the St. Louis and Houston newspapers. After all the paperwork was signed, the family was able to view his body. The home had placed him for viewing in a private room. He was cleaned up, and candles were lit.

Richard had been in the refrigerator. He was so cold!

"I'm sorry, Richard, I'm so sorry," I cried.

"You did nothing wrong," Emily assured me, and hugged me.

The boys stood close, and quiet. I kissed Richard's cold forehead goodbye. His cheeks and eyes were sunken, his face grizzly with stubble, and a scratch was on his face. He was not smiling and he did not look peaceful, just quiet, napping the coldest of naps. I could not feel his presence. There was no holy spirit appearing to me, reassuring me; there was just his cold, cold corpse.

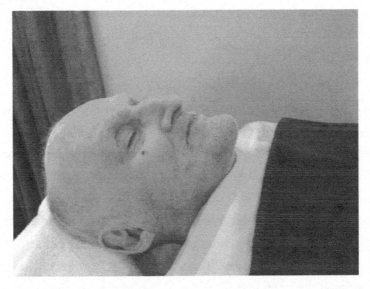

I used to believe in an afterlife and in life before life. I believed that we entered our bodies at birth, reluctantly, because our spirits knew that life was hard and the lessons we learned in life were painful. These thoughts eased me through the pain of the miscarriage I suffered before getting pregnant with Emily, and through those fearful days when I thought that I was losing her, too. I rationalized that her spirit decided that, despite her fears and reluctance, she chose to be born to me because I could help her to fulfill her mission in life. When my father died, I gave a talk at his memorial in which I shared that he did not believe in an afterlife but I did, and that there would be quite a homecoming in heaven when he reunited with Mom and my brother Roger. Boy, wouldn't he be surprised at what was waiting for him that he did not expect!

But it was when I saw Richard there, so cold that I could not feel his presence, that I doubted that there was any energy of him left anywhere in the universe. There were no angels comforting me, save my daughter and stepsons. He did not come and tell me it was all right, just as he had never greeted me in the nursing home to say, *Hey, where've you been? I've been wanting to talk to you or see you.* He'd been gone for so long, and now he would be gone completely. He had been leaving my life, atom by atom, for so many years, and now he was all gone. Gone, and my memory of him was clouded with the dusty residue of my guilt for not having been there for him in his final days.

Yet I wanted to celebrate his life and remember all that he had been and all that he had done for so many people, in his work in schools in Maine, Missouri, Colorado, and Texas; in his work on boards of directors for organizations that served children with autism and learning differences; in his joyful work with Boy Scouts; at his summer camp in the Ozarks; in his work as commodore of his yacht club in Illinois. I wanted Webster College to acknowledge all that he had contributed to building the teacher education and master's programs there, and all the teachers who were better because of him. I wanted the parents of Rainard students to recognize how he loved their children and showed it in so many ways. I wanted the Brookwood Community and Yvonne, its founder, to acknowledge his critical role in the building of that community and how he was loved by its residents.

I reached out to St. Louis University, Webster, and Brookwood. I heard nothing from any of them. I suppose we had not contributed enough money. Bastards.

It was Christmas soon after Richard's death, and I spent it with Emily and her kids. Back in Houston, I arranged for her and I to meet with Rainard School's director and two other friends associated with the school, Kathy and Jodi. I asked for their help in arranging for a Celebration of Life to be held at the school on a Sunday morning, February 26. I scheduled it more than two months after his death because I wanted to give time for family members around the country to make arrangements to be there. My friend Kathy would handle the catering and Tara, the school director, would arrange my request for a proper New Orleans jazz group to play a New Orleans jazz funeral. Richard had loved New Orleans jazz, and he would strut to "When the Saints Come Marching In" whenever it played. Jodi would take care of local arrangements and coordinate with Kathy. They would get the word out locally.

Kathy and her sons, who were my former students, cooked up an amazing brunch buffet for the guests. Tara brought in a trio from the High School for the Visual and Performing Arts, and they played smooth jazz—not at all New Orleans style, which was a big disappointment, but I was grateful for the effort. The tables were decorated Mardi Gras style, and there was even a birthday cake for little Bluebelle, who turned one year old that same day. Folks gathered outside at the picnic tables, enjoying the mild weather and pretty playground. There was a microphone set up, and we took turns talking about our memories of Richard. Scotty Campbell gave an especially beautiful tribute. Rainard teachers were there, and half a dozen families who remembered him. A few former students came. It was nice to share the sweet memories. Phil did not come; he said that the pizza party at his house the night after we visited Richard's body was his memorial, and he did not need any more. Peter could not come because I had carelessly scheduled the memorial for the same weekend as a huge feast day in his Baha'i community, one that he had planned to host for a long time. I regret not having discussed dates with him in advance. But Steve, Judy, and Dani drove all the way from Pensacola, and we had a lovely time together. My sister flew in and was a huge support. My best friend Joni couldn't come because she was very ill. My eldest brother sent a donation to the school, but neither of my other brothers made any effort to come, nor to donate in his memory or to send flowers. I'm still miffed about that. None of Richard's surviving nieces or nephews sent any flowers or donations either.

One weird thing that happened at the memorial was that my friend Jodi left early. She told somebody that she wasn't feeling well. I had greeted her warmly and asked where her son was, but she said he wasn't coming. I expressed disappointment and complimented her on the party decorations. I never heard from her again. She had been a huge support to me and a confidante the last seven years over many a phone call. I had stayed in her home. I tried to call her after the memorial, but my calls were refused. I wrote to her and apologized for I knew not what, but if she could tell me what I did wrong, I would try to make it up to her. I got no response. I reached out to her son, my former student, and asked if he could help. She finally texted me back that she wanted no further contact at this time, and to keep Edward out of it. I was and remain baffled, but now I am angrier that as a friend, she could not confront me and tell me how I had screwed up—if I had. I remain clueless.

Richard's cremated remains were not at the celebration. The doctor at the nursing home had neglected to sign the death certificate, then left the country for a month. The funeral home could not cremate him until the certificate was signed. They reached out repeatedly to the nursing home to forward the document electronically to the doctor for an electronic signature, but they refused to contact the doctor who was on vacation, and no other doctor could do it. Richard's corpse lay in their funeral home's refrigerator for more than a month before they could take care of it. One day, it arrived at my apartment, special delivery with a big, clear label: "CREMATED REMAINS." It had cost $63 to ship the surprisingly heavy, 4" x 4" x 8" package. I put it on the floor at the end of the sofa. He had sat at that end of the sofa for years, so it seemed fitting.

Richard and I had spoken over the years about what do with each other after we died. He insisted that I do whatever was easiest for me, that he did not care. I asked him numerous times over the years if there was a place where he would like his ashes to go. Was there a special place he loved? Yes, he loved his home in Maine. He loved mountains, and he loved the sea. And that is why I decided to scatter his ashes off Hermit Island in Maine and up Mount Katahdin, a hike he had loved in his youth. Emily, our climber, could climb Katahdin in his memory; I disdain climbing, especially the uphill part. I predicted she would not make it to the top, as she was six months pregnant. Richard never met a hill that he did not love to climb. That summer, we would travel to Maine to distribute those ashes. The heavy box was in my suitcase. I predicted it would bring me closure as I sent that burden to the ocean, from whence we all came, and to the winds that take us everywhere and connect us all.

There was no life insurance at the end. I had not paid on the variable whole life policy for years because the cost was getting so high, so we let the corpus be eaten up by not making the payments. When it got close to being completely gone, I contacted the insurance company to see what it would take to make the policy current. However, they chose to delay getting back to me, despite my repeated contacts, until the deadline for reinstatement passed. Screw you, Massachusetts Mutual.

We never thought he would live so long. When I met him, he was taking blood pressure medication and had a volatile personality, both predictors of heart failure. His parents had died by their 80s. He was the eldest of three children, and his younger sister and brother died before he did. He was wild and reckless and drank, but he died at the age of 90. He survived a medical heart conversion, heavy drinking, smoking for years, two major surgeries on his back, both hip replacements, a rollover car accident, and being a belly gunner in World War II. Was his long life because I took good care of him? Was it his fortune to marry a much younger woman? Was it staying active in the field he loved for more than 60 years? Could be, but I think it was his zest for life and love of people that kept him hanging on.

He gave so much to so many, yet so few were there at the end. To be fair, when a person moves around as much as we did, it is not easy in this huge country of ours to get together. Had he stayed in his hometown or St. Louis or even Houston, his final days might not have been as lonely. I might have had more support in my grief. It's as if people don't know what to do with a widow. They treat me as if I was never married, as if I had never loved, as if I am not experiencing a loss—a loss that dragged for years and brought out the best and worst in me. What has been the best? I continued to live a life of adventure and pleasure, despite his not being able to join me. He always fully supported me in seeking love and joy, and for him, it was always about seeing to my happiness. My happiness made him happy. What has been the worst? The worst was that I did pursue the happiness that he wished for me, in ways that I fear may have diminished his own happiness, although he would never admit it.

December 2019

"Mom, I want you do something. I have a challenge for you."

"Hmm. OK, what?"

"When you go away to the cabin to finish your memoir this weekend, I want you to do what it takes to get closure about Randall."

Emily was concerned: I had told her that I had a nightmare about him that week, fourteen years after I had last seen him. I rarely have nightmares, maybe once every ten years, but the man whom I blamed for my ignominious descent after the Michigan debacle had popped up again. I still vacillated between revenge fantasies and a grasping hope that karma had taken care of things for me. Perhaps I should seek out the little Asian healer to recharge that white belly light. Or maybe wrapping up this memoir will do the trick.

Why write a memoir? Maybe it is like working out a sudoku puzzle, but with scenes from our life that might all fit together and make sense when arranged just so. I started this, inspired by NaNoWriMo, the National Novel Writing Month project, which serendipitously commences each November, the month after my devastating exit from the Florida charter school. I was reeling from all I had been through and was still going through, so I hoped that putting it to text would be clarifying and cathartic. After seemingly finishing this, I've punched in a number of times over the years to add to this, so how does it end? With closure? With a cliff-hanger? While the writing may have been useful to me, what can it do for the reader who has made it this far?

While there are those who will read this to see what I have said about them, others may pick it up for the juicy bits. Comrades in Education Land might read it to see a veteran's perspective. After all, my age, if nothing else, gifts me with the status of crone, the old woman with wisdom. Maybe this will serve as a cautionary tale: follow your dreams, 'though the bed be mighty lumpy. Or: beware of heartless bosses with unbridled power. Remember that bureaucracies, such as school districts, unions, and insurance companies, live to feed themselves, not their customers. It's not cynicism if it is accurate, right?

And yet I know that life is sweet and that I am the recipient of grace, of unearned gifts. I have a loving, entertaining family. I have a job that has gotten me out of debt. I have opportunities to walk around in other people's shoes—literally—when I take on roles in community theaters.

It took me years to write this. It started just miles from New Smyrna Beach in Florida, where I could escape when facing my life on the page grew too much. When my life was a big twisted mess, the ocean waves and breezes have always teased out the tangles and straightened things out in my mind. Knots relaxed. Saltwater disinfected and drew out the toxins. At the beach, I am reminded that there is something much bigger than me, something very powerful, from which all life came.

I also had the joy of writing this from my generous nephew Steve's rustic cabin, high atop a hill in the mountains of New Hampshire, looking out over Lake Winipesaukee. His dog kept me company on my solo writing retreats, and Steve patiently led me to a neighboring hill for the pleasure of picking ten pounds of wild blueberries. We took a break with swims in the cool, local ponds and watched the hawks and cedar waxwings.

Some parts I wrote from my basement office in South Dakota, not too far from gorgeous Spearfish Canyon, where I could stand on the bank of the creek and watch the lazy trout in the sparkling waters.

Now I have retreated to a cabin in the Blue Ridge Mountains, close to the Appalachian Trail. The golds and reds of autumn have fallen, but the grass and mosses remain green, and the creek burbles on, whispering comfort.

Jobs and schools may have disappointed me, but I always had nature to renew my love for being on the earth. I am lucky to have had love and this amazing adventure.